Media and Social Justice

Sue Curry Jansen

Censorship: The Knot That Binds Power and Knowledge, 1988.

Critical Communication Theory: New Media, Science, Technology, and Gender, 2002.

Jefferson Pooley

Park, David W., and Jefferson Pooley, eds. *The History of Media and Communication Research: Contested Memories*, 2008.

Media and Social Justice

Edited by
Sue Curry Jansen, Jefferson Pooley, and Lora Taub-Pervizpour

First published in hardcover in 2011 by PALGRAVE MACMILLAN® in the United Statess—a division of St. Martin's Press LLC, 175 Fifth Avenue, New York, NY 10010.

Where this book is distributed in the UK, Europe and the rest of the world, this is by Palgrave Macmillan, a division of Macmillan Publishers Limited, registered in England, company number 785998, of Houndmills, Basingstoke, Hampshire RG21 6XS.

Palgrave Macmillan is the global academic imprint of the above companies and has companies and representatives throughout the world.

Palgrave® and Macmillan® are registered trademarks in the United States, the United Kingdom, Europe and other countries.

ISBN: 978-1-137-33144-1

Chapter 3 is a lightly revised version of a chapter in *Inclusion Through Media*, ed. Tony Dowmunt, Mark Dunford, and Nicole van Hemert (London: Goldsmiths, 2007). Reprinted by permission of Goldsmiths College, University of London.

Chapter 4 is a revised excerpt from *Public Media 2.0: Dynamic, Engaged Publics* (Washington, DC: Center for Social Media, 2009). Reprinted by permission of the Center for Social Media, American University.

Chapter 5 is a combined and expanded version of two articles: William Gamson, "Life on the Interface," *Social Problems* 51, no. 1 (2004): 106–10; and Charlotte Ryan, "Can We be Compañeros?" *Social Problems* 51, no. 1 (2004): 110–13. Reprinted by permission of the University of California Press.

The Library of Congress has cataloged the hardcover edition as follows:

Library of Congress Cataloging-in-Publication Data

Media and social justice / edited by Sue Curry Jansen, Jefferson Pooley, and Lora Taub-Pervizpour.
    p. cm.
    ISBN 978-0-230-10863-9 (hardback)
    1. Mass media—Political aspects. 2. Social justice. I. Jansen, Sue Curry. II. Pooley, Jefferson. III. Taub-Pervizpour, Lora, 1967–

    P95.8.M386 2011
    302.23—dc22   2011002901

A catalogue record of the book is available from the British Library.

Design by Scribe Inc.

First PALGRAVE MACMILLAN paperback edition: May 2013

10 9 8 7 6 5 4 3 2 1

For James D. Schneider (1939–2005)

Contents

Part III: Power Struggles

Part IV: Media Justice

INTRODUCTION

Media, Democracy, Human Rights, and Social Justice

Sue Curry Jansen

Media activism and critical media studies have always addressed social justice issues. Activists work to redress perceived inequities in media access, policies, and representations, while critical media scholars combine teaching, research, and publication with advocacy for democratic media, institutions, and representational practices.

Because most channels for public communication in democratic societies are now dominated by messages produced by commercial media, advertising, and public relations, media activism and critical media studies seek to expand the range and diversity of information, interpretive strategies, and resources available to the public. For example, critical media studies challenge government and market censorship of media and culture; oppose concentrated ownership of media; challenge representational practices that stereotype, marginalize, or "symbolically annihilate" minority views, cultures, groups, or individuals;[1] proactively promote broad access to media resources and media-making skills; encourage development and wide distribution of alternative media; document, publicize, and urge action to counter domestic and global digital divides; use media technologies to expose abuses of power; and develop and promote policy positions to advance social justice.

Critical media researchers pioneered efforts to document and challenge the roles media play in facilitating and rationalizing global inequalities in the distribution of power relations and resources. Many critical media scholars were, for example, advocates of the New World Information Order: the movement, sponsored by the nonaligned nations in the United Nations in the 1970s and early 1980s that promoted a more equitable distribution of global information resources.[2] Some media scholars advocate for recognition of "the right to communicate" as a fundamental human right.[3] Critical media scholarship and activism also operate at local levels in community media projects; these may, for example, involve instruction in media literacy and production with the objective of providing underresourced people with the communication skills and technologies that they need to tell their own stories and stake their own claims for social justice.

Yet critical media scholarship has remained marginal to the interdisciplinary academic field formally designated as social justice studies; social justice studies, in turn, frequently lack adequate theories of media and communication. Greater mutual exposure can enrich both approaches. For example, in his recent, magisterial statement of his comparative theory of justice, *The Idea of Justice*, economist Amartya Sen sees the removal of barriers to free and open discussion, the development of the right ("capability") to communicate, and the institutionalization of an "unrestrained and healthy media" (to give "voice to the neglected and disadvantaged") as essential prerequisites to the pursuit of human justice and security.[4] Despite this foundational claim, even Sen does not offer a theory of media and devotes only three pages directly to the topic. Clearly, both social justice scholarship and activism and critical media scholarship and activism can benefit from greater mutual exposure.

We do not pretend to offer a synthesis of the two areas of inquiry. Our objective is more modest: to offer a provocative collection of essays, which we believe can be useful in starting a long-overdue conversation between the two fields.

Social Justice Scholarship and Activism

Social justice scholarship is, by definition, interdisciplinary and practice oriented, combining academic research and pedagogies with efforts to improve the life chances of marginalized people, communities, and causes. Its intellectual powers are amplified by drawing on the combined knowledge resources of multiple disciplinary lenses; its effectiveness as practice is frequently enhanced by developing applied aspects of this knowledge in partnerships with diverse coalitions of concerned parties.

Whether motivated by intellectual conviction, civic responsibility, ethical imperatives, religious ardor, or loyalty to kin or kind, social justice scholarship shares a common value system rooted in empathy. This value orientation is expressed in the relationship the researcher establishes with the people or practices she studies. At the turn of the twentieth century, the German sociologist Max Weber described that relationship as *verstehen* or sympathetic understanding.[5] More recently and much more expansively, feminists have framed the relationship in moral terms as practicing an "ethics of care."[6] Martin Luther King Jr.'s concept of "the beloved community," which functioned both as a hopeful vision for the future and as a description of an interactional ideal among civil rights activists, takes this ethic out of the academy (and gospel) and into the streets.[7]

Maintaining sympathetic understanding and putting an ethics of care into practice requires activists and scholars to engage in ongoing reflection about the challenges, responsibilities, relationships, and processes involved in representing the lives of others.[8] The scholar must surrender the hubris of the expert and, in so far as possible, become an empathetic partner in the work of the communities and projects she or he seeks to advance while, at the same time, remaining constantly alert to the fragile character of these partnerships. Partnerships formed with and on behalf of marginalized people, cultures, or causes produce moral, ethical, and methodological tensions that require social justice scholars to, in the words of social documentarian Robert Coles, continuously "interrogate" their own "locations": the dispositions, motivations, and expectations they bring to their inquiries and activism as well as the obligations they incur to the people they advocate for and study.[9] These partnerships also require recognition that some boundaries between people may be impermeable and that good intentions do not necessarily produce good outcomes. In short, social justice scholarship and activism can be a risky business. Moreover, its overt value commitments, in contrast to the less visible, naturalized value commitments of dominant research paradigms, makes social justice scholarship a ready target of opportunity for hostile critics of the approach.[10]

Social justice studies, as presently constituted, grew out of the social movements of the 1960s. In the United States, they were extensions of social activism, especially the civil rights movement, the war on poverty, the peace movement, the women's movement(s), as well as broader movements against cultural imperialism and for human rights and global justice. Initial academic arguments for social justice studies were grounded in negation: critiques of claims to value neutrality by the social sciences and analytic philosophy that exposed the unrecognized race, gender, and class biases of established paradigms within academic disciplines and applied forms of expertise.

Social justice scholarship generally embraces the "new history," which recognizes that knowledge is socially constructed and value oriented. The new history seeks to expand the range of knowledge into areas previously neglected or underrepresented by traditional academic disciplines. That is, its mission has been to discover and recover repressed voices and ideas from the past, as well as to create and legitimate opportunities for the views of underresourced peoples and perspectives to be expressed, disseminated, and heard. Realizing this mission usually requires openness to alternative pedagogical approaches, which decenter authority, including feminist approaches and pedagogies that draw on or are inspired by Paulo Freire's *Pedagogy of the Oppressed*.[11]

The appearance of John Rawls's *A Theory of Justice* in 1971 and the many critiques and refinements it inspired served as a second impetus to the development of social justice studies. The most influential philosopher of the second half of the twentieth century, Rawls affirmed the centrality of justice studies to political philosophy, moral theory, law, and public policy. His philosophy of justice as "fairness" established that the capacity to develop a moral character is a sufficient condition to be entitled to equal justice, and, in turn, his theory provided criteria for assessing the failures of contemporary democratic institutions and nation states to achieve justice.[12]

Several international developments added further impetus to social justice scholarship and activism, including the dismantling of European colonial empires after World War II; the emergence of postcolonial art and literature and critical postcolonial studies; the failure of modernization theory, which dominated development policy in the postwar era; the proliferation of international nongovernmental organizations working for (and against) various causes, including social justice; and the emergence of a global feminist movement and its formal recognition, albeit often without requisite support, by international organizations like the United Nations and the European Union. The end of the Cold War and the subsequent global integration of the world economy, which some critics see as modernization theory reconstituted for a new century, also spawned counterglobalization activism, most notably the 1999 protest against the World Trade Organization in Seattle and Naomi Klein's *No Logo* manifesto.[13]

Less dramatically, but more consistently, social justice commitments and values have for decades guided the international work of various religious groups like the Maryknoll Lay Missionaries, who work to provide basic needs to the poor in Africa, Asia, and the Americas. These varied developments, movements, and forms of activism energized fresh forms of thinking about international social justice. Indigenous groups, movements, writers, scholars, and activists effectively rejected Eurocentric intellectual hegemony. Sen, for example, consistently draws on non-Western, especially Indian, perspectives in developing his theory of social justice; however, it must be emphasized that he does so without rejecting essential Western contributions to the development of freedom of expression. In doing so, Sen avoids the trap of identity politics and develops a cosmopolitan approach that is deeply committed to alleviating human suffering and ameliorating global injustices.

Because of the interdisciplinary character of social justice studies, its varied currents generally flow in similar directions rather than flowing together. With some exceptions, overlap is most directly apparent in footnotes, bibliographies, and anthologies. What the various currents have in common is a shared concern for identifying and ameliorating those social forces and structures that systematically undermine the life chances and human dignity of some groups or individuals while creating unfair advantages for others.

Deeper Roots of Social Justice Advocacy

Yet the roots of intellectual advocacy for social justice as well as its links to higher education actually run much deeper in North America than this account of the emergence of social justice studies since the 1960s suggests. The Society of Friends (the Quakers) and the Mennonites protested against America's "original sin" of slavery as early as 1688; however, organized efforts to rally public opinion against slavery did not emerge until the 1830s. Using the "mass" media of the day, the abolition movement established a template for social movements in America; it also served as a springboard for the women's suffrage and temperance movements.

Although it is largely forgotten today, the religious "moral awakening" that provided much of the momentum for abolition also inspired educational fervor. This educational awakening led to the founding of colleges in the newly settled states in the Midwest prior to the Civil War to advance learning and spread the gospel, and in some cases the social gospel, to African Americans, women, American Indians, and the poor.[14] Many of these colleges later abandoned their fervor for social justice but residues of these early visions can sometimes still be found in their mission statements. In the late nineteenth century, the social gospel movement—the social reformist efforts of liberal Protestant sects that sought to improve life on earth as opposed to promising the disadvantaged that they would reap their rewards in heaven—expanded its agendas to redress broader social and economic injustices. The social gospel movement also played significant roles in the development of the social sciences in America, especially sociology and historical economics.[15]

Concepts of labor justice emerged in the 1840s in France and England, contesting "wage slavery." The injustices of unequal relations between owners of capital and workers, and the distribution of income and wealth within emerging capitalist institutions, were called into question by communists, socialists, and social democrats, as well as by many religious leaders who also questioned the increasing role that materialism, money, and market relations played in people's lives. The trade union movement was a response to these concerns: seeking to reverse growing concentrations of wealth and power whether by revolution or reform.

In the late nineteenth and early twentieth centuries, muckraking journalism applied the journalistic imperative to "comfort the afflicted and afflict the comfortable"—sometimes with more ardor than accuracy. Muckrakers sensationalized the social ills that capitalism and modern urban life spawned by exposing threats to public health resulting from unsanitary food processing, exploitation of child labor, dangerous working conditions, urban corruption, and the criminal practices of the "robber barons" of the Gilded Age.

Global struggles for social justice and human rights gained public visibility internationally in the years after World War II, in struggles against colonialism and neocolonialism. These struggles are ongoing, as many of the industrial ills that plagued the United States a century ago have been exported to the developing world, where wages are very low, and unions and government regulation of workplace safety nonexistent. Issues of environmental justice, including global warming, are also, by definition, international struggles.

In all of these movements, media and communication—books, newspapers, leaflets, speeches, sermons, manifestos, slogans, and, more recently, electronic media (Internet, YouTube, Facebook, Twitter)—have played crucial roles in organizing social justice movements and rallying mass support for social change. Media exposure is an essential constituent of all successful social movements; in the United States, for example, muckraking and the progressive reaction to it resulted in antitrust legislation, workplace regulations, food safety inspections, and social welfare programs. Media coverage can also, of course, undermine as well as advance social movements.

In reaction to the successes of campaigns for social reform, corporations organized trade organizations like the National Association of Manufacturers to lobby on behalf of their interests. The public relations industry was born to manage public perceptions of corporations and to frame public issues and legislative agendas in ways that advance corporate interests. By the late twentieth century, media institutions and practices had become so central to the operations of global capitalism that debates about media control, access, policy, law, and representational powers are now primary sites of struggles for social justice.

Media Justice: A Gateway Issue

In what has been called the "New Gilded Age," escalating inequalities in income and access to basic resources—adequate nutrition, shelter, health care, basic education, and a living wage—are now at levels that have not been seen in the United States since before the Great Depression.[16] For example, a recent study shows that the United States ranks forty-second globally, behind Cuba and Malaysia, in mortality rates for children under five; as recently as 1990, the United States had ranked twenty-ninth, which was still a very poor showing for the world's largest economy.[17] The life expectancy gap between rich and poor Americans expanded in recent decades.[18] The "life chances" of children born in the poorest countries of the world have also declined dramatically in the last 30 years.[19] Yet with a few significant exceptions, mainstream and corporate media ignore the new social inequality.[20]

Social justice scholars correctly argue that we need a theory (or theories) of social justice.[21] But unless social justice theorists incorporate adequate understanding of the role that media and communication play in struggles for social justice, their theories will neither possess sufficient explanatory power to advocate successfully for the causes they seek to advance nor be able to explain the potent but often hidden forms of resistance that undermine their efforts. As former US Federal Communications Commission (FCC) commissioner Nicholas Johnson points out, regardless of what your primary area of social advocacy may be, media reform has to be your secondary issue.[22] Without a free, open, diverse, and robust media, democratic social change is virtually impossible.

In his 2007 *Communication Revolution*, Robert W. McChesney strongly affirms Johnson's claim, but he also pushes the argument for critical media scholarship and activism a step further. Drawing on his experience with the media reform group Free Press, McChesney points out that media reform can be a "gateway issue": a first issue that can draw new people into public life, citizen activism, and wider struggles for social justice. Further, he contends—and we heartily agree—that the "fates of media reform and social justice research are intertwined. They will rise or fall together."[23]

Framing Media Activism

Recent efforts to make media reform a first issue and to mobilize media activism into a viable social movement have had limited success in the United States.[24] The use of the Internet as an organizing and mobilizing tool is transforming how social movements are constituted and defined. Online organizing by groups like Free Press in the United States has, for example, been successful in mobilizing the support of millions to petition Congress and the FCC in opposition to policies that would have allowed further concentrations of media ownership. Activism on behalf of net neutrality has attracted support on a similar scale.

In *Remaking Media* (2006), Robert Hackett and William Carroll identify a number of framing devices that have been used in attempts to capture the diverse energies, priorities, issues, and commitments of media activists, including (1) free press and freedom of expression, a frame that implicitly draws on the values of the First Amendment and emphasizes the values of mainstream political liberalism; (2) media democratization, a frame that highlights democracy's deficits and emphasizes participatory democracy, the role of informed citizens, and the responsibility of the press to serve the public interest; (3) the right to communication frame, which emphasizes the importance of communication in relation to other human rights and is most often invoked by activists working in international contexts; (4) the cultural environmental frame, which borrows its trope from the environmental movement and targets toxic cultural fare by opposing the global homogenization of commercial media and market censorship and by advocating for fairness, gender equity, diversity, and democratic decision making in media ownership, employment, and representation; and, finally (5) media justice, which is relatively new and has special resonance in the United States and among minorities. According to Hackett and Carroll, "This frame re-positions the project as one of social justice in a world organized around global capitalism, racism and patriarchy, and directly connotes the need for alliances, even integration, with other social movements."[25] The justice frame is synthetic and inclusive, not only broadly encompassing the concerns of the other frames, but also very intentionally linking to and drawing on historical struggles for social justice and civil rights, including struggles for racial, class, gender, and sexual justice.[26]

In an comprehensive 2007 review of the literature on media activism, Philip Napoli points out that the multiplicity of frames reflect not only the broad range of issues that motivate participants as well as the movement's international reach but also the lack of consensus within the movement.[27] Frames matter. They create collective identities, mobilize, and focus the energies of participants in social movements. Criticism within various factions of the movement voiced dissatisfaction with early framing efforts, claiming they fostered parochialism and misunderstanding. For example, in developing countries, some international media activists view democracy as a loaded word: it can be "a Trojan Horse for capitalist imperialism," according to Aliza Dichter of the Center for International Media Action.[28] Moreover, Hackett points out that within media-policy discourse, market liberals interpret media "democratization" as deregulation and privatization of media.[29] Napoli contends that the media justice frame has developed in response to a general dissatisfaction with more established frames and that the term "justice" is deliberately chosen to link media advocacy to wider struggles for justice and social inclusion.[30]

Our emphasis on the qualifier *social* in social justice is intended to signal solidarity with primary struggles for the creation of *social institutions* that promote human equality, dignity, and fairness. That is, we see media transformation as a necessary, but far from sufficient, condition for creating a just society.

The Social Justice Frame

In embracing the social justice frame for media advocacy, we are not, collectively or individually, endorsing every cause that adopts or co-opts that banner, although we do endorse free and fair access to communicative opportunities for all, in the spirit, though not the letter, of Jürgen Habermas's valiant attempt to articulate ideal standards for democratic communications.[31] We posit no exclusive claims in framing media advocacy within a social justice frame, nor do we recognize or seek to impose any tests of ideological purity on those who may share it. Too often media reform coalitions have been fractured by internal ideological divisions. While divergent views do need to receive fair hearings, coalitions are always fragile and, by definition, sites of limited agreements: strategic goals need to be kept in sight.

Academic study of social justice and media reform are relatively recent developments. In contrast, activists have a long history of involvement in struggles for media justice in the United States. The activism of the Office of Communication of the United Church of Christ (UCC) in the 1960s is generally regarded as the benchmark for the beginning of the contemporary media reform movement.[32] Martin Luther King Jr., in a meeting with one of his Northern supporters, Everett Parker (founder of the UCC's Office of Communication), complained that television stations in the South were not covering the civil rights movement or news of the African American community more generally. In 1963, the UCC petitioned the FCC to revoke the license of WBLT in Jackson, Mississippi, for failing to serve the public interest of its audience, which was about 50 percent African American. The FCC denied the petition, claiming that only companies, not the public, could challenge a license. The UCC took the case to the US Court of Appeals, which found in its favor, establishing the precedent that allows members of the public, either groups or individuals, to petition and hold standing before the FCC and other regulatory agencies. This ruling was crucial to the future of critical media activism addressing broadcasting practices in the United States.

Robert Horwitz sees the UCC effort as a revival of the broadcast reform movement of the 1930s, in which media reformers argued that commercialization of broadcasting runs counter to the spirit and values of a democratic society, and advocated, unsuccessfully, for a nonprofit and noncommercial broadcasting infrastructure in the United States; McChesney has written the definitive history of that struggle.[33] Other scholars have located much earlier precedents for media justice activism. Dan Schiller identified efforts as early as 1894–1919 by trade unions, civic reformers, and academics directed at the development of telephone service infrastructure, calling for universal service and municipal ownership.[34] In my own work, I have uncovered resistance to the emergence of the public relations industry in the early twentieth century by such notables as John Dewey, Walter Lippmann, Upton Sinclair, and Senator Robert LaFollette Jr.[35] Organized labor's advocacy on behalf of "listeners' rights" in the post–World War II era has been chronicled by Elizabeth Fones-Wolf.[36] There are undoubtedly other initiatives that await historical recovery.

Like the UCC, other religious groups have had keen interest in media. Because many of these efforts have been paternalistic, overtly censorious, or both, historians of media reform have tended to ignore them. Secular connotations of media reform, advocacy, and justice in the United States have derived, implicitly or explicitly, from First Amendment precedents and are therefore rightly biased in favor of a free and open media. Yet, as the late George Gerbner, founder of the Cultural Environment Movement, often said, "media activism makes strange bedfellows."[37] In my view, the contributions—for better or worse—of religious groups to media advocacy warrants greater scrutiny by media historians.

One direct offshoot of the Catholic Church's twentieth-century encyclicals on social justice that requires our own acknowledgment here is the pioneering attempt of some members of the Communication Department at Loyola University in Chicago to establish a social justice emphasis or track in their curriculum: Lawrence Frey, W. Barnett Pearce, Mark Pollock, Lee Artz, and Bren Murphy have documented the challenges and pitfalls of such ventures.[38] Elsewhere, I have described in extensive detail my differences with the Loyola group's approach, which builds on speech communication rather than a sociological paradigm.[39] While our own approach emphasizes social-structural, institutional, and political economic analysis of communication, the Loyola group's original efforts and the subsequent support of social justice initiatives and publications by some of its members, especially Frey, warrant recognition for its courage and tenacity. In sum, the editors openly embrace the social justice frame for media activism, scholarship, and teaching precisely because it provides an umbrella broad enough to encompass the efforts of Parker and Frey, as well as Johnson, McChesney, Nichols, and a broadly heterodox mix of others. The merits of all such efforts must, of course, be subjected to rigorous and critical conceptual, methodological, and ethical scrutiny.

Media and Social Justice: A Rationale for Teaching and Scholarship

The mission statement of the Media and Communication Department at the editors' institution, Muhlenberg College, a small liberal arts college, embraces commitments to social justice based on the following rationale. It meets the criteria Sen establishes for social justice; that is, it is a position based on public reasoning that can be sustained reflectively when subjected to critical scrutiny by those who recognize First Amendment legal precedents and international human rights agreements.[40] We share our rationale as one among many possible rationales for this kind of work:

Social justice is a normative term.[41] Attempts to define it are almost invariably contentious: like democracy, it is an "essentially contested term."[42] That is, diverse groups may agree that social justice is desirable, but they frequently disagree about what it is and how to achieve it. The pragmatic solution to this impasse [for us] has been to define social justice plurally and contextually by taking into account the specific histories, legal traditions, social institutions, and cultural values in which claims to social justice are made.

The First Amendment to the U.S. Constitution privileges communication, freedom of speech and freedom of press, and it prohibits overt political censorship. Academic study of communication took root within this context. The first university departments dedicated to the study of communication were established in the United States. As a result, freedom of expression has been a normative value of communication scholarship since its inception.[43]

The Universal Declaration of Human Rights, ratified by the United Nations General Assembly in 1948, lent moral force to claims for a global "right to communicate." Article 19 of the Declaration states, "Everyone has the right to freedom of opinion and expression: this right includes freedom to hold opinions without interference and to seek, receive and impart information and ideas through any media regardless of frontiers." This expansion created the foundations for human rights scholarship, activism, policies, and the development of international laws. It also helped foster a renewal of interest of justice studies, and generated new inquiries into the nature of deliberative democracy and communicative ethics.

The study of media and communication within a liberal arts context requires recognition of these developments and engagement with the intellectual contributions and controversies they inspire. Because communication and information are fundamental sources of power, the right to communicate is increasingly recognized as the fundamental human right upon which other rights depend.[44] It includes rights to participate in public communication (the right to voice), rights to fair representation in and by media, and rights of access to media and media-making technologies.[45]

What this means from a practical curricular perspective is that the study of media and communication from a social justice perspective requires critical scrutiny of media and communication industries, institutions, policies, processes and representational practices. A social justice approach models ethical practices in media making by embracing pedagogies that respect both the human dignity and the communication rights of others. That is, it seeks to equip students with the conceptual tools necessary to monitor how effectively contemporary media industries and public communication practices are facilitating the right to communicate, and it encourages them to engage in communication practices and media making in ways that realize and expand this right.[46]

These values were modeled for us by the life of our late, revered colleague, James D. Schneider (1939–2005), to whom this book is dedicated.

Comforting the Afflicted and Afflicting the Comfortable

Contributors to this volume examine struggles for media justice from a critical perspective. All the authors have been involved in movements for social justice as citizens, scholars, teachers, activists, or as media makers, and many of them are acknowledged leaders in the field.

As we have seen, media activism is a heterogeneous enterprise with diverse politics, agendas, and strategies. The same can be said of the contributions to this volume. For that reason, readers, including the editors of this volume, will not agree with every claim put forth in the following chapters, nor should they if they endorse the premise put forth in the next chapter: that progress toward global justice requires thoughtfulness, reflexivity, and ongoing criticism. Despite their heterogeneity, these chapters have in common an intentional positioning within a social movement frame that insists on a link between media justice and social justice: the strong conviction that you cannot have one without the other.

The first section examines *Frameworks* for transforming media to create conditions that have the potential to advance democratic participation and promote social justice.

Cees Hamelink's "Global Justice and Global Media: The Long Way Ahead" sees the adoption of the Universal Declaration of Human Rights by the international community after World War II as a crucial moment in the human struggle for just social arrangements. He examines the role of global media in the subsequent efforts to realize human rights aspirations and finds that media, as currently configured, are more of an obstacle than an asset, explaining in some detail why news media are ill-equipped to cover human rights. While Hamelink acknowledges that valuable proposals for transforming the media have been put forward by activist scholars, he maintains that they have not yet led to significant changes in the global mediascape. Nevertheless, he cautions against despair, seeing the struggle for human rights as a very long one: a struggle for the development of reflexivity over thoughtlessness. In Hamelink's view, the pursuit of global justice is a long evolutionary process, which will include many setbacks as we slowly make our way through the fog to a destination that is not yet clear.

The conversation with DeeDee Halleck, "Video Activism as a Way of Life," reflects on Halleck's more than five decades of activism around media and social justice issues. Filmmaker, educator, and activist, Halleck has been relentless in her commitment to exploring the possibilities of new media as tools for democratic community action and expression—from community radio to public access television to digital satellite broadcasting. An early advocate for alternative community media, Halleck is at the heart of many major grassroots media initiatives. She is cofounder of Deep Dish TV—recognized as the first national, grassroots satellite network—and the founder of *Paper Tiger Television*, a public access cable series and volunteer video collective. Halleck's work has inspired video artists and media activists around the world. Her reflections on the successes of media and social justice movements in the past provide critical insights for understanding the potential of mobilizing new media tools for ongoing and emerging social justice struggles in both localized and globalized contexts.

In "Media and Democracy: Some Missing Links," Nick Couldry looks at youth and public engagement through the lens of storytelling and its limits. The unequal distribution of media resources generates profound injustices, inflicting "hidden injuries" to self-esteem and self-recognition. Without the ability to share with others accounts of what we feel, remember, think, and propose, democracy itself is rendered anemic. Among other consequences, he contends, the lack of effective access to mediated forms of self-expression opens up a gap between engagement and recognition: talk about public issues is rarely linked to action or even to its promise. Couldry argues that we need broader and more sensitive ways of evaluating whether participatory media projects effectively redress the injustices they identify. He maintains that youth media initiatives, which provide access to symbolic resources, are laudable efforts, but they are not enough. For all the potential of new media and digital tools of media production, distribution, and social networking, what is at stake, in the end, is democracy—effective democracy. Couldry maintains that using media tools to change young people's opportunities to be recognized and heard will only succeed on a wider scale if government and other formal authorities act as if young people and young people's accounts of their lives matter.

Jessica Clark and Patricia Aufderheide's "A New Vision for Public Media: Open, Dynamic, and Participatory" acknowledges that public broadcasting, newspapers, magazines, and network newscasts have played a central role in US democracy, informing citizens and guiding public conversation. However, they point out that the top-down disseminating technologies that supported these media are being supplanted by an open, many-to-many networked media environment. They ask, what platforms, standards, and practices will replace or transform legacy public media? They examine in some depth the answers that are already emerging out of a series of media experiments taking place across legacy and citizen media. After taking a hard look at the "first two minutes" of Web 2.0 experimentation, Clark and Aufderheide conclude that the crucial initial step is to embrace the participatory: that is, the feature that has been most disruptive of current media models. Multiplatform, open, and digital public media will be an essential feature of truly democratic public life as we move forward. They will be media both for and by the public. But, Clark and Afterheide conclude, this will not happen by accident or for free. If we are going to have media for vibrant democratic culture, we have to plan for it, try it out, show people that it matters, and build new constituencies to invest in it.

The second section of this volume, *Collaborations*, explores the potential as well as the challenges involved in creating community partnerships in struggles for media and social justice.

In their chapter, "Sustaining Collaboration: Lessons from the Media Research and Action Project," Charlotte Ryan and William Gamson reflect on their long-running collaboration with social justice activists at the Media Research and Action Project (MRAP) at Boston College. Since the mid-1980s, MRAP has served as a space for collaboration between social movement scholars and policy advocates to the mutual enrichment of both activism and scholarship. Still, MRAP has faced a number of challenges, which Ryan and Gamson explore in the form of a conversation about the project's two constituencies. Aspects of academic culture push fast-track research achievable in a summer, they observe, and thereby minimize relation building. Activists may be alienated by the "secret language" of scholarly jargon and feel pressure to claim early and exaggerated victories rather than share mixed or disappointing outcomes. In addition, chronic funding shortfalls and the labor involved in seeking funds to mixed results can prove demoralizing. Community-university partnerships, in short, usually involve three- or four-way negotiations among community-based organizations, universities, funders, and, sometimes, government agencies. Despite shared goals, each social location has competing agendas, constituencies, timetables, standards, budgets, and space limitations. These factors complicate collaboration. Ryan and Gamson offer lessons from the MRAP experience and highlight the many rewards of joint work for all involved.

Nina Gregg's contribution, "Media Is Not the Issue—Justice Is the Issue," provides a close analysis of several community-based efforts to address media justice in central Appalachia, with a focus on projects supported by the Appalachian Community Fund (ACF), a social justice foundation. ACF, along with a partner organization, convened a Southeast Media Justice Conference in February 2007. The conference was designed as an opportunity for social justice organizations in the Southeast and Appalachia to explore issues of media control, to expand their understanding of media justice, and to share with each other examples of the work already happening in the region. ACF subsequently awarded competitive media justice grants to four community organizations in 2007 and to five community organizations in 2008. Examining several media justice projects, the chapter explores what media justice means to activists in rural Appalachian communities and how they are organizing to challenge media control, develop alternative media institutions and channels, and increase the voices of marginalized communities through analysis, strategy, and skills. Rural media justice organizing offers a perspective on media and social justice that differs significantly from the familiar focus on concentration of media owner-ship and federal communication policy.

In their chapter, "Detours through Youth-Driven Media: Backseat Drivers Bear Witness to the Ethical Dilemmas of Youth Media," Lora Taub-Pervizpour and Eirinn Disbrow examine the assumptions of media scholars, community media educators, and media activists who understand youth media as a vital space of media resistance. Media made by young people is a realm of media practice where it is possible for youth to intentionally adopt positions as media producers. In these acts, young people are seen to confront the deep, proliferat-ing, and pernicious ways in which corporate mass-mediated culture constructs and exploits young people as consumers. In assuming the stance of media maker, it is widely believed that young people acquire agency and engage in acts of resistance. While the authors position their work in solidarity with media researchers whose scholarly activity attempts to fortify youth media-making programs, they also examine the social, cultural, and political-economic forces that shape and constrain the possibilities of young people's media production. Taub-Pervizpour and Disbrow draw on long-term research conducted within a youth media program involving low-income, urban minority teens to suggest the need to scrutinize the particular ways in which marginalized youth and adult media educators collaborate in cultural production, including attending to the relationships and contexts in which young people conceptualize, research, and make media. They remind readers that new digital media technologies are not inherently democratic and argue that merely placing them in the hands of young people, marginalized by class, race, language, or gender, is not intrinsi-cally oppositional.

Mari Castañeda's contribution, "¡Adelante!: Promoting Social Justice through Latina/o Community Media," examines the ways that Latina/o community media promote social justice not only in Latino communities but also within the broader landscape of US civil society. Her chapter analyzes broadcast and print media examples from across the country and the US-Mexican border that demonstrate the important role of such Latina/o community media in creating social change through media justice. Latina/o media in the United States have a long tradition of emphasizing community needs and social justice in their cov-erage of education, politics, culture, and economics. Community media have consistently committed their access to newsprint and the airwaves, observes Castañeda, to addressing pressing issues that affect Latino populations in direct and indirect ways. The rising backlash against Latino immigrants, the shifting US demographics, and the inequities that Latinos continue to experience are issues that make the coverage by Latina/o community media even more critical, especially since they make visible communities that are voiceless and denigrated in mainstream English-language media.

The third section, *Power Struggles*, examines specific efforts to push back against structures of dominances within media and cultural institutions by using media, media critique, or both to challenge attempts to silence or marginalize alternative voices and practices.

In her chapter, "Feminism and Social Justice: Challenging the Media Rhetoric," Margaret Gallagher unpacks the paradoxes of the progress of feminism. Acknowledging that the international women's movement has made significant progress since 1970 as is evident by the fivefold increase in the number of women serving as heads of government in the twenty-first century, Gallagher nevertheless points out that no country has yet achieved gender equality. In fact, gender gaps in health, economic, and political participation have actually expanded in 43 countries since 2008; however, mainstream media narratives routinely suggest that the women's movement has achieved its objectives and is no longer relevant. In many of these narratives, there is an explicitly negative critique of feminism as a social movement. Gallagher maintains that challenges to the feminist movement have become increasingly sophisticated and resistant to criticism, as feminism has become part of the cultural vocabulary that media narratives draw on. With few exceptions, the feminist discourse that mainstream media invokes is conservative; emphasizing individualism and consumerism, it fits perfectly within the grammar of neoliberalism. Incorporation of feminist ideas into media discourses that serve to deny the politics of feminism as a social movement makes the pursuit of social justice for women especially challenging today. Gallagher examines how this discourse works in specific contexts, including advertising, policy, access to information and communication technologies, and media reform. She identifies new strategies that are necessary to open up spaces for women's agency in the new media environment, arguing that what is actually needed today is wide-scale social transformation of media in which women's rights and women's "right to communication" are respected and implemented.

Brian Martin's contribution, "Defending Dissent," identifies some enduring struggles involving defamation laws as well as the new opportunities that the Internet has opened up for resisting attempts to suppress dissent. Media organizations constantly face threats of lawsuits, which lead them to avoid stories that may make them vulnerable to legal action. Individuals, especially individuals who express controversial views that challenge powerful people or organizations, may also face legal threats or action, which have the effect of inhibiting free speech. As president of Whistleblowers Australia, Martin created a website, "Suppression of Dissent," where whistleblowers and others could tell their stories and post supporting documents. He shows how the Internet can be used to evade defamation threats by ensuring that the material is widely circulated, so that legal action—rather than hiding the material—actually makes it more widely known. In essence, he argues, the Internet can serve as a "defamation haven," analogous to tax havens. He describes the forms of resistance that are most effective in evading suppression and defending dissent. This experience also led to his research on how to make censorship backfire so that it would damage censors instead of their intended targets. Martin sees the Internet as a new arena for resisting suppressions of free speech, but one with quite a different topography than the traditional venues. He argues that the ground is tilting toward free speech, but that it is important to know how to take advantage of the opportunities.

In his chapter, "Software Freedom as Social Justice: The Open Source Software Movement and Information Control," John L. Sullivan maintains that free, open source software (FOSS) advocacy can be increasingly characterized as a broader movement for social justice. He tracks the emergence and development of FOSS efforts such as the GNU/Linux operating system and the GNU Public License (GPL), noting that advocacy of open source software has expanded beyond the relatively small community of software programmers to encompass a larger group of nonexpert users and related organizations. Sullivan shows that the interests of FOSS advocates have begun to merge and overlap with the interests of the free culture-digital commons advocates in the past half-decade, with increasing cross-fertilization across these two groups. These issues more closely align the current aims of FOSS with other digital rights initiatives, suggesting the emergence of a larger umbrella movement for cultural and software freedom on the horizon that advances social justice efforts.

In "Watching Back: Surveillance as Activism," Mark Andrejevic explores the appropriation of monitoring technologies by social activists who turn the surveillance cameras back on the authorities as a means of holding them accountable to public scrutiny and the legal system. He focuses on the work of I-Witness and the Glass Bead Collective, both based in New York City. The two groups assemble amateur and professional videographers to monitor public rallies, marches, and other politically oriented demonstrations in order to document abuses by law enforcement agencies. They have had success in getting charges dropped against activists and others who were arrested and charged on false pretenses, but they have also been targeted by the authorities, most notably during the 2008 Republican National Convention in St. Paul, Minnesota. Andrejevic explores both the democratic political potential of techniques of reflexive surveillance—activists filming themselves in order to document police abuse—as well as the potential drawbacks of the approach.

The last section, *Media Justice*, examines struggles for justice in media policy, foundation funding of research, and media reform efforts themselves using historical analysis as well as ethnographic and experiential knowledge of activists doing media democracy work and monitoring media censorship.

Christina Dunbar-Hester's chapter, "Drawing and Effacing Boundaries in Contemporary Media Democracy Work," profiles a movement that emerged in the wake of the Telecommunications Act of 1996 and that seeks to change the media system in the United States. The movement developed in light of such factors as a regulatory environment favoring national broadcasting networks and corporate media consolidation, embedded practices of community media production and pirate radio, Indymedia and the transnational "antiglobalization" movement, and the emergence of "new media" including the Internet. Dunbar-Hester maintains that due to the heterogeneity of participants in the movement and the way in which it overlays other, related social justice agendas, the media democracy movement represents a diverse, even chaotic field of activism. She identifies key sites of intervention, including radical activist, reform, and academic agendas based on ethnographic research on low-power radio activists and the groups with whom they interact. The chapter also examines the difficulties involved when diverse groups, who nominally share the same goals of democratic social change through critique, seek to collaborate.

In his chapter, "From Psychological Warfare to Social Justice: Shifts in Foundation Support for Communication Research," Jefferson Pooley compares and contrasts the Ford Foundation's recent foray into media research and policy reform with earlier interventions by American foundations. As with the previous initiatives of the Ford and Rockefeller Foundations, Ford's recent efforts have been linked to its wider public policy goals. The difference is that Ford's objectives, for the first time, largely align with those of social justice activists. In other words, Ford's $20 million outlay from 1998 to the present has supported—rather than thwarted—media and social justice campaigns. Pooley traces this remarkable shift by comparing earlier foundation interventions (Rockefeller funding in the 1930s and Ford's programs in the 1950s) with Ford's collaborative grantmaking to media academics, activists, and policy researchers over the last decade. He argues that Ford's recent activities challenge overly rigid assumptions made by the large critical literature on foundations, social science, and the status quo.

Mickey Huff and Peter Phillips's chapter, "Media Democracy in Action: Truth Emergency and the Progressive Media Reform Movement," critiques the tendency of mainstream media to marginalize, through ridicule or inattention, major stories and story angles that fall outside a narrow range of acceptable media discourse. They discuss the process by which some stories and interpretations earn respectful treatment from corporate media, while others do not, by drawing on over a decade of experience at Project Censored, which labors each year to publicize the stories that the mainstream press ignored. Examples from Project Censored's book series, along with reflections on the project's evolution, inform Phillips and Huff's argument that activists and scholars need to creatively redefine what journalists establish as legitimate news. They conclude that mainstream media is contributing to "a truth emergency," which undermines the viability of democracy.

Notes

1. "Symbolically annihilate" appears in George Gerbner, "Violence in Television Drama: Trends and Symbolic Functions," in *Media Content and Controls*, ed. George Comstock and Eli A. Rubenstein, vol. 1, *Television and Social Behavior* (Washington, DC: US Government Printing Office, 1972), 44.
2. Sean MacBride, *Many Voices, One World: Report by the International Commission for the Study of Communication Problems* (Paris: UNESCO, 1980).
3. "The right to communicate" movement has been active since 1974, when UNESCO launched its formal work in this area. UNESCO has no means of enforcing this right, but several international organizations have passed nonbinding resolutions that have established a "common understanding of the rights to communicate," which often includes a course of action. For a summary of these resolutions, see the Right to Communicate Group, "The Right to Communicate," http://www.right tocommunicate.org. See also Cees Hamelink, this volume; Hamelink has been one of the leaders of this initiative.
4. Sen's effort both builds on and departs from John Rawls's theory of justice. Sen's approach could be accurately described as a theory of social justice because his approach is nontranscendental and comparative, focusing on how people actually behave, rather than justice as an abstract ideal, with a primary focus on meeting basic human needs and human rights: hunger, medical neglect, poverty, torture, injustices based on race and gender exclusions, and so on. Sen's approach seeks more justice than currently exists rather than perfect justice. Despite only brief attention to media and media freedom, Sen's approach incorporates many communication-related ideas and assumptions, including communication competence ("capability"), criteria for public reasoning (which overtly recognizes some kinship with Habermas's work), and more, all of which warrant unpacking—so much so that I dare to read it as a communication theory as well as an approach to justice. Amartya Sen, The Idea of Justice (Cambridge, MA: The Belknap Press of Harvard University Press, 2009), 336–37.
5. Max Weber, *From Max Weber*, ed. H. H. Gerth and C. Wright Mills (New York: Oxford University Press, 1946). Weber's contemporaries, Wilhelm Dilthey and Georg Simmel, pushed the concept of sympathetic understanding even further than Weber; still, Weber is cited here because his concept has much broader currency in contemporary social science discourse.
6. Carol Gilligan, *In a Different Voice* (Cambridge, MA: Harvard University Press, 1982).
7. After the March on Montgomery in 1966, King, who was deeply impressed by the diversity of the marchers, described their solidarity: "As I stood with them and saw white and Negro, nuns and priests, ministers and rabbis, labor organizers, lawyers, doctors, housemaids and shopworkers brimming with vitality and enjoying a comradeship, I knew I was seeing a microcosm of the mankind of the future

in this luminous and genuine brotherhood." Martin Luther King Jr., *Where Do We Go from Here: Chaos or Community?* (New York: Harper and Row, 1966), 9, quoted in Kenneth L. Smith and Ira G. Zepp Jr., "Martin Luther King's Vision of the Beloved Community," *Christian Century*, April 3, 1974, 361–63, http://www.religion-online.org/showarticle.asp?title=1603.

8. Elizabeth Barret offers a profound exploration of the moral dilemmas involved in representing the lives of others in her film, *Stranger with a Camera*, a film produced by Appalshop and KET Public Television, 2000.

9. Robert Coles, *Doing Documentary Work* (New York: Oxford University Press, 1997).

10. At the most basic level, value commitments violate the normative ideal of objectivity. Add advocacy for social justice, and controversy is, and perhaps should be, inevitable. See Ronald L. Cohen's introduction to *Justice: Views from the Social Sciences* (New York: Plenum Press, 1986), 1–10, for a brief but informative discussion of social justice as a contested concept.

11. Paulo Freire, *Pedagogy of the Oppressed* (New York: Herder and Herder, 1970).

12. John Rawls, *A Theory of Justice* (Cambridge, MA: Harvard University Press, 1971). It is impossible to identify all the activists and scholars associated with social justice studies, but in addition to Rawls and Sen, some prominent contributors are Bruce Ackerman, Brian Barry, Seyla Benhabib, Joe Feagin, Andrew Kuper, Martha Nussbaum, Thomas Nagel, Thomas Pogge, and Thomas Scanlon.

13. Naomi Klein, *No Logo: Taking Aim At the Brand Bullies* (New York: Picador, 2000).

14. For an eloquent, thought-provoking discussion of this educational movement, see Marilynne Robinson, "A Great Amnesia," *Harper's*, May 2008, 17–21. While many Protestant denominations were involved in this movement, of special interest from a social justice perspective were the liberal Protestant sects who sought to improve life on earth as opposed to promising the poor that they will reap their rewards in the next life. They preached a social gospel that supported settlement houses for immigrants, social services, and good works.

15. Sociology, for example, was largely conceived in the United States as a form of applied Christianity; in the view of the social gospelers, theology attended to the first commandment while sociology addressed the second, focusing on labor injustices and the other pathologies of industrialization and urbanization. Similarly, historical economics was posited as counter to classical economics and laissez-faire and exposed the inequitable distribution of surplus value produced by labor. To our ears, this may sound like vintage Marxism, but it was largely a homegrown response to the rapid development and national expansion of capitalism in the post–Civil War era. See Charles Howard Hopkins, *The Rise of the Social Gospel in American Protestantism, 1865–1915* (New Haven, CT: Yale University Press, 1940); and Dorothy Ross, *The Origins of American Social Science* (New York: Cambridge University Press, 1991).

16. For an exhaustive statistical analysis of escalating social inequality in the United States, see Larry M. Bartels, *Unequal Democracy: The Political Economy of the New Gilded Age* (New York: Russell Sage Foundation and Princeton University Press, 2008). See also Joe E. Feagin, "Social Justice and Sociology: Agendas for

the Twenty-First Century: Presidential Address," *American Sociological Review* 66, no. 1 (2001): 1–20.

17. J. T. Rajaratnam et al., "Neonatal, Postneonatal, Childhood, and Under-5 Mortality for 187 Countries, 1970–2010: A Systematic Analysis of Progress Towards Millennium Development Goal 4," *Lancet* 375, no. 9730 (2010): 1988–2008.

18. In 1980, the gap was 2.8 years; by 2008, the gap had increased to 4.5 years. Robert Pear, "Gap in Life Expectancy Widens for the Nation," *The New York Times*, March 23, 2008, http://www.nytimes.com/2008/03/23/us/23health.html#.

19. The concept of "life chances," originally coined by Weber, is used by Brian Barry to illustrate the way that deliberate policy choices—what he calls "the machinery of social injustice"—made by rich countries and international institutions like the International Monetary Fund can have devastating effects on the life chances of people in poor countries. See Barry, *Why Social Justice Matters* (Cambridge: Polity, 2005); and Feagin, "Social Justice and Sociology."

20. A notable exception is the *New York Times*'s Nicholas Kristof, who apparently has carte blanche to cover stories of his own choice and focuses primarily on social justice issues. See *Reporter*, directed by Eric Daniel Metzgar (HBO Documentary Films, 2008).

21. Barry, *Why Social Justice Matters*.

22. Nicholas Johnson, quoted in Robert W. McChesney, *Communication Revolution: Critical Junctures and the Future of Media* (New York: New Press, 2007), 149.

23. McChesney, *Communication Revolution*, 158, 220. McChesney's entire book presents a compelling argument for the interdependence of critical media scholarship, media reform, and social justice.

24. The media reform movement has had greater success in some other nations, such as Canada. See Robert A. Hackett and William Carroll, *Remaking Media: The Struggle to Democratize Public Communication* (New York: Routledge, 2006).

25. Hackett and Carroll, *Remaking Media*, 79.

26. Ibid.

27. Philip M. Napoli, "Public Interest Media Activism and Advocacy as a Social Movement: A Review of the Literature," McGannon Center Working Paper Series, Fordham University, 2007, http://fordham.bepress.com/mcgannon_working_papers/21.

28. Aliza Dichter, quoted in Hackett and Carroll, *Remaking Media*, 79.

29. Robert A. Hackett, "Taking Back the Media: Notes on the Potential for a Communicative Democracy Movement," *Studies in Political Economy* 63 (2000): 61–86, cited in Napoli, "Public Interest Media Activism."

30. Napoli, "Public Interest Media Activism."

31. That is, we salute Habermas's quest but recognize the limits of its idealism in a mediatized world.

32. Robert B. Horwitz, "Broadcast Reform Revisited: Reverend Everett C. Parker and the 'Standing Case' (*Office of Communication of the United Church of Christ v. the Federal Communication Commission*)," *The Communication Review* 2, no. 3 (1997): 311–48.

33. Horwitz, "Broadcast Reform Revisited"; and Robert W. McChesney, *Telecommunications, Mass Media, and Democracy: The Battle for the Control of U.S. Broadcasting, 1928–1935* (New York: Oxford University Press, 1993).

34. Dan Schiller, "Social Movement in Telecommunications: Rethinking the Public Service History of U.S. Telecommunications, 1804–1919," in *Communication, Citizenship, and Social Policy*, ed. Andrew Calabrese and Jean-Claude Burgelman (Lanham, MD: Rowman and Littlefield, 1999), 137–55.

35. Sue Curry Jansen, "International Public Relations: Neo-liberal Fixer and Diplomat without Portfolio," in *Propaganda and Public Persuasion in Liberal Democracies: Political Economy and Culture*, ed. Gerald Sussman (New York: Peter Lang, forthcoming).

36. Elizabeth Fones-Wolf, *Waves of Opposition: Labor and the Struggle for Democratic Radio* (Urbana: University of Illinois Press, 2006).

37. George Gerbner, communication with the author.

38. Lawrence R. Frey et al., "Looking for Justice in all the Wrong Places: On a Communication Approach to Social Justice," *Communication Studies* 47, nos. 1–2 (1996): 110–27; and Mark A. Pollock et al., "Navigating between Scylla and Charybdis: Continuing the Dialogue on Communication and Social Justice," *Communication Studies* 47, nos. 1–2 (1996): 142–51. Frey coedited, with Kevin Carragee, two large volumes of reports of social justice studies undertaken by speech communication scholars and activists: *Communication for Social Change*, vol. 1, *Communication Activism* (Cresskill, NJ: Hampton Press, 2007); and *Media and Performative Activism*, vol. 2, *Communication Activism* (Cresskill, NJ: Hampton Press, 2007).

39. Sue Curry Jansen, "Rethinking Social Justice Scholarship in Media and Communication," *Communication, Culture and Critique* 1, no. 3 (2008): 329–34. The review also included a third collection, also written from a speech communication (rhetorical) perspective, Omar Swartz, ed., *Social Justice and Communication Scholarship* (Mahwah, NJ: Lawrence Erlbaum, 2006).

40. Within Sen's comparative approach, the "impartial stranger"—one who has no vested interest in the outcome of a particular problem—is posited as a mediator. She or he (perhaps most often, they) is not posited to be completely objective nor a transcendent judicious ideal but rather more-or-less the best we fallible humans can hope for in the kind of social worlds we actually inhabit. He borrows the concept from Adam Smith and points out that, unlike contemporary market fundamentalists who claim Smith's legacy, Smith never argued that the market could deliver justice. To the contrary, Smith believed that market theory needed to be accompanied by moral theory. Sen, *The Idea of Justice*, 125.

41. Science itself, it should be noted, is also a normative practice, with established procedures for assessing appropriate observational practices, forms of measurement, standards for assessing validity and statistical significance, and so on. Recent human rights scholarship has articulated public norms for assessing the objectivity of social justice claims within a comparative framework, including the ability of such claims to survive critical scrutiny by "impartial spectators" and the capacity to meet tests of public reasoning. See Sen, *The Idea of Justice*.

42. W. B. Gallie, "Essentially Contested Concepts," *Proceedings of the Aristotelian Society* 56 (1956): 167–98.

43. This does not mean, of course, that all communication scholars have lived up to the demands of these norms. To the contrary, we know that some of the founders of the field paid lip service to them in public even as they were deeply involved in

secret Cold War–era government-sponsored research on techniques to advance the effectiveness of propaganda and psychological warfare. See Christopher Simpson, *Science of Coercion: Communication Research and Psychological Warfare, 1945–1960* (New York: Oxford University Press, 1994). See also Jefferson Pooley, "The New History of Mass Communication Research," in *The History of Media and Communication Research: Contested Memories*, ed. David W. Park and Jefferson Pooley (New York: Peter Lang, 2008), 43–69.

44. Sen, *The Idea of Justice*; see also Ronald Dworkin, *Is Democracy Possible Here? Principles for a New Political Debate* (Princeton, NJ: Princeton University Press, 2006).

45. See the Center for Communication Rights, http://www.centerforcommunication rights.org.

46. We believe that our rationale meets Stanley Fish's well-known objections to social activism in academe on two grounds. First, liberal arts colleges, especially private colleges, with social justice or religious histories are, by definition, value-oriented; Fish specifically excuses them from his indictment. Second, even Fish presumably does not object to scholarship based on the First Amendment or the Universal Declaration of Human Rights in the classroom, especially when it is secured, as Sen requires, by public reasoning. See Stanley Fish, *Save the World on Your Own Time* (New York: Oxford University Press, 2008).

PART I

Frameworks

CHAPTER 1

Global Justice and Global Media
The Long Way Ahead

Cees J. Hamelink

The aspiration toward just social arrangements has kept thinkers and activists busy for much of recorded human history. At the beginning of the twenty-first century, we must conclude that all our philosophical and political deliberations have not delivered a just global system.

Yet after the Second World War, the international community made a serious attempt to break through this unsatisfactory state of humanity: through the adoption of the Universal Declaration of Human Rights, it solemnly pledged that the twentieth century's unprecedented barbarism would never happen again. This did constitute a crucial moment in contemporary history since the Declaration embodied fundamental principles of morality that from 1948 onward would guide the "human family" in its treatment of all the members of the human race.

The most essential notion in the Declaration was "everyone": nobody was to be excluded from the rights and freedoms in the Declaration. In its (often forgotten) Article 28, the Declaration provided for the right of everyone to a "social and international order in which the rights and freedoms set forth in this Declaration can be fully realized." In these words, the drafters of the Declaration gave the world a sense of what global social justice could mean: a global society in which all people would matter and enjoy protection of their dignity, equality, freedom, and security. Global social justice could now be defined as a global human rights culture: a world where no one would be humiliated, discriminated, disempowered, or unwillingly harmed. If we take this vision as point of departure, the key questions for an essay on media and social justice become the following: Can (global) media contribute to the realization of the entitlement Article 28 proposes? Can media assist humanity in learning the values that underpin a human rights culture, cooperation, compassion, communality and nonviolence?

Consulting the literature on media studies that has developed over past decades, the tentative answer to this question is not very encouraging. Most certainly one can conclude that the contribution of media to human rights awareness and human rights activism has been wanting. If one takes a fundamental human rights value such as human cooperation, it is striking that modern mediascapes are significantly characterized by forms of human competitive strife. In general, competition between human beings is seen to make better news than cooperation. Through polemical debates and myriad forms of contest (from beauty pageants to science quizzes), there is an almost permanent exposure to competitive behavior, which suggests that human life is about winning more than anything else.

Another human rights value is inclusiveness: "all people matter." This standard does not fare very well when media aggravate human divisions and amplify *us* versus *them* constructions. Worldwide, media gave a global podium to Samuel Huntington's *Clash of Civilizations* as a convenient construction that made numerous people believe that the world can be divided into "our" and "their" civilization and that the two are at war.[1] Although the thesis was never taken very seriously by scholars in matters of international and intercultural relations, it was generously incorporated into media news discourses after 9/11. Illustrations can be found in influential media such as *The New York Times*, *The Wall Street Journal*, *Newsweek*, and the major television networks. For many media organizations around the world, the thesis became the key guide to reporting and interpreting the 9/11 events. The Huntington thesis was also frequently used in Norwegian and Danish newspapers in connection with the controversy around the Mohammed cartoons. The thesis reflects strongly *us* versus *them* thinking and suggests that *them* are dangerous to *us*.

Human rights and media have not been able to come to a happy marriage. In terms of news reporting, for example, most media are, by and large, ill-equipped to adequately deal with human rights violations. The prevailing style of news reporting emphasizes the sensational and focuses on the sound bite. Evidently, the standard news values that affect news reporting in general also shape human rights reporting. Human rights reporting typically needs background, context, and in-depth analysis. Because most news reporting favors the incidental event, many chronic human rights violations go unreported. Occasionally, violations occur as a sensational event that suits the timing needs of the media, but more often human rights violations involve long-term structural processes. The media's emphasis on event rather than process tends to hamper a sufficient understanding of what specific violations are really about. As a result, events caused by basic human rights violations (such as in the case of massive poverty) are often presented as "natural" disasters.

There is the additional problem that the victims of human rights violations are often the forgotten social actors because they do not belong to the world's newsmaking elites. Moreover, as with all other events, media select in biased ways what is newsworthy and what is not. As a result, not all human rights violations are considered equally newsworthy. It should also be realized that serious reporting of human rights violations is hampered in many countries by forms of state censorship, intimidation from fighting factions, and real dangers for journalists.

Another consideration concerns the fact that in most media, the area of human rights is not recognized as a special field of reporting. Few, if any, media have a human rights beat. To this should be added the observation that media themselves may, in their performance, undermine human rights provisions, such as the right to the protection of privacy, or the right of the presumption of innocence. Most seriously, there is the very real possibility that media are party to the public incitement to genocide (like in the Rwandan civil war in the 1990s), and thus become perpetrators of crimes against humanity.

For those of us who have been actively engaged in developing alternative news networks, in setting up people's communication movements, or in pleading for people's right to communicate, the perplexing challenge remains: How to realize media structures and contents that mobilize people to resist global injustice? How to overcome the prevailing (near perfect) match between mainstream channels of information and entertainment and the "Disneyfication" of sociopolitical and cultural life?

Unfortunately, such questions have not been a top priority for the global media and communication research community, as assembled in such organizations as the International Association for Media and Communication Research (IAMCR) and the International Communication Association (ICA). Most of its members are kept occupied by their universities producing peer-reviewed research that will not rock the boat of the epistemological conservatism of those who hand out funds and tenure tracks.

Even so, some academics have refused to be discouraged and have given us insightful critical analyses about the structural shortcomings of the dominant information and entertainment channels in modern societies. Their findings provide strong support for the claim that media need reform. And indeed, the call for a global human rights culture does suggest that societies need alternative structures of media ownership, new conceptions of professionalism, more accessible media, broad participation in the creation of media content, and stronger forms of protection against political and commercial censorship. By and large, however, such valuable proposals have not led to significant changes in the global mediascape.

Other academics have proposed that the fundamental obstacle to radical media reform is not only the supply side but particularly the demand side. Their contention is that since societies receive the media they deserve, prevailing formats of information and entertainment production could only change if their audiences demanded a difference. This school of thought offers proposals for media education in schools, for the participation of children in media production, and for social movements of critical media consumers such as the People's Communication Charter.[2] The realization of such laudable projects has not so far had a deep global impact.

These depressing observations are countered by those academics who expect that the so-called new media will bring about the desired reforms in both media production and media consumption. The advent of new technologies does indeed bring expanded capacities for mobilization and participation as they liberate us from the oligopolistic control by barons of culture—the industrial moguls that gatekeep information and entertainment. There is, however, no guarantee that an expanded and differentiated number of media producers will actively promote the core human rights values. The notion of "new" suggests advances not only in technologies but also in human behavior. This reflects a crude technological determinism that is not supported by human realities. It also has to be asked how far the "new" has really overtaken the "conventional." It could be argued that the conventional, mainstream media continue today to be the grand players in global communication

Is all of the above reason for despair?

We learned from Darwinian biology that processes of evolution in which species seek more adequate mechanisms to adapt to their environment may take millions of years. As Charles Darwin suggested, his discoveries in human biology promised new insights in human psychology. One of these insights is that human culture, as the nongenetic adaptation to the environment, evolves its strength and diversity over long stretches of time.

Certain thought patterns and behavioral constructs that evolved among our savanna ancestors and that have served human survival and reproduction well may become dysfunctional in other environments, but they may not easily disappear! An example that is instructive for aspirations toward a global human rights culture is the "tribal instinct" that was essential to survival in the Stone Age but that today obstructs global respect for human rights. Tribalism is a powerful force that has shown its devastating potential in recent times in the former Yugoslavia, the Russian Federation, and Rwanda. The "tribal instinct" represents the strong belief that the members of our own clan (which could be our family, our ethnic group, or our national state) deserve the protection of basic rights and freedoms but that these entitlements cannot be equally extended to include the "outsiders."

Tribalism is only one illustration of how our Stone Age minds and our technological potential do not keep the same pace. Modern technology develops exponentially at a speed that the human mind can only follow if it transcends its biological limitations.[3] This means that we have arrived at an essential cultural crossroad where we need to decide to either slow down technological development (but can we?) or upgrade our mental faculties through artificial intelligence (but do we want to?).

There is a story about Australian aboriginals that tells us that whenever they cover great walking distances, they stop before reaching the destination so their souls can catch up with their bodies! Could this be a way to deal with our predicament?

We have developed media of communication that span the globe, offer instant global exposure to local events, and provide unprecedented possibilities for human interaction, but we lack the mental capacity to use them in cooperative, compassionate, and communal ways. Obviously there are small pockets of creative resistance that seem to prove the opposite—but then the resistance movement did not protect us in the West against the commission of crimes against humanity in Iraq and Afghanistan, nor save thousands of small children in those countries from death, physical destruction, or traumatization. All the impressive critical documentaries made by top filmmakers and journalists did not change the bankers' greed and governments' compliance with a financial system that took all the benefits and outsourced the costs to society at large.

If we take evolutionary thinking seriously, then we know that our march through history is a slow procession. It has the character of the famous *Echternach* procession in which the participants take two steps forward and one step backward. Eventually, though, the procession reaches its destination. On the way, we will have time to reflect, acquire patience, and develop the mental capacities needed to realize a global vision for the pursuit of social justice. There is a long way ahead!

Is this a defeatist position? Not necessarily! The "long march ahead" liberates us from overheated expectations of radical social change and the inevitable disappointments of not achieving a just world in our own lifetimes. Does it leave us with inertia and passive waiting for Godot and thus permit the status quo to remain undisturbed?

On the contrary! There is much work to be done during the procession. Let us by all means continue to write and act for media reform. Let us continue to make plans for audience mobilization and global media consumer action. While on the road, let us use the opportunity to engage in reflection about our uncertainty on what to do. Maurice Merleau-Ponty has given us this image:

"We walk together in a thick fog to a destination that we do not know and that may not even be there; and on our way we are uncertain about what to do."[4]

Here we encounter what is arguably the most fundamental clash in today's world: between reflexivity and thoughtlessness. This is a collision of mindsets that is more fundamental than rifts between cultures, ethnic backgrounds, or religions. The reflexive mindset tells us that all claims to validity—be they political, moral, or religious—are open to examination and critique. Reflexive minds are willing to test all ideas in public, listen to those who criticize them, and remain open to the need to revise earlier convictions. The core of the reflexive mindset is the urge to examine life. When Socrates stood before his judges in Athens he admonished the court that "the unexamined life is not worth living."

The refusal or incapacity to make time and space for the development of a reflexive mindset makes us act in thoughtless ways; throughout history this has caused more harm than the malicious intentions. As Susan Neiman writes, "Thoughtlessness can be more dangerous than malice; we are often more threatened by self-serving refusal to see the consequences of conventional actions than by defiant desires for destruction. For whether they're restrained by cowardice or by something nobler, most people refrain from acting those desires out."[5]

Ironically, for this essential reflexivity, the mainstream media do provide essential input. Whatever biases and omissions there may be in the global news coverage, the media do confront us with a world we should be thoroughly embarrassed about. Even if media cannot be expected to be the pioneering leaders of a global movement toward global social justice, they do provide their audiences with a strong challenge to reflect about the meaningfulness of the long march. There is not likely to be instant satisfaction in the realization of global justice. However, we do have agency to mobilize all our human communicative talents, all our words and images, and all our media of expression to steer our common procession away from thoughtlessness toward full confrontation with global injustice. To render the long march ahead a meaningful experience we have to expose ourselves—through all the media at hand—to the pain of others lest we remain locked up in eternally dense fog.[6]

Notes

1. Samuel P. Huntington, *The Clash of Civilizations and the Remaking of World Order* (New York: Simon and Schuster, 1996).
2. See People's Communication Charter Home Page, http://www.pccharter.net.
3. Ray Kurzweil, *The Singularity Is Near: When Humans Transcend Biology* (New York: Viking, 2005).
4. Maurice Merleau-Ponty, *Éloge De La Philosophie* (Paris: Gallimard, 1965).
5. Susan Neiman, *Evil in Modern Thought: An Alternative History of Philosophy* (Princeton, NJ: Princeton University Press, 2002), xii.
6. Susan Sontag, *Regarding the Pain of Others* (New York: Farrar, Straus and Giroux, 2003).

CHAPTER 2

Video Activism as a Way of Life

An Interview with DeeDee Halleck

DeeDee Halleck and Lora Taub-Pervizpour

For media reform activists and scholars, DeeDee Halleck needs no introduction. DeeDee's efforts were integral to building community broadcasting from the ground up in the United States. Most famously, she is the cofounder of the public access cable series *Paper Tiger Television* and cofounder of Deep Dish TV, the first grassroots community television network in the United States.[1] More recently, in 2001, DeeDee developed the TV version of the renowned *Democracy Now!* radio show. The host of that program, Amy Goodman, is certainly not the first to describe DeeDee as "the mother of public access in the U.S." and credits DeeDee with the ability to "make us all believe that everything is possible."[2] She has served as a trustee of the American Film Institute, Women Make Movies, and the Instructional Telecommunications Foundation and was president of the Association of Independent Video and Filmmakers from 1977 to 1982. Between 1986 and 2001, DeeDee taught in the Department of Communication at the University of California, San Diego (UCSD), where she is now professor emerita. At UCSD, her courses ranged across the subjects of telecommunication history and policy, television production, and the history of community media in the United States. DeeDee's teaching was legendary, profoundly democratic in its organization and pedagogy, and set many hundreds of students—myself included—on a path of media and social justice advocacy. In DeeDee's work we see powerfully represented the intersections of media advocacy, education, and cultural production. From teaching undergraduates and testifying before Congress to demonstrating and documenting media justice movements with video camera in hand, DeeDee has been indefatigable in her efforts to protect, promote, and expand the right to communicate. In this short interview, conducted by phone in May 2010, the independent filmmaker, media activist, and educator shares her sense of the current state of media and social justice.

In 2002, your book **Hand-Held Visions: The Impossible Possibilities of Community Media** *was published.[3] Since then, how has your thinking about the "impossible possibilities of community media" changed or grown?*
Right after the book was published, I got very involved with the World Summit on the Information Society, or WSIS, as a venue where community media and access to communication infrastructure could be discussed.[4] I had been a member of the MacBride Round Table on Communication, which was created in 1989 as an attempt to keep alive some of the potential that had been expressed in UNESCO's MacBride Report calling for a New World Information and Communication Order (NWICO) in the late 1970s.[5] As president of the Association of Independent Video and Filmmakers, I felt it was very important that the AIVF support that effort in some way because the MacBride Report had been so maligned in the American press and because independent producers in the United States were just as locked out as Third World countries in terms of access to broadcasting infrastructure. The US State Department saw NWICO as a big threat to US telecommunications corporations. If you read the research papers that were done in connection with NWICO, and later on the MacBride Report itself, there were statements and suggested policies that actually supported independent production, media literacy, and a lot of the things that I've spent my life trying to propose. Back in the 1970s, we had a meeting at my house in Willow, New York, and we made a declaration, called the "Willow Declaration," stating that we, as academics and independent producers and media teachers, supported many of the aims of the NWICO. So when I saw that this UNESCO/ITU [International Telecommunication Union] World Summit was coming up in 2003, I felt that this was also an international venue that should be taken seriously by people in the United States. I attended several of the PrepComs [Preparatory Committees] and was very involved in helping draft the "Civil Society Declaration," which I still think is an important communication rights document.[6] That happened after the book came out, so I was busy for three years going to UNESCO meetings in Geneva and Paris, taking an active role in their community media sector.

Right now, I've been putting together some of the contacts I made in those discussions for a video series about these issues from a global perspective. Around the world, people are making their own media, their own networks. People are much more aware about the need for communication rights. It's much more on people's radar now than it was in the 1970s. Now is a good time not only to think about the problems but also to learn about the wonderful projects people are doing all over the world. In some countries, there are even some quite forward-looking national regulations, although there have been setbacks. I visited South Korea and saw a terrific effort there with a media center called MediACT that was a great hub of activity. They were just starting a big campaign to promote local media literacy, but the right-wing government that came into power recently saw this as a threat to free trade and neoliberal deregulation and closed down the TV station and the MediACT media center, which had been vital to independent media production in South Korea since 2000.[7] They had a 24-hour television channel showing all kinds of wonderful things—lots of youth media, media by disabled people, immigrant workers; marginalized people had a space and an infrastructure to make their voices heard. I just received an email informing me that they're reopening now in a different location to continue this important work. It has been quite a beacon of hope for many of us around the world involved in community media. A few steps forward and a few steps back, but we'll persist.

Hope and possibility have been ever-present in your work, even in the face of no shortage of setbacks. What keeps that hope and sense of possibility alive for you?

Just seeing the inspiring work that people are able to do. For example, I am in contact with a group of women in India from the Deccan Development Society.[8] They've made over one hundred films dealing with many issues, on specific problems with agriculture, food security, and the struggle to oppose genetic modification, Monsanto Corporation, and BP Cotton. They've also addressed the need for children's daycare and the mistreatment of women and children. The quality of their work and their clear articulation of why community media is important inspires me. Victoria Maldonado is my partner on this project to survey community media around the world. She sent the Deccan Development Society a group of questions so they could choose a few to answer, but they answered every single one. Their responses, which we have translated for the series and web page, are very clear about the need for their own media. To me, that's the bottom line. Electronic media are the means of expression in our world and people need to learn to express themselves and have the means to do that. One of our questions was "How do people sustain themselves?" Even though Deccan started out with some assistance from a nongovernmental organization (NGO), they now are at such a level that they are commissioned to create video by different groups. They proudly stated that they even lent out a camera to another organization. Before, they were in the position of having to borrow cameras, and now they are lending them to others. This is a very positive development as far as they are concerned.

In the United States, the work of Prometheus Radio has been spectacular.[9] They have been able to help communities develop radio stations that are very community oriented. Local people actually *build* the station, in the tradition of "barn raising" within farming communities of the nineteenth century: barn-raising parties because you need many hands to raise a barn, especially the barns made with pegs and tongue-and-groove. You need someone to hold the uprights while someone else slides in the joints. In that same spirit, Prometheus is raising radio stations, bringing together carpenters, people who know how to solder, and mentors who show local people how to do the interviewing and research to create news programs. It is an intense community-building effort in just a few days. I always thought that "barn raising" was just a metaphor until I actually saw Prometheus Radio in action in Northampton, Massachusetts, in August 2005. The whole thing started with clearing out a bare-bones basement that was sooty and full of junk. Walls were painted and one big wall was cut through to make a screen for seeing between the control room and studio. A workshop was held to teach people how to make cable. The community made all of the cable; none was bought ready-made.

Pete Tridish, one of the founders of Prometheus, recognizes that this kind of barn raising is not the most efficient way to make a radio station, but it's the most efficient way to build a community around radio. Every person who made a cable—and there were hundreds of cables—now feels that they have materially contributed to the station. It becomes a sense of proprietary community right to the station. At the same time as the cable workshop, there were workshops in news-gathering and antennae-building. Several hundred local people were engaged in the activities, alongside a dozen or so experts from beyond the community. It wasn't that these experts came to do the work for the community. Their whole mode of working was to facilitate the effort and support people's learning to produce radio themselves. Some were working on software programs, with free and open source software, showing people how to create a playlist of radio songs.[10] It was very inspiring. I hope to go to another one this summer in Catskill, New York. The work is so energizing, so hopeful. Those who get involved are the people who will do the programming and run the station. They feel a proprietary sense of what the radio is. In Northampton, after building all day Saturday, they raised the antennae Sunday morning and were transmitting by Sunday afternoon. Leading up to this, they paraded through town to the studio with posters with slogans like "low power to the people" and signs with the radio call letters. At the studio, they had a giant papier-mâché switch and with great fanfare, with as many people's hands as possible, they pulled the switch and went on air. There were kids and old people and three Buddhist monks who wanted to do a show and helped solder cables. Prometheus has a wonderful way of bringing a sense of empowerment through communications that I have never seen before.

As your student at UCSD in the late 1980s, if there was one lesson I took from your class, it was all about empowerment through communications. As a teacher myself now, I often think about some of the things you did in your signature course, Communication General 100. In that enormous lecture hall, with nearly two hundred undergraduates, you tried to create conditions for students not only to experience their own media empowerment but also to develop a sense of what it's like to not be able to exercise their right to communication. I'd like to hear your perspective on teaching media in a university setting. What were you trying to do?

Above all, the essential lesson for students is that they can be part of the process. At UCSD, I was given the chore of teaching a large lecture course called

Com Gen 100. When I realized that it was in a giant lecture hall and that I was to lecture to 180 students who would sit and take notes, I just thought that this was not the way to learn communication. But I had to teach the class, so I tried to turn it into a workshop that gave students a voice and access to whatever communication tools were available. In some cases, it was chalk on the board that teachers usually control or making posters. Phil Donahue actually inspired how I taught this course. I called it the Donahue class because we put microphones on long cables throughout the so-called audience so that students' voices were amplified to fill a very large lecture hall. What made Donahue so popular is that he actually physically gave people the microphone. Phil and I had a discussion about this once. With all of the other talk shows, Oprah and Jerry Springer, people don't feel empowered in the same way because they're not actually holding the microphone.

I also wanted students to make their own videos and to realize how hard it is to make a news report. In a lottery style, groups of students picked a letter and then chose a country beginning with that letter. Their assignment was to create a short news story on something happening in relation to that country within the previous three weeks. This was before Google. It was not really possible to do a quick Internet search on places like Qatar or Indonesia. The very first lesson in the project was realizing the difficulties in gathering information about countries that are unrepresented in the mainstream media. The second lesson is how difficult it is to make a three-minute video given the paucity of information. Students often resorted to producing comical reports based on cliches and stereotypes. A news report for an Arab country, for example, featured a student dressed up with a towel on his head making an allusion to oil magnates in the Middle East. The *real* hard work of the project was to have students watch each group's video and really assess it themselves, defending and discussing it. The discussions were intense, even in a room of 180 students, as they talked about why they resorted to stereotypes. If they could see this at work in each other's news projects, maybe the same thing was happening on the evening news? Looking back, the projects almost predict the rise of Jon Stewart because humor inevitably seemed to be the way that students could look at these issues. It was a learning experience for me as well as the students.

How did your colleagues, administrators, and students respond to this experiment? Was there push-back from any direction?

Reception was mixed. Certainly there were some in the Communication Department who understood what I was trying to do. The graduate students, who were my teaching assistants, were at first resistant and bewildered. But the more they realized what was happening, and why it was happening, the better they liked it and became a part of it. It was very threatening to the quiet academic model of teaching and learning. Looking back, I realize I made mistakes. I could have been more aware of the difficulties that the course raised for the audiovisual people who helped out. I could have brought them in more effectively so that they didn't feel so harassed and besieged. From an AV perspective, it was a difficult class to handle and I could have been more supportive. A number of students claim that it was a transformational class. Now that I'm on Facebook, I hear from former students who say things like, "Com Gen 100 changed my life!" At times, students made Com Gen 100 T-shirts. It was somewhat legendary and students were proud of having gone through it.

The class also upset many students. Students who were used to taking notes and fulfilling all of the usual expectations of education especially struggled. They would ask, "Well, what should I study? I don't understand. Can you give me the notes? Are you going to have a midterm?" They expected to do what they normally do to be able to get their normal grades. Certain things about the class served as a kind of a leveler, so that students who had done poorly or who weren't usually "A" students all of the sudden grasped this class, got excited about the subject, made more of a contribution and maybe became "A" students for the first time. In other cases, some of the "A" students, although they were the ones who anxiously complained at first, finally realized that "wow, this is a different kind of learning with something that maybe I can really benefit from." There were a variety of reactions, but always at the end we had a big party and performance day. Students would do heartfelt performances that were sometimes very emotional. For instance, there was a group with a student who was disabled and the way that the group integrated him and his problems into the performance at the end was very moving. I have tapes of those performances and someday I want to put them together.

Readings were another important dimension of Com Gen 100. Many of the students opted for communication classes because they imagined being the weather girl, or because they wanted to go into public relations or corporate communications. I took it as my challenge to have them develop their potential and move beyond what I felt were very limited aspirations. In their communication courses, students were assigned books and articles that were classics, insightful, quite wonderful, but it seemed to me that students were reading this work in a cursory way. They would just highlight a few sentences and hope that they would not be asked about them on test, or maybe use them in quotes in a pro forma paper at the end of the semester. They didn't engage with those texts. The goal was to get the students to actually think about those ideas and that history. So we devised a final project in Com Gen 100 that was almost like a game show. All the titles of course readings were put into a hat and each group of students picked two titles. Readings included "The Work of Art in the Age of Mechanical Reproduction" by Walter Benjamin, *Ways of Seeing* by John Berger, Roland Barthes's "The Great Family of Man," and Allan Sekula's *Photography Against the Grain*.[11] It was a great mixture of texts, and the students would have to do a skit that utilized both of the readings that they had picked from the hat. The project required them to engage with that writing in a way that they hadn't before, putting two authors in dialogue with each other. Sometimes the works might not seem relevant to each other, but the students had to discover how they were related. Some of the connections they made were astounding. They were finally reading in an engaged and participatory way rather than saying, "Let me highlight this or that sentence because it might be on a test."

One of the people who really helped me think about reading deeply was a friend who I had worked with at *Paper Tiger*, Martha Rosler, a brilliant writer and activist. She was teaching at UCSD in the Visual Arts (VA) Department at the time and invited me to come to one of her courses. I was interested in seeing her teaching. She was a popular teacher with the VA grad students. The class was very long, scheduled for three hours, but I remember it went on for four or five hours, with the whole class intently reading and talking about one page of a Roland Barthes essay. Martha spent the entire time going over every single sentence in the essay, having students talk about it, think about it, and it just went on and on. The discussion got very deep, difficult, and funny! It was a wonderful class. Afterward, I was talking with Martha, and we agreed that the problem with students at a place like UCSD is that they have no idea *how* to read. They approach their readings, with highlighters in hand, but they don't *think* about what the author is saying. Martha felt that the best contribution she could make to students' learning was to take one essay and show them some of the things they could think about the next time they read a Barthes essay. It really impressed me.

It's amazing to hear you talk about this class. It wasn't really until I began thinking about this interview that it became clear to me just how deeply these lessons as a student in Com Gen 100 really shaped the way I teach and the goals that I have for students in the courses I teach. And listening to you, I think about some of the goals I share with you now in terms of wanting students to connect deeply to readings, to see them not just as books to be sold back at the end of the semester! So I wonder how many other students in the class went off to pursue careers that were beyond their initial aspirations to become the weather girl or the PR rep.

I should start a Com Gen 100 Facebook page. It would be fun to see. I've had many students write me and describe how important the course was to them. Part of the success of the class was the quality of the TAs. We had wonderful graduate students in the department, and the course would not have worked without them. It was very demanding. One of the biggest demands was simply keeping up with and commenting on all of the course discussion happening over email. The first Com Gen class I taught (with Alessandro Duranti) was in 1987, long before PCs were ubiquitous. I required everyone in the class to post their comments on the Internet. No one had an email until they got one through the class—it was a test of computer access at UCSD. I observed some of the computer labs on campus and only saw guys. There were no women in the computer rooms. In planning the course we considered that "the big problem is going to be getting the women involved, they aren't going to want to get near the computer." One of my former students, Jill Small, said she would never have gotten into computers without the course, and she went on to head up the Women's Project at GreenNet in London. Jill was terrified of computers. But the class required total immersion; you had to get involved and engaged with the computers.

What do you think about the space of the university today as a site for the struggles to broaden people's right to communicate? What do you think about higher education as a site for this kind of media and social justice work?

It's incredibly important. There are so many different disciplines and programs that are deeply forward thinking and progressive. I think of visual arts, certainly communication, and history, which all have abiding concerns with social justice. But there is also so much that has changed within higher education just in the last 15 years that it is hard to predict where things are going. With the economic crash, many universities are struggling now more than ever and are resorting to raising fees, eliminating departments, and reducing the role of tenured faculty. Many young people now are adjuncts and being totally exploited by work that maybe 20 years ago would have enabled them to get a full-time faculty position. One of the scariest things is that in the face of this economic crisis, universities have to search for what to me seem like nefarious sources of funding. Right now, near my new apartment close to Columbia University, the university is taking over 17 city blocks of the uneven but recently vibrant community of Manhattanville. Columbia has falsely designated it as blighted and is attempting to take it over through eminent domain so that they can build a huge extension to the university.[12] Where, in this economic climate, are they getting money for a project of this scale? A lot of the funds are coming from federal bioterrorism grants, which are currently one of the few sources of available funding.[13] Similarly, Bard College, traditionally a liberal arts college, with a not particularly impressive or well-developed science entity, just built a very elaborate science building. I don't know the total details on financing, but I do know that their math department received a grant from the Department of Defense. We are seeing in higher education the same forces that have transformed other parts of our society, where the manufacturing and factories that survive are benefitting in some way from money from defense or national security. Situated in a military town, UCSD has received military grants all through the years of the university's existence. As funding from these sources increases, it becomes harder for universities and colleges to address issues of social justice and social empowerment. As a system, that's not where higher education is currently heading.

When I first called you for this interview, you were at a demonstration. We could barely hear each other over the sounds of the protesters. Are you concerned that we're so plugged in today that we don't get off our computers very much and get out into the street enough? Are you worried that our engagement in online publics becomes a replacement for engaging in the public outside our door, in the streets of our communities?

The demonstration was in protest against a new immigration law in Arizona. The issue is that the law requires officers to report anyone that they think might be an illegal immigrant. This brings back to my mind Com Gen 100, where we showed *Sesame Street* in Arabic and asked students to consider what kind of lessons it was teaching. There was always someone in the class who spoke Arabic and I would ask if they understood what Bert or Ernie or Cookie Monster was saying. The student would take the microphone and translate into English for the rest of the class. In the climate today, I wonder if I could still do that in a class, or if students would be afraid to admit they speak Arabic, or even Spanish! We are in such a situation that admitting you know Spanish can be risky. The fact that this kind of repression is coming down can really inhibit that kind of simple classroom expression. It's a wonder. The demonstration I went to was so full of energetic young people from many different countries. It was so spirited and very hopeful. Immigrants and others were marching the same day in cities around the United States by the thousands and thousands. This is definitely not going away. The repressive laws are being questioned, and at the same time, they're not just questioning the errors in the law, but people are really beginning to think about the contributions that immigrants have made in this country. Just last night I heard on the radio that a San Diego Padres baseball player will refuse to play in the All-Star Game if it occurs in Arizona. Sometimes you find responses from unexpected corners. The baseball players are going to be a big part of the reaction to the Arizona law.

Getting students motivated and involved in social justice activism is difficult. Their world has been post-9/11. The bigger problem for this generation of students, I think, is the sense of hopelessness that they feel about global warming. I see this in my grandson. He's sure that the world is going to end in his lifetime and it makes him very, very sad. It's hard to even begin to talk to him about it because he gets so emotional. And he is ten years old. He says to me, "Well now I'm two digits old. I'll never be three digits old." The future for him is something that is full of terror. Not terror in terms of bombs or terrorists or kidnapping—but in the sense of not having a world to live in, with the animals and trees that he loves.

Notes

1. *Paper Tiger Television*, http://papertiger.org; and Deep Dish TV, http://www.deepdishtv.org.
2. Jonathan Lawson, "Media Hero: DeeDee Halleck," *Yes!* March 10, 2005, accessed January 8, 2010, http://www.yesmagazine.org/issues/media-that-set-us-free/media-hero-deedee-halleck.
3. DeeDee Halleck, *Hand-Held Visions: The Impossible Possibilities of Community Media* (New York: Fordham University Press, 2002).
4. In 1998, the International Telecommunication Union was at the forefront in recognizing the need for a global discussion aimed at bridging the digital divide, which was considered an imperative step toward achieving the United Nations' Millennium Development Goals (MDGs). Following a proposal from the government of Tunisia, the ITU resolved at its Plenipotentiary Conference in Minneapolis in

1998 to hold a World Summit on the Information Society (WSIS) and to establish the summit on the UN's agenda. In 2001, the ITU Council determined to proceed with WSIS in two phases: the first phase took place December 10–12, 2003, in Geneva, followed by meetings in Tunis November 16–18, 2005. The UN General Assembly endorsed the plan, charged the ITU with a leadership role, and recommended that the summit agenda be determined through an open-ended intergovernmental Preparatory Committee (PrepCom) that would also determine how other stakeholders would participate and finalize a draft Declaration of Principles and draft Plan of Action. The objective of the Geneva phase was to "develop and foster a clear statement of political will and take concrete steps to establish the foundations for an Information Society for all, reflecting all the different interests at stake" ("Basic Information: About WSIS," accessed May 14, 2010, http://www .itu.int/wsis/basic/about.html). The Geneva phase was attended by nearly 11,000 participants from 175 countries, including nearly 50 heads of state or government, high-level political officials, and representatives from international organizations, the private sector, civil society, and media. The Tunis summit drew nearly twice as many participants. See *Geneva Declaration of Principles* (Geneva: WSIS, 2003) and *Geneva Plan of Action* (Geneva: WSIS, 2003), *Tunis Commitment* (Geneva: WSIS, 2005) and *Tunis Agenda for the Information Society* (Geneva: WSIS, 2005), accessed May 14, 2010, http://www.itu.int/wsis/documents/doc_multi .asp?lang=en&id=2266|2267. General information and background on WSIS can be found on the International Telecommunication Union website, accessed May 14, 2010, http://www.itu.int/wsis/basic/about.html.

5. The MacBride Round Table was created to sustain and promote discussion of the issues central to the International Commission for the Study of Communication Problems (known as the MacBride Commission), a UNESCO panel established in 1977 and presided over by Nobel Peace Prize laureate Seán MacBride to establish recommendations concerning a wide array of global media and communication issues that had been raised in the 1970s in the movement over a New World Information and Communication Order (NWICO), in particular the imbalance of media flows between the global North and South. See William Preston, Edward S. Herman, and Herbert I. Schiller, *Hope and Folly: The United States and UNESCO, 1945–1985* (Minneapolis: University of Minnesota Press, 1989). The MacBride Commission produced in 1980 a controversial report, *Many Voices, One World: Towards a New More Just and More Efficient World Information and Communication Order* (Paris: United Nations; London: Kogan Page; and New York: Unipub, 1980), articulating a right to communicate. For detailed accounts of these struggles over policy to shape a more equitable global communication environment, see Hamid Mowlana and Colleen Roach, "New World Information and Communication Order: Overview of Recent Developments and Activities," in *Few Voices, Many Worlds: Towards a Media Reform Movement*, ed. Michael Traber and Kaarle Nordenstreng (London: World Association for Christian Communication, 1992), 4–17; Milton Mueller, Christiane Page, and Brenden Kuerbis, "Civil Society and the Shaping of Communication-Information Policy: Four Decades of Advocacy," *The Information Society* 20, no. 3 (2004): 169–85; and Mueller, Kuerbis, and Page, "Democratizing Global Communication? Global Civil Society and the Campaign for

Communication Rights in the Information Society," *International Journal of Communication* 1 (2007): 267–96.

6. *Shaping Information Societies for Human Needs: Civil Society Declaration to the World Summit on the Information Society* (Geneva: WSIS, 2003), accessed May 15, 2010, http://www.itu.int/wsis/docs/geneva/civil-society-declaration.pdf.

7. MediACT grew out of a proposal by the Association of Korean Independent Film and Video to the Korean Film Commission in 2000 to build theaters exclusively for independent films and a media center. MediACT officially opened in 2002 to promote public access and independent film. See "What is the Media Center?," accessed May 15, 2010, http://www.mediact.org/web/eng/info_01.php.

8. Deccan Development Society, accessed May 15, 2010, http://www.ddsindia.com.

9. Prometheus Radio Project, accessed May 15, 2010, http://prometheusradio.org. See Christina Dunbar-Hester, this volume.

10. See John L. Sullivan, this volume.

11. Walter Benjamin, "The Work of Art in the Age of Mechanical Reproduction," in *Illuminations* (New York: Harcourt, Brace and World, 1968), 217–52; John Berger, *Ways of Seeing* (Harmondsworth, UK: Penguin, 1972); Roland Barthes, *Mythologies* (New York: Hill and Wang, 1972), 100–102; and Allan Sekula, *Photography Against the Grain: Essays and Photo Works, 1973–1983* (Halifax, Canada: Press of the Nova Scotia College of Art and Design, 1984).

12. For background on Columbia University's Manhattanville initiative, see Kim Kirschenbaum, "Year in Review: Uncertainty for Manhattanville," *Columbia Spectator*, May 8, 2010, accessed June 7, 2010, http://www.columbiaspectator.com/2010/05/08/year-review-uncertainty-manhattanville.

13. See Coalition to Preserve Community, "Columbia's Plan: Biotech Hazard on the Hudson," StopColumbia.org, September 26, 2006, accessed June 7, 2010, http://www.stopcolumbia.org/content/view/42/58.

CHAPTER 3

Media and Democracy

Some Missing Links

Nick Couldry

I call our system a system of despair, and I find all the correction, all the revolution that is needed . . . in one word, in Hope.

—Ralph Waldo Emerson[1]

E merson was writing about education in 1840s America in a fast-changing society that had a long way to go toward an effective representative democracy. This, after all, was before the US Civil War and the abolition of slavery, before the struggles to create trade unions, before the civil rights struggle for excluded black citizens in the 1950s and 1960s—and before America's recent crisis over corporate and military influence on the federal administration of George W. Bush. But Emerson's basic idea—seeing, for what it is, the *despair* written into the world around us and imagining "that something else is possible"[2]—is still relevant to today's United States and to today's Britain. It is still relevant to ask what might be the links between how we treat young people and address or ignore their hopes and the type of society we can expect in the future; it is still worth asking what resources might make a positive difference to those young people's hopes and the society that for all of us emerges.

In fact, for those who want to build hope, this may be a particularly important moment, in Britain at least. For young citizens' despair at the workings of British democracy is starting to come to the surface, where it can no longer be ignored. In the three most recent general elections in 2001, 2005, and 2010, voter turnout among 18- to 34-year-olds—that is, among those who are in or

Thanks to Tony Dowmunt, Mark Dunford, and Nicole van Hemert, the editors of *Inclusion through Media* (London: Goldsmiths, 2007), where this chapter was originally published in very similar form.

have recently left full-time education—was *below* 50 percent. This is hardly surprising when in a recent survey *only 27 percent* of the UK adult population agreed with the statement "I have a say in how the country is run."[3] And the British government is beginning to get worried: quite rightly, because unless those who were 18–34 earlier in the decade start voting in greater numbers, Britain will cease to be a working democracy in the next decade or two. In 2001, for the first time in a modern peacetime election, fewer than 60 percent of voters turned out to vote. So British governments need to listen to their young citizens better or risk losing their legitimacy.

If governments need to listen, what should they be told, or perhaps reminded of? For one thing, in case we forget it, they should be reminded that Britain has become more, not less, unequal over the past two decades; for another, that local government in Britain has lost, not gained, power and resources over the same period, which means, inevitably, that the experience of effective democracy is much more distant from people than before. It is important to be clear that the issue is not voter apathy: as the *Power* report published in March 2006 argued, drawing on a lot of recent evidence and picking up a growing trend in the literature on political engagement, people in Britain are not uninterested in politics in principle; they do not have, or find, places where they can go to be listened to and have their views and ideas taken into account when government policy gets made and implemented.[4] Or as my colleagues and I put it in a recent London School of Economics "Public Connection" study, the problem with British democracy is not a lack of public engagement on the part of its citizens but a lack of *recognition of* that engagement *by governments.*[5]

I'll be drawing on the Public Connection study later, but this chapter is not mainly about political engagement, or even as we put it there about "public connection," the basic level of *orientation* to a world of public issues on which any potential interest in politics depends. I want to focus instead on a problem within British democracy and a dimension of social injustice that even more rarely sees the light: I mean the undemocratic nature of the *media*, not the political process.

No one would deny the importance of the freedom that British media generally enjoy: the freedom to publish that once was severely restricted by government in various ways. No one would deny that this freedom is important to the very possibility of democracy. But that is not the same as saying that media institutions themselves are democratic, in the sense of taking account of the views of the citizens affected by what they publish or broadcast. Yet if media—vital institutions of democracy as they are—themselves operate in a way that is not open to democratic challenge, this is a democratic deficit too.

There are two ways of thinking about remedying that deficit. First, by making the process of media production more open to citizen intervention or, as the political philosopher James Bohman has put it, "widen[ing] the circuit of influence over the means of communication";[6] discussing this leads into media ethics and media regulation and would take me too far afield. The second way is by making fairer the distribution of the resources on which media rely— the resources to make media or, more simply, to tell stories *and be listened to*. It is this second route—challenging the injustice in how society's storytelling resources are distributed—that I want to discuss here.

I am not a media practitioner; I am a media and social theorist. But my work in researching and thinking about media and media's relationship to democracy—the conditions of democracy—has focused from the start on the unjust distribution of society's resources for storytelling, or, more technically, the unequal distribution of "symbolic power."[7] Because I'm not a practitioner, I do not claim expertise in putting that injustice right; instead, I will try to explain why, and how, I think this injustice matters, and in that way I hope to contribute something to the debate on why we need more media and social justice projects and what it would mean for such projects to succeed.

Hidden Injuries

Others will have other stories, but my first real understanding of these issues started with reading the American sociologist Richard Sennett's book *The Hidden Injuries of Class*.[8] Countless books have been written before and since on the economic and status injustices linked to class in the United States, Britain, and elsewhere, but until then few if any writers had focused on how class differences "feel": the psychic pain they cause and the difficult routes people take in dealing with that pain. Sennett had done interviews with working-class people in Boston, and his book brings out how people internalized their low position in the society, as a way of coping with it, until they came to feel in subtle ways that they deserved it—that those who were better off or had higher status deserved those greater rewards because they had qualities those "below" them did not. An unequal class system, in other words, in addition to inflicting material injuries through poor housing, poor wages, and long working hours also inflicted "hidden injuries" on its victims, injuries to self-esteem and self-recognition. In this way, the justice of the class system seemed natural even to those who had most to gain from challenging it; as a result, it was almost immune to change, until at least those hidden injuries were grasped more clearly.

Over the next three decades, similar and just as powerful studies of "hidden injuries" were told by writers investigating other dimensions of inequality. So Carol Gilligan and many other feminist writers wrote about the damage to women's self-esteem caused by the internationalization of gender hierarchies in the education system; Stuart Hall, David Theo Goldberg, and others, drawing on the classic early work of W. E. B. DuBois and Frantz Fanon, wrote of the psychic damage done by racism and race-based social systems; and more recently, Michael Warner, Judith Butler, and others have written about the hidden injuries inflicted by societies where one norm, and one norm only, of sexuality—heterosexuality—is imposed as a grid to regulate men and women's much greater range of sexual orientations and practices.

In all those different ways, we have come to see how so-called "material" inequalities—in money, physical assets, legal rights—are matched by "symbolic inequalities." These symbolic inequalities amount to more than being represented unfairly by others, crucially important though that is. These hidden injuries eat away also at individuals' own symbolic resources, their ability to represent themselves, to tell their stories effectively and with confidence. In the controversial context of the current "war on terror," new forms of hidden injury and symbolic inequality are emerging, linked with intercultural differences; some replay older forms of racism and others are directly linked to the unequal treatment of, and respect for, different religions. The problem of "hidden injuries" is, in other words, a large and ever-changing one.

Correcting these symbolic inequalities might seem to be a matter simply of giving greater respect to individuals in our interactions with them. But in *mediated societies*—societies where media institutions have a dominant role and most, if not all, of our information about what's going on beyond our immediate locality comes from media—it is impossible to separate the recognition individuals get from each other and the way that media resources are distributed. Another American sociologist, Todd Gitlin, expressed this beautifully when he wrote, "What makes the world beyond direct experience look natural is a media frame."[9] Yet not everyone has access to the resources of media institutions that build that frame. This means that *who* has access to media resources affects whether *my* experience can make sense or seem interesting and important *to you*. Media, Raymond Williams once wrote, provide "images of what living is now like"—or not, as the case may be.[10] If your life is the type of life that is *not* regularly represented in media, it is liable to be cast into the shadows, making it harder for you to get others to listen to your story of what life is like for you. This is where we can see the hidden injuries of media power working, shaping our expectations of whether others would even be interested if we were to tell them our story.[11]

It is not surprising, then, that just getting your hands on media resources—a digital camcorder, for example—can be a "hook" to get people involved in a community project. *That* this is such a hook is part of the wider problem, since it is the flipside of people *not* normally having such access to media tools. The "glamour" of media—useful attraction though it is—is the other side of an injustice. So projects that try to correct that injustice by giving effective access to media tools are of enormous importance: I'll come back to what counts as effective access later.

Often those projects involve technical training: media skills are now inseparable from web skills because the dispersed nature of the web makes it a colossal resource for telling stories and sharing information. However technical the issues of digital technology skills become, it is vital not to lose sight of the basic point, and the basic injustice being addressed, which always comes down to our ability to exchange with others our accounts of what we feel, remember, think, and propose. Storytelling feeds back to the ways in which we recognize and respect each other as individuals, as the founder of the Center for Digital Storytelling, Joe Lambert, explains: "We all pre-judge, and label, and disregard folks before we know that much about them. Story sharing and listening creates compassion, and offer a huge does of humility. While opinions may not change, certainly a deeper civility can be engendered, a kind of civility that is rapidly disappearing from our culture."[12] Or as the leader of another much less well-known collective storytelling project in Chile has put it, "It is necessary that all voices are heard in the concert of life."[13]

There are of course many forms of injustice: fundamental are failure to sustain a fair distribution of food, housing, basic amenities, health, and education. Among these huge lacks "civility" and mutual respect might seem rather incidental, but as the development economist Amartya Sen points out, being able to participate in how things that affect you are decided is part of living a life that is worthwhile and worthy of a human being, and democracy in this broad sense contributes both to development and to freedom.[14] We are gradually coming to realize that there is no rigid boundary between "hard" questions of economic resources and "soft" questions of recognition. As the American political philosopher Nancy Fraser has pointed out, each of us needs resources—not just a basic standard of living, but the tools to make ourselves heard—if we are to be recognized: injustice of "resources" and injustice of recognition are part of the same larger story.[15] Which means, to recap, that in mediated societies, the fair distribution of media's narrative resources—remember, we call them "media" resources because, for so long, they have been concentrated in media *institutions*, but it could be otherwise—is part of a wider social justice.

The implications of this insight continue to grow as more and more people cross national borders looking for work or fleeing war, yet often fail to get recognition—politically or socially—in their new host countries and as growing economic inequalities within nations are forgotten by affluent elites beneath a story of economic success and market flexibility. This is why the social justice projects have much wider implications than for the particular communities they directly affect. They are challenges to a wider and usually hidden injustice:

the injustice of access to the "medium" through which we see the social world around us.

General principles, however, only take us so far. In the rest of my chapter, I want to think more specifically about how such projects can work, drawing first on a few insights from the Public Connection project mentioned earlier.

Some Implications of the Public Connection Project

Our aim in this project was, in a way, very simple: to test out, by listening to people's voices and accounts, whether the bottom line of most political science and media research is true.[16] That bottom line is the assumption that, whatever their dissatisfaction from the details of politics and whatever the growing debates about the exact stuff of politics should be about, nonetheless citizens in a complex democracy such as the United Kingdom are *oriented to*, potentially attentive to, a world of public issues and public affairs where, in principle, politics goes on and political issues are decided. We call that basic orientation "public connection." A linked assumption is that people's uses of media—their media consumption—sustains that public connection, so people's "public connection" is mediated. But what if that were not the case? Then all the efforts of politicians and other public commentators would be wasted because people would already be turned in another direction.

We had a special reason for asking this question in 2004 and 2005 because of growing uncertainties about what politics should now be about and what exactly—beyond turning up to vote—citizens should do. This uncertainty is common among academics, but our hunch was that it would be shared by citizens more generally, and that we could tap into it by giving people the space to reflect over time on what they had followed each week in the public world and how media had helped them follow it. We left it up to our diarists to define what they counted as of "public" concern. We obtained fascinating reflections from 37 diarists aged 18–69 across Britain in 2004, interviewed them before and after their diary, and then in mid-2005 commissioned a nationwide survey on the issues raised from the diary research.

You can read our wider findings elsewhere.[17] Here I just want to pick out some points that seem most relevant. Our general finding was that most people in the United Kingdom *do* have public connection and that media help sustain it. But this was only the start of a much more complex story.

First, when we looked at our survey results—which get closer to the average population (inevitably, since if you ask someone to produce a diary, you are weighting things a little toward those who are already engaged in some sense, although not necessarily toward politics)—we found a significant minority for whom media did not work to engage them. You were more likely to be disengaged if your socioeconomic status was lower as well as more likely to lack a sense that you can affect things locally. Turning to media, disengagement was predicted both by an interest in celebrity and by a sense that media are often irrelevant to one's life: in other words, by a paradoxical disengagement from media as well. If you were manual working class (where levels of disengagement are much higher in any case), then the more television hours you watched, the more likely you were to be disengaged, although this was not true for other social groups. This illustrates that media consumption in itself is not a route to engagement: watching large amounts of television may be a feature of disengagement, and strikingly disengagement from media as much as from politics. If media contribute to engagement—and by and large they do—it is only as part of a broader balance of consumption and activity within people's lives.

Second, we found among our diarists that even those who are most engaged—people who both followed the news closely and were civically active—had few, if any, outlets for taking action on public issues. Indeed, although people generally had plenty of places where they could talk about public issues, it was rare to find anyone report a link between talking about an issue and taking action on it: this is symptomatic, we believe, of what political scientists have called a weak "deliberative culture" in Britain.[18] This is exactly the gap between engagement and recognition that I noted earlier. This suggests a larger issue: that the lack of opportunities for citizens and media consumers to participate effectively in political decisions or policy generation is not something that better media or better engagement in media can remedy by itself. As one of our diarists, a 47-year-old senior health protection nurse from the rural Midlands, put it, "It's all right having a duty and following things but is there a point if there's nothing at the end of it?"

This links to a final and broader point that emerged in many forms in our study: that to assess the wider consequences and meanings of particular habits or activities (watching a TV news bulletin, reading the paper, going online, or indeed picking up a camcorder), it is not enough to study them in isolation; it is essential to find out how those habits are connected up with other habits, as part of wider practices—or perhaps are *not* connected up with anything else in a person's life. In fact, it was the wider, "joined-up" practice of citizenship that, ironically, was *missing* in New Labour Britain as reviewed in our study. This suggests that it is the *articulations* of what young people do in particular projects with wider contexts *to durable habits and practices* in daily life that we need above all to review in assessing the effectiveness of projects where media resources are, temporarily, passed into their hands.

Media and Social Justice in Action

Several studies illustrate many inspiring ways in which the basic inequality in the distribution of symbolic resources—the resources for giving an account of one's life—can be addressed. Inevitably there are many solutions because if the aim is to redress a lack of recognition, we must realize that "recognition" comes in many forms and from many directions. Holding a camcorder in your hand is one way; posting a diary on a social networking site may be another, providing people have the time to read it attentively; so is learning how to edit a mass of footage of yourself and your friends into a well-shaped narrative or having the story of lives like yours represented with sensitivity for the first time by others through mainstream cinema or television. Outcomes will, and should be, variable.

There is also an inevitable conflict about "audit." Audits are accounting processes that measure "value." Audits at some level are necessary as a way of sustaining basic trust in those who distribute funds. But as the leading sociologist of audit culture Michael Power has pointed out, there is a danger in audit culture that it ends up measuring only what it wants to measure, while being blind to the distortions that audit tools introduce into the practices it claims to regulate: "The audit process requires trust in experts and is not a basis for rational pubic deliberation. It is a dead end in the claim of accountability . . . more accounting and auditing does not necessarily mean more and better accountability . . . and [yet] *it expresses the promise of accountability . . . but this promise is at best ambiguous*: the fact of being audited deters public curiosity and inquiry . . . Audit is in this respect a substitute for democracy rather than its aid."[19] More bluntly, "value for money"—accounting value—is not the same as value for life; economic measurement and moral-ethical norms intersect in the one word "value" without any clear resolution since they face in opposite directions. Yet projects that address injustices in the distribution of symbolic resources are, in the end, defined not by accounting ends but by their aim to make society more just and so more livable.

At the same time, it is reasonable and fair that projects that use scarce resources are held to account for the likely consequences of how they spend that money. Whatever the wider doubts about the overextension of audit culture in contemporary Britain, the more important issue in the short term may be how we introduce into the evaluation process a more nuanced "account" of how, over time, the skills in which projects involve their participants are plausibly linked with enduring habits and practices in those participants' daily lives. Why not use narrative—the tools of narrative placed in the hands of participants by projects—as a means to encourage them to tell their evaluation story at a later date, by telling how, looking back, they see the projects as having affected or not affected their daily lives? In this, and many other respects, the huge expansion of online resources and skills provide new opportunities for recording and exchanging reflections and diaries, for creating discussion fora, and for channeling participants' proposals for new projects and new uses for the skills they have learned. Indeed, that longer-term process of social archiving may *itself* be an important form of self-respect, given the much wider democratic deficit in Britain that I noted earlier. I leave open the question of how we can rethink the purpose of "evaluation" in such a way that time becomes available for former participants and former project leaders to reflect, and have policymakers register those reflections, in an effective way.

This leads me to my final point. The aim of social justice projects, as I understand it, is to redress injustices and in that way alter lives. The term "participation" is potentially a slippery one—not just, I would add, in the context of "participatory video," but in the whole history of democratic politics.

So along with building broader and more sensitive ways of evaluating whether participatory media projects effectively redress the injustices they identify, we need to be realistic. For all the potential of new media and digital tools of media production, distribution, and social networking, what is at stake, in the end, is democracy—an effective democracy. Change through media tools young people's possibilities to be recognized and be heard will only succeed on a wider scale if, from the other direction, government and other formal authorities act as if young people and young people's accounts of their lives mattered. In this respect, I suspect, our thinking and practice about what democracy might mean has still a long way to go.

Notes

1. Ralph Waldo Emerson, "Education," in *The Portable Emerson*, ed. Mark Van Doren (New York: Penguin Books, 1977), 256.

2. Alain Badiou, *Ethics: An Essay on the Understanding of Evil* (London: Verso, 2001), 116.

3. Electoral Commission, *An Audit of Political Engagement 4* (London: Electoral Commission, 2007), http://www.electoralcommission.org.uk/__data/assets/pdf_file/0007/65284/Audit-4-Report-Web-2007-03-27.pdf.

4. Power Inquiry, *Power to the People: The Report of Power: An Independent Inquiry Into Britain's Democracy* (London: Power Inquiry, 2006), http://www.powerinquiry.org/report/documents/PowertothePeople_002.pdf.

5. Nick Couldry, Sonia M. Livingstone, and Tim Markham, *Media Consumption and Public Engagement: Beyond the Presumption of Attention* (New York: Palgrave Macmillan, 2007), 189.

6. James Bohman, "The Division of Labour in Democratic Discourse," in *Deliberation, Democracy, and the Media*, ed. Simone Chambers and Anne N. Costain (Lanham, MD: Rowman and Littlefield, 2000), 60.

7. See Nick Couldry, *The Place of Media Power: Pilgrims and Witnesses of the Media Age* (New York: Routledge, 2000); and Couldry, *Media Rituals: A Critical Approach* (New York: Routledge, 2003).

8. Richard Sennett and Jonathan Cobb, *The Hidden Injuries of Class* (New York: Knopf, 1972).

9. Todd Gitlin, *The Whole World is Watching: Mass Media in the Making & Unmaking of the New Left* (Berkeley: University of California Press, 1980), 6.

10. Raymond Williams, *Drama in a Dramatised Society: An Inaugural Lecture* (Cambridge: Cambridge University Press, 1975), 9.

11. Nick Couldry, "The Hidden Injuries of Media Power," *Journal of Consumer Culture* 1, no. 2 (2001): 155–77.

12. Joe Lambert, *Digital Storytelling: Capturing Lives, Creating Community*, 2nd ed. (Berkeley, CA: Digital Diner Press, 2006), xxi.

13. Ysern de Arce and Juan Luis, "Presentación" in *Enciclopedia Cultural de Chiloé* (Chiloé, Chile: Fundación Radio Estrella del Mar, 2003).

14. Amartya Sen, *Development as Freedom* (New York: Knopf, 1999).

15. Nancy Fraser, "Rethinking Recognition," *New Left Review* 3 (new series): 107–20.

16. Funded under the ESRC/AHRC (Economic and Social Research Council/Arts and Humanities Research Council) Cultures of Consumption program (project number RES-143-25-0011),whose financial support is gratefully acknowledged. I would emphasize that the particular "cultural studies" interpretation that I give to the project here is mine, rather than necessarily a collective view.

17. Couldry, Livingstone, and Markham, *Media Consumption and Public Engagement.*

18. C. J. Pattie, Patrick Seyd and Paul Whiteley, *Citizenship in Britain: Values, Participation, and Democracy* (Cambridge: Cambridge University Press, 2004), 274.

19. Michael Power, *The Audit Society: Rituals of Verification* (Oxford: Oxford University Press, 1997), 127; emphasis added.

CHAPTER 4

A New Vision for Public Media
Open, Dynamic, and Participatory

Jessica Clark and Patricia Aufderheide

Public broadcasting, newspapers, magazines, and network newscasts have played a central role in our democracy, informing citizens and guiding public conversation. Now an open, many-to-many networked media environment is supplanting the top-down dissemination technologies that supported them. What platforms, standards, and practices will replace or transform legacy public media?

Answers are already emerging out of a series of media experiments taking place across legacy and citizen media, which we examined in depth in *Public Media 2.0: Dynamic, Engaged Publics*—a Ford Foundation–funded white paper released in February 2009 at the Public Media conference in Atlanta.[1] After taking a hard look at this "first two minutes" of public media experimentation, we concluded that the first and crucial step, for media providers with public purpose, is to embrace the participatory—the feature that has been most disruptive of current media models.

Since then, we have continued our research into participatory public media 2.0 experiments—via the September 2009 report *Scan and Analysis of Best Practices in Digital Journalism In and Outside U.S. Public Broadcasting*, a series of in-depth case studies, and our Public Media 2.0 Showcase.[2] In each case, our analysis relies on an analytical reframing of the term "public media," outlined in a later section, which asserts that the core mission of public media projects is to support the formation of publics around contested issues.

This article was originally excerpted from the white paper *Public Media 2.0: Dynamic, Engaged Publics*, published by American University's Center for Social Media in February 2009 (www.futureofpublicmedia.net). A version of this excerpt was published by *The American Prospect* on April 30, 2009, http://www.prospect.org/cs/articles?article=will_public_media_survive.

This reframing of public media has proven influential. The white paper has informed current high-level thinking among funders, journalistic organizations, and public broadcasters about next steps for public media and solutions for the journalism crisis. The Knight Commission report, *Informing Communities: Sustaining Democracy in the Digital Age*, quotes the white paper liberally and builds on a number of its core concepts to assert that public engagement is crucial to transforming the sector.[3] The report was cited in the Federal Communications Commission's National Broadband Plan[4] alongside citations of comments submitted by Rutgers University Professor of Law Ellen Goodman, who drew on the public media 2.0 framework to argue for rewriting the Public Broadcasting Act.[5] Clark also recently participated as a respondent during the drafting process of three other major research efforts: (1) the Station Resource Group's *Grow the Audience* project;[6] (2) *The Reconstruction of American Journalism*, the widely discussed 2009 report by Michael Schudson and Leonard Downie Jr.;[7] and (3) *The Big Thaw: Charting a New Future for Journalism*, commissioned by The Media Consortium.[8] Harvard policy scholar Yochai Benkler, author of *The Wealth of Networks*, wrote in *The American Prospect*'s TAPPED blog that "Jessica Clark and Pat Aufderheide have written the best current analysis of how we can pursue the core values underlying support for public media in the new, networked environment."[9]

What's the Big Idea?

We argue that multiplatform, open, and digital public media will be an essential feature of truly democratic public life from here on in. For the first time in modern democracies, public media will be media both for and by the public. While such media may look and function differently from public service broadcasting, it will share the same goals as those that preceded it: educating, informing, and mobilizing users.

But public media 2.0 will not happen by accident or for free. The same bottom-line logic that runs media today will run tomorrow's media as well. If we are going to have media for vibrant democratic culture, we have to plan for it, try it out, show people that it matters, and build new constituencies to invest in it.

This would not be the first time. In the post–World War II boom, the shallowness and greediness of consumer culture appalled many people concerned with the future of democracy. Commercial media, with few exceptions, mostly catered to advertisers with lowest-common-denominator entertainment. How could people even find out about important issues, much less address them?

In the United States, this concern inspired such initiatives as the Hutchins Commission, the Carnegie commissions on public broadcasting, the Poynter

Institute, and other journalistic standards and training bodies. Foundations also supported media production and infrastructure, including the Ford Foundation's commitment to public broadcasting and the Rockefeller Foundation's investment in independent filmmakers. Some corporations also created public media for a mass-media era: for instance, the burgeoning cable industry offered C-SPAN as a service particularly interesting to legislators. Guided by public interest obligations, commercial broadcasters grudgingly supported current affairs programming and investigative reporting. Taken together, these efforts placed the onus of enlightening the public on media makers and owners. Public service was incentivized through regulation, tax exemptions, taxpayer dollars directly to public media institutions, often-ignored chances for citizen review of broadcast licenses, and limited input to media through mechanisms such as ombudsmen, letters to the editor, and community ascertainment meetings designed to match local coverage to local concerns.

This concern also drove the passage of the Public Broadcasting Act of 1967, which created US public broadcasting as we know it today and a range of other policy initiatives that generated pockets of noncommercial electronic media and protection for daily journalism. Public media 1.0, like parkland bordering a shopping mall, inhabited a separate zone: public broadcasting, cable access, and national and international beats of prestige journalism. These media occasionally played major roles (showcasing political debates, airing major hearings, becoming the go-to source in a hurricane), while also steadily producing news and cultural enrichment in the background of Americans' daily lives.

Throughout the second half of the twentieth century, public media 1.0 was accepted as important but rarely loved—politely underfunded by taxpayers, subsidized weakly by corporations, and grudgingly exempted from shareholders' profit expectations. It was often hobbled by the inevitable clash between democratic debate and entrenched interest. In public broadcasting and in print journalism, partisan and corporate pressures distorted—even sometimes defanged—public discussion. Cultural battles sapped government funding for socially relevant arts and performance.

Public media 1.0 was also limited in generating vigorous public conversations by the one-to-many structure of mass media. Carefully culled op-ed pages aired carefully balanced views but created limited participation. The same was true of talk shows and town-hall forums. Print and broadcast inevitably functioned in a top-down fashion.

And then came the Internet, followed by social media. After a decade of quick-fire innovation—first web pages, then interactive Flash sites; first blogs, then Twitter; first podcasts, then iPhones; first DVDs, then BitTorrent—the individual user has moved from being an anonymous part of a mass to being the center of the media picture.

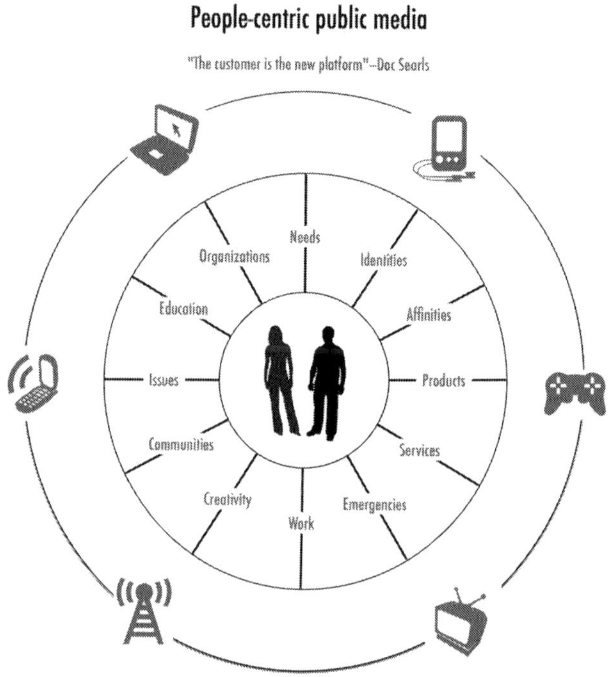

People-centric public media

"The customer is the new platform"—Doc Searls

Figure 4.1 People-centric public media

Commercial media still dominate the scene, but the "people formerly known as the audience" are spending less time with older media formats.[10] Many "digital natives" born after 1980 (and a number of us born before) now inhabit a multimedia-saturated environment that spans highly interactive mobile and gaming devices, social networks, and chat.[11] People are dumping landlines for cell phones and watching movies and TV shows on their computers. Open platforms for sharing, remixing, and commenting on both amateur and professional media are now widely popular—hastening the demise of print subscriptions and so-called appointment television. There's more choice, more chance for conversation and curation, more collaboration with media makers and much more creation by users.

Media producers' habits are evolving, too. Video is now ubiquitous, databases serve as powerful engines for content management and visualization, social networks are increasingly common platforms for distribution, and more and more place-based media are available on local platforms. And trends suggest that connectivity, participation, and digital media creation will only increase along with growing access to broadband and mobile devices. All of these shifts set the stage for the rise of public media 2.0 projects, which leverage participatory media technologies to allow people from a variety of perspectives to work together to tackle a topic—to share stories and facts, ask hard questions, and then shape a judgment on which they can act.

Here are a few examples from the *Public Media 2.0* white paper:

- *The Mobile Report*: Media Focus on Africa Foundation worked with the Arid Lands Information Network to equip citizen reporters in Kenya with mobile phones to report on violent election conditions, which were then aggregated on an online map that served as a reference point for reporters and election observers.[12]
- *10 Questions Presidential Forum*: Independent bloggers worked with *The New York Times* editorial board and MSNBC to develop and promote the 10 Questions Presidential Forum. More than 120,000 visitors voted on 231 video questions submitted by users. Presidential candidates then answered the top ten questions via online video. The top question was also aired during the MTV/MySpace "Presidential Dialogue" featuring Barack Obama.[13]
- *Facing the Mortgage Crisis*: As foreclosures began to sweep through the United States, St. Louis public broadcasting station KETC launched "Facing the Mortgage Crisis," a multiplatform project designed to help publics grappling with mortgage foreclosures. Featuring invited audience questions and on-air and online elements that mapped pockets of foreclosures, the project directed callers to an information line managed by the United Way for further help. Calls to the line increased significantly as a result.[14]

What unites such diverse, multiplatform projects? People come in as participants and leave recognizing themselves as members of a public—a group of people commonly affected by an issue, whatever their differences about how to resolve it. These projects have provided a platform for people to meet, learn, exchange information, and discuss solutions. They have found each other and exchanged information on an issue in which they all see themselves as having a stake. In some cases, they take action based on this transformative act of communication.

This is the core function of public media 2.0 for a very simple reason: Publics are the element that keeps democracies democratic. Publics provide essential accountability in a healthy society, checking the natural tendency of people to do what's easiest, cheapest, and in their own private interest. Publics regularly form around issues, problems, and opportunities for improvement; they are not

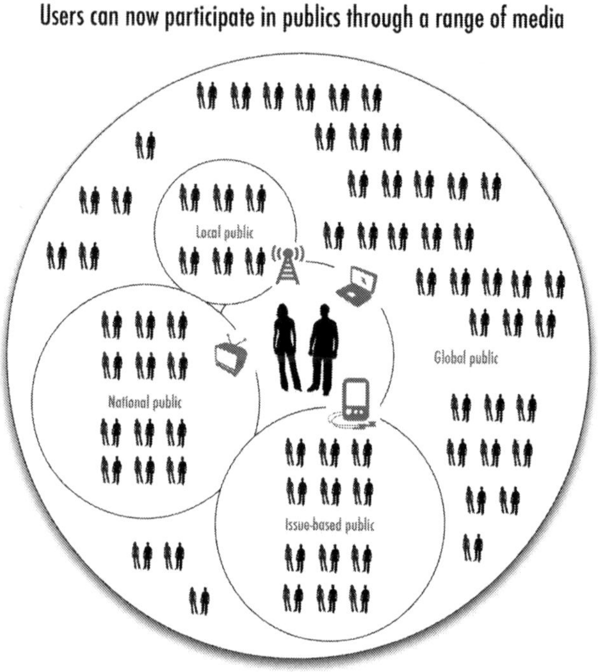

Users can now participate in publics through a range of media

Figure 4.2 Users can now participate in publics through a range of media

aggregations of individual opinion or institutionalized structures. Such informality avoids the inevitable self-serving that happens in any institution. Publics are fed by the flow of communication.

This is the kind of media that political philosophers have longed for. When Thomas Jefferson said that he would rather have newspapers without government than government without newspapers, he was talking about the need for a free people to talk to each other about what matters. When American philosopher John Dewey argued that conversation was the lifeblood of a democracy, he meant that people talking to each other about the things that really affect their lives is what keeps power accountable. When German social theorist Jürgen Habermas celebrated the "public sphere" created by the French merchant class in the eighteenth century, he was noting that when nonaristocrats started to talk to each other about what should happen, they found enough common cause to overturn an order.

It is important to note that public media 2.0 is not synonymous with partisan or activist media. Social media tools can be used for rabble rousing or for engagement across difference. Partisan and activist media have as strategic goals targeted actions, and they typically use the most powerful persuasive tools they can to do that job. While such media projects can effectively engage and mobilize their users around issues, they do not serve the same broad civic function as public media projects, which provide information, framing media, and platforms for debate, discussion, and negotiation of contested issues in a democracy. Public media establish, earn, and draw on their legitimacy by observing standards and practices that signal to users their accuracy, timeliness, utility, and reliability. Public media actively engage users, allowing them to critique and address those in power, but do not dictate a particular ideological approach. At their best, they do serve as social justice media projects, speaking across social, cultural, and class difference—or cultivating translation and other mechanisms to help self-expression translate across those divides—so that diverse stakeholders can communicate effectively about issues that require public deliberation and action.

This is important because publics are often formed not of cliques or communities but of people drawn out of those comfort zones by the issues they face in common with people they normally do not talk to. Media that facilitate public life have to be media that address people across inequality and inexperience. The lifelong work of John Dewey—both in his writing and in his practice—was testimony to this concept. While Dewey was committed to face-to-face interaction, he worked and thought before the era in which people Twittered and text messaged across a room. In *Dewey on Democracy*, William R. Caspary summarizes Dewey's approach: "Dewey's ideal is a high level of citizen participation in public discussion and decision-making: 'a responsible share according to capacity in shaping the aims and policies of the groups to which one belongs.' Access to participation is to be free and equal, 'without respect to race, sex, class or economic status' . . . Dewey envisions vital dialogue that includes elements of empirical investigation, interpretation, critique, narrative, ethical deliberation, conflict, and conflict-resolution. Such discussion, however, is continuous with political contestation, not isolated in a separate, ideal public space."[15]

Public media and democratic governance are mutually reinforcing. In strong democracies, as discussed by Benjamin Barber and others, there are correspondingly strong policies for media for public life, including dedicated support for robust communication infrastructure, policies for privacy, freedom of expression and access, and education for self-expression.[16] In this country, among the incentives for independent media are nonprofit postal rates, nonprofit tax laws, the First Amendment, and support for public broadcasting (funneled through a nongovernment organization, the Corporation for Public Broadcasting). Commercial media can serve some public media functions, but there are no guarantees. Conversely, if a government only supports state media and provides no incentives for independent media, that is another blow to civil society. Samizdat, informal, and tactical media are all ways that people communicate under the radar of repressive governments. Nourished with appropriate policies, standards, and support, such outlets and practices can bloom into public media as political conditions shift.

We now have the digital tools to facilitate participatory public media, but we do not yet have the policies, nor do we have the public will. In fact, we are now barely seeing the glimmers of what is possible. And yet, now is the time to act to secure public media 2.0 for future generations. The initial period of individualistic experimentation in participatory media is passing, and large institutions—including political campaigns, businesses, and universities—are now adopting social media forms, such as blogs and user forums. With greater use comes consolidation in tools, applications, platforms, and ownership of them. Every step of consolidation forecloses options, creates powerful stakeholders, and also establishes new, much needed business models.

Of course, as new business models emerge, the heady days of experiment will cede to the familiar terms of power and profit. Some media and legal scholars see big trouble in this consolidation. Jeff Chester thunders against corporate greed;[17] Jonathan Zittrain fears that Apple will make our digital lives easy by taking away our creative choices;[18] Siva Vaidhyanathan worries that Google's tentacles will reach into every aspect of our lives while making it ever easier for us to do our work with its tools;[19] Cass Sunstein is sure we are losing our social souls.[20] All of these are issues worth taking seriously. They are reasons why the terms of public media 2.0 are so important.

Public media 2.0 can develop on the basis of the platforms that are the winners of the consolidation currently taking place and with the help of policy that supports it within that environment. But it will not happen by accident. Commercial platforms do not have the same incentives to preserve historically relevant content that public media outlets do. Building dynamic, engaged publics will not be a top agenda item for any business. Nor will tomorrow's commercial media business models have any incentive to remedy social inequality. Participation that flows along today's lines of access and skill sets will replicate past inequalities. If public media 2.0 looks less highly stratified and culturally balkanized than the public media of today, it will be because of conscious investment and government policy choices.

Inclusion is not just a side issue in public media. In order to function well, public media projects and platforms designed to engage stakeholders around issues must be both accessible to and representative of the entire population. The current public broadcasting system has often failed in this regard, as has the mainstream news system. Open technological architecture can help to diversify participation, but further measures need to be taken to engage underserved users. Inclusion must therefore be a top priority when creating policies and infrastructures for the new public media; otherwise the system will have failed from the start.

These ideas are not new; they are just easier to implement given social media technology. Community media outlets have been championing this inclusive, participatory ethos for decades; the lessons they have learned and the facilities they have fought to build should be valued and incorporated more explicitly into any emerging public media system. But in order to meaningfully inform public debate, public media projects must also operate within the same news and information ecosystem as more influential and high-profile outlets. Right now, many projects designed to bring new perspectives into circulation—cable access centers, independent media projects, low-power FM (LPFM) stations, outlets serving communities of color—suffer from a lack of resources, low visibility, and a dearth of connections to even the marginally better-supported public broadcasting outlets in their communities. Similarly, public broadcasting organizations are fragmented, often working in opposition and hoarding resources. As platforms and funding streams converge into digital forms, new policies and incentives should emphasize collaborative approaches, open platforms, modular content, and shared system resources.

Leadership for Public Media 2.0

Who will lead the charge to define and support public media 2.0? There are plenty of organizations that now perform at least experimental versions of public media 2.0. But who will turn those experiments into broadly accepted social habits? That question has already generated a wide range of proposals, from creating a Digital Future Endowment,[21] to establishing a National Journalism Foundation,[22] to funding a "public-media corps,"[23] to reviving the Carnegie Commission's call for a Public Media Trust.[24]

There are two outstanding needs: (1) *content* and (2) *coordination* that builds capacity for engagement. We believe it is important to separate these functions in understanding the needs for leadership:

Content has been the glory of mass media, and there already is a deep pool of high-quality content via mass media journalism, public broadcasting, and the many content entities—including a welter of freelancers and independent producers—that serve them. Many of these entities face a grave long-term challenge as old business models collapse. But there are still plenty of them today, from prestige newspapers and magazines to media production houses to such institutions as National Public Radio.

What is needed for the future of high-quality content is at least partial taxpayer support for the many existing operations and for innovative new projects.

A federal body committed to promoting media production would fund both institutions and individuals who make, curate, and archive public media, functioning much as the National Endowment for the Arts does today. Such a federal body would address the maintenance of high-quality news and information, documentary resources, and the historical record. It would invest in the maintenance and accessibility of the content pools that have already been created and that will grow with public participation. It would be structured to fund either commercial or noncommercial entities, so long as they made or enabled the making of public media. Alternatively, one might assign existing cultural and research support agencies responsibility for public media support.

Coordination that builds capacity for participation in public media 2.0 will pose a new challenge—distinct from the work of legacy media organizations and untested as yet in the digital era. Functions of a coordinating body would include

- providing an accessible and reliable platform for public interaction,
- providing a toolset for public participation,
- setting standards and metrics to assess public engagement,
- developing a recommendation engine to identify and point to high-quality media,
- committing staff at local and national levels primarily to building public engagement with media and to partnerships to make it happen,
- tracking emerging technologies and platforms to assess and secure their potential for public media 2.0.

The resulting platform would not be the only way or place for public media 2.0 to happen, but it would offer a default location for engagement. It would not be the source of public media content, though its recommendations might legitimize such content. Rather, its staff would be charged first and foremost with promoting public life through media.

Who would do that? A coordinating body of this sort might be created from whole cloth. It is also possible to imagine the linked organizations that make up the public broadcasting system—with their federal public service mandate, local stations, and national programming outlets, the public broadcasting stations reach almost every community in the nation—playing such a role.

But public broadcasters face significant challenges to joint action. Well known and profound structural problems, rooted in public broadcasting's decentralized structure, its mixture of content production with distribution functions, and its multiple-source funding, impede collective efforts.[25]

Public broadcasters might well identify roles for themselves both in content provision and in coordination. Such an approach would require restructuring and separating out content provision from coordination functions. This would require incentives from the federal government and a clear mandate to the Corporation for Public Broadcasting to execute the change. But such an approach would also reclaim a multibillion-dollar public investment in public media and avoid the challenge of creating a new structure that would have some overlapping functions.

If the public gets a chance to build public media 2.0, it will not be merely because of structures such as a coordinating body and content funding. Government policies vital to building participatory capacity must be enacted at the infrastructure level. For instance, broadband needs to be accessible across economic divides and available to public media on equal terms with more commercial media for a vigorous, expandable digital network of communication to thrive. Policy makers should mandate that network developers use universal design principles so that people of all levels of enablement can access communication and media for public life. Users need privacy policies that safeguard their identities as they move across the digital landscape.

In short, there are big questions about how to develop public policies to support public media 2.0, and they are important to engage because public policy will be crucial in turning isolated experimentation into pervasive public habit.

Notes

1. Jessica Clark and Pat Aufderheide, *Public Media 2.0: Dynamic, Engaged Publics* (Washington, DC: Center for Social Media, 2008), accessed March 16, 2011, http://www.centerforsocialmedia.org/future-public-media/documents/white-papers/public-media-20-dynamic-engaged-publics.
2. Pat Aufderheide, Jessica Clark, Matthew C. Nesbitt, and Carin Dessauer, *Scan and Analysis of Best Practices in Digital Journalism In and Outside U.S. Public Broadcasting* (Washington, DC: Center for Social Media, 2009), http://www.centerforsocialmedia.org/future-public-media/documents/white-papers/scan-and-analysis-best-practices-digital-journalism-and-o; and Center for Social Media, "Public Media 2.0 Showcase," accessed March 16, 2011, http://centerforsocialmedia.org/future-public-media/public-media-showcase.
3. Theodore B. Olsen and Marissa Mayer, *Informing Communities: Sustaining Democracy in the Digital Age* (Washington, DC: The Aspen Institute, 2009), accessed March 16, 2011, http://www.knightcomm.org/read-the-report-and-comment.
4. Federal Communications Commission, *Connecting America: The National Broadband Plan* (Washington, DC: Federal Communications Commission, 2010), accessed March 16, 2011, http://www.broadband.gov/plan.
5. Ellen P. Goodman and Anne Chen, "Digital Public Media Networks to Advance Broadband and Enrich Connected Communities" (working paper, SSRN [Social Science Research Network], November 6, 2009), accessed March 16, 2011, http://ssrn.com/abstract=1569677.

6. Public Radio Audience Growth Task Force, *Public Radio in the New Network Age: Wider Use, Deeper Value, Compelling Change* (Takoma Park, MD: Station Resource Group, 2010), accessed March 16, 2011, http://www.srg.org/GTA/Public_Radio _in_the_New_Network_Age.pdf.

7. Leonard Downie Jr. and Michael Schudson, *The Reconstruction of American Journalism* (New York: Columbia University Graduate School of Journalism, 2009), accessed March 16, 2011, http://www.cjr.org/reconstruction/the_reconstruction _of_american.php.

8. Tony Deifell, *The Big Thaw: Charting a New Future for Journalism* (Chicago: The Media Consortium, 2009), accessed March 16, 2011, http://www.scribd.com/ doc/21342457/The-Big-Thaw.

9. "Public Media 2.0 Roundtable: Creation and Curation," TAPPED, the group blog of *The American Prospect*, April 30, 2009, accessed March 16, 2011, http://www .prospect.org/csnc/blogs/tapped_archive?base_name=public_media_20_round table_cre&month=04&year=2009.

10. Jay Rosen, "The People Formerly Known as the Audience," PressThink blog, June 27, 2006, accessed March 16, 2011, http://journalism.nyu.edu/pubzone/weblogs/ pressthink/2006/06/27/ppl_frmr.html.

11. John Palfrey and Urs Gasser, *Born Digital: Understanding the First Generation of Digital Natives* (New York: Basic Books, 2008).

12. Media Focus on Africa Foundation, "Kenya Elections 2007: Media Campaign," accessed March 16, 2011, http://mfoa.africanews.com/site/page/mobile_report.

13. Personal Democracy Forum, "What is 10Questions.com?" accessed March 16, 2011, http://www.10questions.com/2010/about.

14. KETC, "Facing the Mortgage Crisis," accessed March 16, 2011, http://www .stlmortgagecrisis.org.

15. William R. Caspary, *Dewey on Democracy* (Ithaca, NY: Cornell University Press, 2000), 8–9.

16. Benjamin Barber, *Strong Democracy* (Berkeley: University of California Press, 1984).

17. Jeff Chester, *Digital Destiny: New Media and Future of Democracy* (New York: The New Press, 2007).

18. Jonathan Zittrain, *The Future of the Internet and How to Stop It* (New Haven, CT: Yale University Press, 2008).

19. Siva Vaidhyanathan, "The Googlization of Everything," accessed March 16, 2011, http://googlizationofeverything.com.

20. Cass R. Sunstein, *Republic.com 2.0* (Princeton, NJ: Princeton University Press, 2007).

21. Michael Calabrese and Cheri Carter, *Digital Future Initiative Final Report: Challenge and Opportunities for Public Service Media in the Digital Age* (Washington, DC: New America Foundation, 2005).

22. David Sasaki, "Toward a National Journalism Foundation," MediaShift blog, November 17, 2008, accessed March 16, 2011, http://www.pbs.org/idealab/2008/ 11/toward-a-national-journalism-foundation005.html.

23. Jeff Chester, "Memo to Obama Administration: Time for a 'Public Media Corps,' [or the WPA Meets the Digital Age]," Digital Destiny blog, November 23, 2008, accessed March 16, 2011, http://www.democraticmedia.org/jcblog/?p=692.

24. Lauren J. Strayer, "Corporation for Public Broadcasting: Building a Digital Democracy Through Public Media," in Change for America online project, Center for American Progress, accessed March 16, 2011, http://www.americanprogressaction.org/issues/2008/changeforamerica/pdf/pbs.pdf.

25. Pat Aufderheide and Jessica Clark, *Public Broadcasting and Public Affairs: Opportunities and Challenges for Public Broadcasting's Role in Provisioning the Public with News and Public Affairs* (Boston: Berkman Center for Internet and Society, 2008), accessed March 16, 2011, http://cyber.law.harvard.edu/pubrelease/mediarepublic/downloads.html.

PART II

Collaborations

CHAPTER 5

Sustaining Collaboration
Lessons from the Media
Research and Action Project

Charlotte Ryan and William Gamson

In this chapter, we reflect on an academic-activist collaboration that we founded at Boston College in 1985, the Media Research and Action Project (MRAP).[1] During its 25-year history, MRAP has worked to forge a shared "safe space" where scholars, advocates, and social movement groups exchange strategies, theories, and experiences.[2] At the beginning, we focused on issue framing (the way that journalists or organizations package messages), with the assumption that media sociology and advocacy campaigns could mutually inform one another. In practice, MRAP has been many things—a proving ground for graduate student projects, a site for strategy workshops and formal media training, a meeting place to brainstorm about how social justice voices navigate a for-profit media system. Along the way we have been trying to do what Michael Burawoy described, nearly a decade after MRAP's founding, as "public sociology."[3]

When we introduce MRAP and its range of activities, we describe two overlapping wings with interrelated projects. The more formal academic wing has helped participants "bake" doctoral dissertations, papers, books, and lectures. The translational research and action wing has offered a strategizing and training space for activists; in workshops and capacity building programs, we have worked with nonprofits, advocacy, community, labor, and other social movement groups to deepen their ability to strategically frame and disseminate messages that enhance their organizing efforts.

This chapter is a combined and expanded version of a pair of previously published articles: William Gamson, "Life on the Interface," *Social Problems* 51, no. 1 (2004): 106–10; and Charlotte Ryan, "Can We be Compañeros?" *Social Problems* 51, no. 1 (2004): 110–13.

The relation between the two wings is critical; the action wing does apply theories developed in the academic wing, but it also explores theoretical gaps that arise in practice. In turn, the value of the academic wing rests not only in its theoretical offerings but in its capacity to reflect with activists on their practice. The seminar offers organizers needed distance and also provides comparative experiences and ideas from other times and places.

The metaphor of "wings" could overstate the division; many MRAP members have played both roles, each project demanding a different blend of theory-informed practice and practically informed theorizing. Our individual histories and strengths determine where we most often fall in recurring cycles that link action and reflection through dialogue. The wings' interdependence is more important than their differences. Here the metaphor is fitting: by working synergistically, the wings achieve their shared purpose.

The dialogue between academics and activists has been mutually rewarding, even as tensions arise from time to time around priorities, pacing, language, and other issues. In all this work, we have applied Freirian, constructionist, and feminist theories stressing dialogue. And we've learned volumes. While our learning is largely stored for now in personal files and journals, we present some key lessons in the sections that follow.

One Mission: Three Phases

Within sociology, we have worked primarily within one subfield, political sociology—more specifically political discourse—to explore how social movements and marginalized constituencies "talk politics" under conditions not of their own making. Our choice of media as an entry point reflects our understanding of mass media as our historical period's master forum—the arena in which groups commonly engage in political discourse. How we advance this mission has varied with resources. Finding sufficient resources to create sustainable infrastructure has been an ongoing struggle, and we have been forced to adapt our agenda again and again.

To condense a long and complicated history into a few paragraphs, MRAP has gone through three phases since the mid-1980s. At first, we were a weekly breakfast seminar, meeting during the academic year, which served as a kind of incubator for doing public sociology focused on the mass media and social movements. Graduate students developed public sociology projects focused on strategies of change, various faculty from sociology and other departments and universities used the seminar to present their work, and staff members from advocacy groups or campaigns would join us to reflect on their experiences, strategies, or both.

Eager to bridge the academic-activist divide, we approached activists, asking them to share with us successful experiments in "talking politics."[4] We would often run one- or two-day workshops and other training exercises on the media for various groups during this phase. To create a workshop curriculum, we blended activists' identified best practices with social movement scholars' lessons from the civil rights, antiwar, women's and gay liberation movements. We modeled ourselves after Aldon Morris's "movement half-way houses," building intentional relations between academic social movement theorists and social movement practitioners.[5] In our first several years so operating, we ran workshops for close to two hundred local and regional organizations.

Our frustration with one-shot training exercises as vehicles for building effective media strategies propelled us into a second phase in the mid-1990s. This community outreach phase involved actively seeking outside funds and building long-term relationships with a smaller number of organizations. The two most important projects in this phase were an ongoing relationship with the Rhode Island Coalition Against Domestic Violence and a multiyear Media Fellows program. The Media Fellows were community activists, nominated by their organizations, who spent several days a month over one to two years working with MRAP staff to strengthen their groups' media capacity. One of us (Ryan) took the lead and provided the central energy to make these programs happen.

At the turn of the century we encountered a perfect storm of resource challenges. First, the economy tanked, with the dot.com crash being of particular import in our case. September 11 catalyzed an added shift in foundation and state spending that destabilized many of our partners. Finally, foundations expressed little interest in the type of sustained regional capacity-building MRAP championed. Facing its own financial pressures, Boston College pressed MRAP to become self-sufficient. As the federal government went on a war footing and cut social spending, we made the very hard decision to mothball MRAP's outreach program in 2003. This decision signaled the opening of a third phase in which MRAP returned to its origins as a research seminar and incubator of public sociology.

A word is in order about public sociology. Just as MRAP entered its third phase, noted ethnographer Michael Burawoy was elected to the 2004 presidency of the American Sociological Association (ASA) on a public sociology platform. Burawoy's definition of public sociology embraced all efforts by sociologists to work in the public interest broadly conceived. MRAP's work fell easily within this big tent definition, and we were gladdened that the American Sociological Association had chosen to focus on the profession's social responsibilities. While many have debated Burawoy's delineation of four quadrants—traditional or professional scholarship, policy work, critical theory, or direct engagement with marginalized communities—we share the view that mutually respectful synergy among the quadrants is critical.[6]

The Rewards

In each phase, the MRAP seminar and our participation in practical projects such as the Media Fellows have provided us with enormous intellectual resources. Our experiences have informed and shaped our professional sociology writing over the past 20 years. It is exhilarating to both see the practical usefulness of our ideas about media framing processes and at the same time confront the multiple ambiguities, limiting conditions, and taken-for-granted assumptions in the professional sociology on this topic, including our own. MRAP's public sociology has helped to keep our professional sociology grounded in the real world. A concrete example will serve to illustrate. After the first general session with the Media Fellows, we gave them an assignment: set up a media committee in the organizations they represented before our next monthly meeting. We offered little instruction on how to do this and, to be honest, had not thought through what this might involve.

At the next meeting, they reported on their multiple problems. Our Media Fellows were younger than the typical board members and leaders of the organizations that they represented. Furthermore, they were more likely to be women. Older male leaders in some organizations seemed wary that the Media Fellows would become the public face of the organization, siphoning off their own status and power. Other leaders of the organizations were eager to dump media work on the fellows so that they would not themselves have to worry about it. The fellows found it difficult to answer such apparently simple questions as, why do we need a media committee?

In facing the first problem, we quickly came to the collective conclusion that one needed to analyze the power dynamics in the organization before trying to set up a media committee. The role that the Media Fellows would need to play in being a catalyst for organizational growth had to be understood in order to make such a committee effective. Setting up a media committee requires conscious attention to organizational dynamics and should not be done casually or haphazardly.

The same lesson was true for the second problem of dumping media work on the MRAP fellows. For us, this violated a central MRAP principle: that media strategy should be a part of a larger organizational strategy, not divorced from it. But this kind of strategic thinking came naturally to neither the Media Fellows nor the potential members of a media committee in their organizations. Thinking strategically was something that the fellows needed to understand well enough to be able to communicate why a media committee was desirable and what it would do strategically. By the end of the session, we decided to make setting up a media committee a long-term goal toward which we would work together.

As public sociologists, we work with collective actors to apply theoretical constructs to an actual situation. Working as a team, we attempt to draw insights and directions from existing social movement paradigms. To impose theories on activists would be to ignore the fact that all human beings theorize. Subjected to practice, only the most robust theoretical constructs survive. Most theoretical models are underdeveloped, offering a vague sense of relationships between ideas, sometimes little more than a direction for future inquiry. In practice, one quickly learns which concepts are underspecified. Far more easily than intellectuals working alone, we, in tandem with collective actors, link concepts into workable and transferable paradigms and related transformative practices. The "framing caucus" is one such transformative practice that evolved through collaboration.

Springboarding from the sociological literature on the social construction of meaning, MRAP developed framing tools to help groups "talk politics." With our community partners, however, we came to a deeper understanding of framing as a collective actor's reflexive process of "real talk"—the term used by Mary Belenky and her coauthors for dialogue that stresses listening and grounded knowledge.[7] Many of these insights came through our sustained work with the Rhode Island Coalition Against Domestic Violence (RICADV). As they prepared for media appearances, the coalition staff crafted MRAP's framing concepts into a caucus format. The framing caucus, says Karen Jeffreys, RICADV organizer, allows RICADV members to collaboratively "think for the organization."[8] Individuals work as a team, their shared understanding allowing them to function, metaphorically speaking, as the collective actor's "brain."

When sociologists reserve theorizing as the proper function of academics, we deny the publics we serve access to a source of power and pleasure—thinking. The various movement groups with whom MRAP collaborates describe the process of talking about ideas—in framing caucuses and informally over lunches—as both pleasurable and meaningful. Three RICADV interns, Titus Dos Remedios, Mao Yang, and Sarah Cataldo, describe participation in the framing caucuses as life changing: "Anyone can develop a message and put it out, but here it matters. Our individual opinions matter; we're part of making the group message. And the group message matters. Our group is part of a movement, part of something bigger. Our message gets out and has real power. People need to feel like they're part of something bigger."[9]

Shared Space, Complementary Roles

As codirectors, the two of us have carved out distinct if complementary roles at MRAP, and our experiences hint at the range of public sociology engagement. One of us, Gamson, has been a kind of vicarious public sociologist, with the other, Ryan, doing the public sociology as what Burawoy (echoing Antonio Gramsci) calls the organic intellectual. She has been the creative force behind the numerous collaborations with grassroots community groups on using the mass media to achieve a more just society. Gamson has had the privilege of being able to go along for the ride, watching and bringing into the discussion some insights and techniques from professional sociology and using his standing in the profession as a past president of the American Sociological Association to open doors in the university.

Rather than being an advocate, Gamson sees himself as a potential resource for those groups who share the values and preferred framing of the social and political issues that interest him. Being a resource here means doing first-rate professional sociology. One owes this to one's partners—the advocates who are attempting to create a more just world. They need to be able to assess with some accuracy the nature of the opportunities and constraints they face, the weaknesses and strengths of their adversaries, the dynamics of the contest in which they are engaged, and their own internal problems in carrying out their mission. The sociologist in this partnership has a responsibility to help the advocate partners to be objective in the following sense: separating their desires that the world ought to be a certain way from a tough-minded assessment, based on the best available evidence, of whether it actually is that way.

Ryan's involvement with MRAP grew out of a desire to reflect on years of organizing in union, community, and international settings. The tough-minded assessment of existing conditions is essential but not sufficient to guide movement strategies. To craft strategy, movements also need to assess themselves in light of those conditions, to tap wisdom from other movements, and to establish routines that support self-reflection, strategic positioning, and knowledge production. Our activist partners came to appreciate our combined skills, the whole of MRAP being far more useful than any single person or element.

The Challenge of Sustainability

The type of collaboration that we have described assumes that both scholars and the activist organizations can, over time, build infrastructure that facilitates interaction, reflection, and the sharing of learning from one engagement to the next. Boston College, as an institution, has provided a supportive environment for MRAP and for both public and critical sociology. At Boston College, the idea of a value-engaged rather than a value-free way of being a sociologist is completely legitimate and positively supported. We have found that old battles to defend the legitimacy of a value-engaged critical or public sociology against those who would disparage it as "journalism" or "ideology" were not relevant. All four of Burawoy's sociologies (professional, policy, critical, and public) were legitimate and desirable and, far from being marginalized or merely tolerated, public sociology could make the claim of furthering the special mission of the institution as a Jesuit university, to advance social and economic justice with a thoroughly ecumenical spirit.

Yet the MRAP enterprise, in spite of its institutional legitimacy, has faced a number of difficult challenges and frustrations. During a seminar at Boston College, Burawoy was discussing doing public sociology as "organic intellectuals" in contrast to those who do it as "traditional intellectuals." Someone from the audience wisecracked, "Yeah. Those are the ones who get paid." We exchanged glances and a rueful smile.

The wisecrack was a reminder of how, even in the mostly favorable and supportive environment at Boston College, it has been extremely difficult to institutionalize the kind of public sociology pursued by Burawoy's organic intellectuals. The experience has sensitized us to additional tensions between professional sociology and public sociology beyond the false dichotomy between scientist and advocate.

During the community outreach phase of MRAP, the university supplied both in-kind support in the form of office space and, for about four years, a half-time salary for Ryan as codirector. But Boston College aspires to be the leading Catholic research university, and the research university ideal is Harvard's "Every tub on its own bottom." Ultimately, the MRAP community outreach program would have to compete for sponsors with more conventional professional and policy sociologies. Our experience in seeking external, long-term funding for operational costs has been a discouraging one.

It is possible to frame what MRAP does in ways that are acceptable to nonprofit and public sector programs and we made such attempts—we accepted contract work from nonprofits, wrote grants, and responded to federal requests for proposals. A brief account of one such attempt will illustrate one of the central problems. MRAP participant Bill Meinhofer, an experienced grant writer, worked with eight of our community partners to respond to a Commerce Department request for proposals to address the digital divide: the program proposed to help low-income communities, particularly communities of color, increase their uses of new technologies, including the Internet.

Building on the groups' participation in our Media Fellows program, we requested funding for computers, database creation, website development, and training in new technologies, the goal being to increase the groups' overall communications capacity. In our proposal, we made the point that none of the organizations had sufficient staff and resources to achieve such a capacity on their own since they were almost all small organizations with budgets of $500,000 a year or less. Each group expressed eagerness to participate.

We received a high rating, just below the funding level for that year, and were encouraged to resubmit. The kicker was in the content of the reviews regarding how to improve our proposal. The reviewers, were concerned about the stability and survivability of the grassroots organizations with whom we had developed working relationships. We were likely to be funded, we were told, if we made the same proposal with a large, well-established statewide nonprofit such as the United Way. A public sociology dedicated to helping grassroots change organizations with limited resources increase their capacity and, therefore, their chances of survival, was not fundable; but working with an established charitable organization would be. We did not resubmit.

Our efforts to achieve funding from private foundations were more promising and successful. The Boston Foundation funded the Media Fellows program for a few years and we had a number of other small grants for specific projects. Often these projects consumed more resources than they provided, since large portions of them went to the community groups with whom we were collaborating; program implementation required a considerable amount of uncompensated work on top of what was covered in the budget.

We found that foundations are happier to provide seed money for projects that promise to become self-sustaining but have unrealistic expectations about the speed with which this can be accomplished. Furthermore, foundations with a social-action orientation are often distrustful—for good reasons—of university-based projects with community "partners" who are more like clients than collaborators.

The Challenge of Multisector Negotiations

Collaboration is fine in principle but not so smooth in practice. Community-university partnerships usually involve three-way or four-way negotiations among community-based organizations, universities, funders, and, sometimes, government agencies. Despite shared goals, each social location has competing agendas, constituencies, timetables, standards, budgets, and space limitations. Accrued, these complicate collaboration.

From the professional sociologist's standpoint, dialogic social movement theorizing is risky business. We have found that it takes five to seven years for a full-fledged collaboration to bear fruit. Yet the nomadic academic marketplace makes it difficult for sociologists to make long-term commitments. With tenure track as the pacesetter, academic culture pushes fast-track research achievable in a summer. Academics need sure bets: stalled collaborations or disagreements over findings represent lost publications—not heavenly opportunities to deepen theory. And so academics gravitate toward quick ways to harvest data that minimize relation building.

The pressure to publish work that contributes to existing paradigms also results in academics writing in language impenetrable to nonspecialists. For instance, social movement theory devolves into a private language of social movement scholars. Collective actors who do not speak that language are seen as atheoretical or as sources of raw material in the colonial tradition. This hurts relation building. Activists rarely see social movement theorists honor their ideas, much less recognize that activists theorize constantly.

Perceiving theorists as being more interested in each other than in front-line experience, activists withdraw as well. That activists could have been theorists' collaborators and have been given the short end of the academic whooping stick is obscured. A self-fulfilling prophecy is at work, with each side retreating to a stereotype of the other.

Some theorists have tried to collaborate but feel undercut by the pragmatic, antitheorizing bent of many schools of movement organizing. To complicate the most engaged theorist's tasks further, collective actors themselves are responding to many external rhythms—city hall hearings, legislative cycles, funding cycles, and contract negotiations. Each arena—politics, philanthropy, education, economics, health care—introduces unique rules of play and evaluation standards and boasts its own specialized languages, demands, and criteria for success. Organizers fear that acknowledging weaknesses will erode a hard-won reputation, destabilize a coalition, or undercut foundations' interest.

To gain funding, for instance, the collective actor may code-switch; a project denied funding when called "infrastructure" is funded when labeled "capacity building." They may feel pressured to claim early and exaggerated victories rather than share mixed or disappointing results. In failing to learn from valiant but unsuccessful experiments, the natural cycle of learning through action and reflection is disrupted.

Collective actors need to be convinced that academics' or foundations' invitation to reflect on practice will be worth the effort and will not be used against them. Activists explain that they are working hard just to hold the fort. To evaluate their organization critically is to risk not getting a grant renewed. And yet activists simultaneously express a need for safe spaces to talk and reflect. While MRAP never had adequate resources, we had enough to begin—space for reflection, access to libraries, the Internet, and an institutional sponsor so that we could approach foundations. The space we gained was tenuous at best; many of our academic peers dismissed our work as traditional professional "service." We have never achieved sufficient institutional stability—the very process of establishing partnerships and delivering tangible results often exhausts more resources than are allotted. As a result, we learn a great deal, but consolidate our lessons incompletely.

Lessons Learned

As we write, MRAP is rapidly approaching its twenty-fifth year. Perhaps like many silver anniversaries, we find the experience bittersweet; our quest to advance media justice has not escaped the growing pressure on universities and nonprofits from market forces. We have seen individuals and far too many organizations come into and leave the media justice field. While not ignoring the steady expansion of transnational media conglomerates in these decades, we have also observed, and in a modest way contributed, to the rise of a global communication movement. Lawrence Frey and Kevin Carragee's anthologies of *Communication Activism* suggest the breadth and richness of that movement.[10] We have also witnessed increased attention to communication justice by all social movements. Now communication is increasingly included in human rights charters.

MRAP's primary objectives have been twofold: (1) to document structural inequalities in media institutions and (2) to collaborate with social justice movements to address these media inequities. While we are far from having achieved those objectives, we have learned much about how to build media justice collaborations between scholars and movement organizations. We would stress the need to attend to the following factors:

- *Sustained working relationships between scholars and justice groups.* Relationships need to be long-term and not terminate at the end of a contract or grant. And they are not personal; they are intended to "build the work" of media justice.
- *Collaboration that seeks mutual benefit in the pursuit of a shared justice goal.* The collaboration between activist researchers and social movement organizations needs to be democratic in nature, with open and reflective communication between both parties that reflects their respective knowledge and experience.
- *Creation of communication infrastructure (in the academy or the community) that permits the justice organization to gain standing as a consistent, reliable, and dependable actor in communication arenas.*

- *Engagement in learning cycles so activists and scholars distill lessons from practical campaigns.* (A favorite MRAP aphorism is that "experience is not the best teacher; reflection on experience is the best teacher.")
- *Establishment of archives for storing and disseminating movement learning.* Social movements often have short lives, making it all the more imperative that institutional memories be organized, stored, and shared with other generations and other movements.

While the decision by scholars and collective actors to engage in the work described may be costly and slow both the activists' agenda and academic work, the ultimate result is infinitely superior. Given limited space, a story may best illustrate this. One of our community partners, Project RIGHT, complained repeatedly to local TV news stations regarding negative portrayals of their community and Boston's communities of color as crime ridden. They asked not that crime reports be stopped but that news coverage of communities of color put crime in economic and political context—for instance, that youth crime be covered in the context of public and private disinvestment in jobs, education, and so on. Working together, the Boston Association of Black Journalists, MRAP, Project RIGHT, and other organizations surveyed community needs, documented weaknesses in coverage, and developed proposals for change that they presented to general managers of local TV stations. Having researched and strategized carefully, we were able to counter the media outlets' token responses and push beyond them. While our long-term impact was modest, the experience thrilled all involved. For us, it represented public sociology at its best, synergistically linking uncommon partners to deepen knowledge and equalize social resources.

A tough-minded assessment of the safe space MRAP created would force us to recognize that we also benefit from distinguishing between wishes and reality. MRAP scholar-activist partnerships fall short of their full potential: in the absence of sufficient resources to develop infrastructure, sustain working relationships, and amass learning, how could we expect otherwise? MRAP's participants struggle, often unsuccessfully, to bridge the often lonely divides of American academia and American life.

For the kind of public sociology represented by MRAP to survive in a university, perhaps the institution must incorporate a larger vision of the value of such engagements. Not every tub can stand on its own bottom. Programs committed to addressing structural inequalities may not always be able to be self-sustaining. The issue of short-term costs versus long-term benefits arises: would not liberal education including academic sociology benefit from long-term investments in a more equitable society?

As tough-minded assessors, we consider the alternatives—the corporatist drift of much of the academy versus the costs of collaborative scholarship that resists that drift. In our judgment, the effort has been worth it. Our shared strengths bolstered individual weaknesses. Together with partners, we managed at times to use ideas and community to launch strategic challenges to media inequalities—"to put a heart where a gash has been," in the words of radical planner, Mauricio Gaston. For us, the imperfect whole has far exceeded the imperfect parts.

Notes

1. Media Research and Action Project, http://www.mrap.info. Recently, the project's name was changed to Movement/Media Research Action Project.
2. William Gamson, "Safe Spaces and Social Movements," *Perspectives on Social Problems* 8 (1996): 27–38.
3. Michael Burawoy, "2004 ASA Presidential Address: For Public Sociology," *American Sociological Review* 70, no. 1 (2005): 4–28.
4. Doug Bevington and Chris Dixon have documented that most activists do not utilize academic social movement theory. Bevington and Dixon, "Movement-Relevant Theory: Rethinking Social Movement Scholarship and Action," *Social Movement Studies* 4, no. 3 (2005): 185–208.
5. Aldon Morris, *The Origins of the Civil Rights Movement: Black Communities Organizing for Change* (London: Free Press Collier Macmillan, 1984).
6. For an excellent, historically grounded introduction to the public sociology debates, see Robert Kleidman, "Engaged Social Movement Scholarship," in *Handbook of Public Sociology*, ed. Vincent Jeffries (Lanham, MD: Rowman and Littlefield, 2009), 341–56.
7. Mary F. Belenky, Blythe Clinchy, Nancy Goldberger, and Jill Tarule, *Women's Ways of Knowing: The Development of Self, Voice and Mind* (New York: Basic Books, 1986), 144.
8. Karen Jeffreys, communication with authors, July 7, 2005.
9. Sarah De Cataldo, interview by authors, June 5, 2007.
10. Lawrence Frey and Kevin Carragee, *Communication Activism: Communication for Social Change*, 2 vols. (Cresskill, NJ: Hampton Press, 2007).

CHAPTER 6

Media Is Not the Issue

Justice Is the Issue

Nina Gregg

When media activist Malkia Cyril told a roomful of attendees at the 2007 Southeast Media Justice Conference in Knoxville, Tennessee, that "media is not the issue . . . justice is the issue,"[1] she was relaying a message that had been partly born in Tennessee five years earlier. Cyril, director of the Youth Media Council (now the Center for Media Justice) in Oakland, California, participated in an invitation-only gathering on media justice at the Highlander Research and Education Center in Tennessee in August 2002.[2] That meeting, funded by the Ford Foundation and organized by community media consultant Nan Rubin, set in motion several initiatives, among them Ford's support of a new Media Justice Fund (MJF) at the Funding Exchange (FEX)[3] and the participation of FEX member funds around the country in media justice grant making.[4] The MJF, which closed down in 2009, was "grounded in the belief that social and economic justice will not be realized without the equitable redistribution and control of media and communication technologies. The MJF supports leadership of people of color, low-income families, LBGT and youth, working within marginalized communities to organize around media and communication technologies to affect media accountability, infrastructure and policy change."[5]

FEX had been making grants for film, video, and radio projects through the Paul Robeson Fund for Independent Media for more than 20 years.[6] The new MJF emphasized influencing federal communication policy and promoted community media collaboration and capacity building rather than production—reflecting the composition of the 2002 Highlander meeting and Ford's commitment to media policy reform.[7] The group assembled at Highlander was concerned about changes in federal communication policy and wanted to support the emergence of organizations prepared to challenge deregulation of the media sector. Participants were "asked to look at the current issues in media policy and the needs for strategic organizing."[8] The group agreed on two very basic political principles:

1. *Technology and Media should serve all people*—Each of us has an individual commitment based on the core values of social justice and equality, and the institutions that control and shape our media must be transformed in order to realize this goal.

2. *Local communities, especially those that are marginalized, should have some ability to decide how media resources are created, used and allocated*—As the major target of mass media and technology, the public has a strong interest in both the structure and content of its media. There must be accessible mechanisms to promote public voices, participation and involvement in how media is used and governed.[9]

The Media Justice Fund at the Funding Exchange

"Compared to other social justice issues . . . the field was undernourished and under-resourced," Hye-Jung Park, an FEX staffer, reflected later. "Media justice was another galvanizing issue within the larger vision of social justice."[10] However, tension between the objective of elevating media policy reform as a social justice issue and social justice activists' strategic interest in shaping coverage of their issues and producing their own content emerged as one of the key challenges in the meeting and would surface later in media justice grantmaking both nationally and among FEX's member funds.[11]

The MJF announced three goals:

1. To support (1) work carried out by media activist and reform groups that organize around social justice principles and (2) work carried out by social justice organizations that engage in media activism and reform as a component of their core work through strategic funding.

2. To impact Media and/or Telecommunications policy; expand and/or establish infrastructure within a given community; or promote and advocate corporate and industry media accountability encouraging collaboration between organizations with a media focus and organizations with a broader social justice perspective.

3. To facilitate the creation of regional collaborations of media justice and social justice organizers and activists by involving Funding Exchange member funds in the overall process.[12]

FEX (in consultation with Ford) outlined Community Media Collaborations, Media Justice Toolkits, Immediate Response Grants, and regional meetings as activities eligible for grants.[13] Funding was also available for traveling to regional and national conferences on media reform. The MJF developed a comprehensive communication and information campaign, the Media Justice Community (a web-based platform for ongoing networking within the media justice community), and the Knowledge Exchange, an innovative collaboration with Consumers Union, a national consumer advocacy organization, to "identify the community impacts of national media policy, as a critical step in building a more just and diverse media landscape."[14] Over six years (2003 through 2009) the fund distributed more than $2 million, nearly $1 million of which was distributed to member funds for their grantmaking programs. Ten percent of the distribution to member funds was allocated for administration.[15]

This chapter focuses on media justice grants made by the Appalachian Community Fund (ACF), a member of FEX, through the lens of Malkia Cyril's assertion that media is not the issue, justice is the issue. The aspirations and expectations of the group that met at Highlander and the needs and realities of community organizers and social justice activists were different but not incompatible. By considering how media justice was understood by grant recipients and tracing how they used the media justice grants, this chapter explores both the opportunities and challenges of fulfilling the vision of media justice.

The Appalachian Community Fund

ACF was founded in 1987 as a publicly supported, nonprofit grantmaking organization providing resources to grassroots organizations working to overcome the underlying causes of poverty and injustice in Central Appalachia (east Tennessee, eastern Kentucky, southwest Virginia, and West Virginia). The history of Appalachia is one of economic and environmental exploitation as well as organized and grassroots resistance.[16] Over 20-plus years ACF has awarded over $5 million to more than 300 community-based social justice organizations.[17] Many of ACF's grantees work in small communities far from urban centers and across large geographic regions, without mass transit and with limited or inconsistent Internet service. In its large area and low population density, the region served by ACF differs from the locations of most other FEX funds.

ACF had not previously defined media justice activities as a funding priority. When FEX launched the MJF, Gaye Evans, executive director of ACF, saw an opportunity: "We know groups in the region are doing media justice work, and there's the history in Appalachia of people trying to tell their stories themselves instead of others telling their stories. We wanted to raise the discussion and analysis to a different level by convening people to share what they are doing."

ACF partnered with the Fund for Southern Communities (another FEX member) to host the February 2007 conference. "The MJF opened this up for us—we wouldn't have arrived at this level of engagement and analysis without the new resources," Evans said. ACF planned to apply to FEX for funding to make media justice grants; one rationale for the conference was "to educate ourselves about who might be applying."[18]

The 2007 Southeast Media Justice Conference was designed as an opportunity for social justice organizations to expand their understanding of media justice work in the South and Appalachia, to deepen understanding of issues around media control and media justice, and to explore places for further work and collaboration.[19] "The MJF and Ford emphasized the importance of media policy issues (ownership and control) for social justice, but our conference had a broader scope, reflecting the experiences and needs of groups in our region," explained Evans.[20] In their evaluations of the value of the conference, participants shared new understandings and identified next steps with their organizations, including the following:

- I learned a lot about "Media Justice," how it is more: (1) fighting the media to get your story told; (2) being able to have access to media/media tools; (3) coming up with a strategy to get through the media by being courageous and demanding.
- I will take home a new understanding of Media Justice and how it affects the work we do. I will start a conversation w/ Board about media justice and how or should it be integrated into our strategic plan.
- A deeper appreciation of the need for true justice versus more access.[21]

After the conference, ACF circulated a request for proposals and encouraged community groups to think more strategically about the relationship of media to their social justice agendas. The need for media strategy was already understood by these groups. The region has a long and well-documented history of pervasive stereotypes[22] as well as cultural traditions using music, drama, poetry, and film to tell its stories, but the availability of grants from ACF to support media activity as part of social justice work was new—and not just for ACF. The Media Justice Fund was "the first fund to deliberately connect smaller, grassroots social justice organizations with those who do more traditional media policy work."[23]

In addition to the national media justice grants awarded through the MJF, for three years FEX made media justice monies available to member funds to disburse through their own activist-led grant making. During two funding cycles (2007 and 2008), ACF awarded $54,000 in media justice grants from $5,000 to $7,500 in two categories: (1) Media Justice Toolkits, which were "popular education materials for social justice activists and the general public on media justice issues" and (2) Community Media Collaborations, described as "projects that address media policy, infrastructure or accountability within the context of a social justice issue or campaign."[24] Tennessee Health Care Campaign, the Appalachian Institute for Media Justice, and the Community Media Organizing Project received grants for Toolkits; the Ohio Valley Environmental Coalition, the Center for Rural Strategies, Appalshop, South Central Educational Development, and Citizens for Police Review received grants for Community Media Collaborations. Most were one-time awards; the Community Media Organizing Project and Ohio Valley Environmental Coalition received grants both years.

The Toolkits funded by ACF incorporated hands-on training for members and allies in public speaking, developing media strategies (framing, messaging, and best practices for events and different media), and introductions to new technologies. Media policy issues were addressed but skills and strategy were prioritized. All the Community Media Collaborations emphasized new content production and new producers, with variations that reflected the missions, locations, scope, and needs of each organization. Citizens for Police Review, inspired by Deep Dish Network and the independent radio news program *Democracy Now!*, aimed for the "'technical empowerment' of residents which can in turn lead to community and political empowerment"[25] by encouraging increased production of community access programming by African American residents of Knoxville; Appalshop's project was designed to bring ten organizations into the online community through radio webcasting; and South Central Educational Development planned to train youth and members of the lesbian, gay, bisexual, transgender, questioning (LGBTQ) community and others without voice in southern West Virginia counties in webcasting and to provide the organizational and studio infrastructure for their webcasts. The Ohio Valley Environmental Coalition embarked on a long-term strategy to develop an alternative grassroots media network for distribution of local citizens' stories of fighting for community survival with increasing numbers of individuals and policy makers, to place community media stories to positively influence policy decisions, and to strengthen the base of community activists in the region and beyond who are working for a sustainable future.[26]

Tennessee Health Care Campaign's Community Media Toolkit

Tennessee Health Care Campaign (THCC) offers a representative example of the adaptation of the MJF's vision of Toolkits to the realities of a grassroots organization's mission and needs. A core element of THCC's identity is a commitment to participation of the people most affected by health care policy in the shaping of public policy: "By involving and developing leaders from those most affected by public policy, THCC enables the faces and voices of the disenfranchised to be seen and heard, and helps everyday people to engage in civic participation—often for the first time."[27] This commitment complements the visions of media justice that were circulating at the 2007 Southeast Media Justice Conference.

THCC began in 1989 with a mission to ensure guaranteed affordable choices in health care for everyone. The organization relies on volunteers throughout Tennessee to be the faces and voices of health care advocacy, and the grant from ACF enabled THCC to provide education and training in an area of the state that was key to THCC's organizing strategy.[28] The purpose of the ACF grant, according to Susan McKay, THCC's communication and development director, was to "change the dynamic of how low-wealth, uninsured people were covered by the local news media. We also wanted to have those impacted by health care policy, especially the uninsured, reclaim their voice by learning how to engage media." Media justice, McKay explained, "means having ordinary people have a voice in creating and shaping news and information in their communities . . . Part of our mission is about getting those directly impacted by health care policy directly involved in advocating for themselves and within their communities, so our mission and our idea of media justice go hand in hand."[29]

Three training components occurred over nearly a year: two workshops on media framing and messaging, followed by six months of monitoring local media to document the presentation of health care (content, points of view, and who spoke), and finally, engaging the media through radio interviews, newspaper stories, and letters to the editor. The foundation laid in 2007–2008 appears to have paid off, as THCC is now deeply engaged in the national health care debate and volunteers remain active in this region of Tennessee. However, McKay noted that one-time funding "makes any significant results hard [to sustain]."[30]

Ohio Valley Environmental Coalition's Mountain Reporter Network

The Mountain Reporter Network illustrates the integration of the MJF's vision of Community Media Collaborations (addressing media policy, accountability, or infrastructure within the context of a social justice issue or campaign) into an ambitious, long-term strategy that is as much an engagement with the existing media system as an attempt to bypass it. With objectives similar to those of THCC, the Ohio Valley Environmental Coalition (OVEC), in partnership with the Center for Rural Strategies, launched the Mountain Reporter Network. OVEC is "dedicated to the improvement and preservation of the environment through education, grassroots organizing and coalition building, leadership development and media outreach." Active throughout West Virginia and portions of southern Ohio and eastern Kentucky, OVEC members address environmental concerns including clean air and water, the economic and environmental impacts of coal mining, sludge safety, alternative energy, and clean elections. In recent years, OVEC has become nationally recognized for education and organizing to halt mountaintop removal coal mining.[31] OVEC's partner, the Center for Rural Strategies, "seeks to improve economic and social conditions for communities in the countryside and around the world through the creative and innovative use of media and communications. By presenting accurate and compelling portraits of rural lives and cultures, we hope to deepen public debate and create a national environment in which positive change for rural communities can occur."[32]

When ACF awarded a media justice grant to OVEC, the organization had been working on communication strategies for quite some time.[33] The Progressive Technology Project provided OVEC with a camera and sound recording equipment, which were used in trainings to raise confidence levels of members as expert spokespeople. "We are constantly being asked by media to put them into contact with individuals," said OVEC staff member Vivian Stockman. "We have a visually compelling story, an extensive list of traditional media and bloggers, and organize several events each year that draw media attention. When our organizers meet new people, if they have stories to tell, we encourage them to talk to the media."[34]

With the grant from ACF, OVEC held eight training workshops with members and youth leaders on framing, messaging, and digital media production skills. The organization, according to its report to AFC, had identified a need to "make and distribute our own media . . . to take advantage of the increasing web-based communications that by-pass Big Media . . . and to produce our own radio actualities and film clips" for radio and TV stations. "We operate on the principle that social change can happen when ordinary citizens feel personally powerful and see themselves as agents of change . . . If people hear their neighbors on local radio or on the Internet, they understand both the importance of the issue and the power available to those who make their own media."[35]

OVEC began exploring the use of new media technologies to provide coverage free of coal industry influence as an alternative to local media's dependence on industry.[36] Through the partnership with the Center for Rural Strategies, OVEC trained members in community and web-based radio and PlaceStories, a digital storytelling and communications system, as part of their effort to develop the Mountain Reporter Network as an alternative, community-based media project.[37] Community reporters, who have been trained as both spokespeople and citizen journalists, "become leaders, and they model leadership behavior to people they interview as well as to other members."[38] As OVEC's Vivian Stockman admitted, "We're having a harder time [building a Mountain Reporter Network with digital media than with traditional media] because of the digital divide."[39] In some counties where OVEC is active, there is no high-speed Internet access and not everyone has computers. After PlaceStories trainings, people are eager to create and share their stories but often need assistance to get them onto the network. Mimi Pickering, who led PlaceStories trainings, described a man who "stayed up all night to baby his computer while it downloaded the software" and who parks outside a fast-food restaurant to log on to their wireless network. He created a PlaceStory but was unable to upload it to the website.[40]

Stockman made virtually the same point as Susan McKay of THCC about what media justice means for their members and their issues. "It's essential people be allowed to tell their own stories and be heard without a corporate lens," Stockman said. "It's empowering for people in the coalfields to hear their neighbors on NPR; the role model of speaking up enables the next person down the holler to speak up, to be affirmed that 'what I've learned and gone through is real. I should be respected when I stand up and be heard. I count and my opinion counts.'"[41]

OVEC's media strategy goes beyond individual affirmation. "The training deconstructs the media," explained Pickering. "It enables people to become more engaged as activists and citizens." Pickering described another community organization that recorded stories of people trying to continue their education while enrolled in a workfare program. "They brought the recorded stories to the state capitol and gave copies to legislators who were able to see constituents they'd never see otherwise. When the stories of affected people come to life, they can change policy."[42] Stockman and Pickering see the PlaceStories web platform and the digital stories as tools for community building and outreach, the building blocks of an online community of people of similar interests telling their stories to each other nationally and internationally. PlaceStories is "a way to get around corporate media gatekeepers."[43]

Communicating about Justice

The centrality of controlling and producing content as a component of MJF grantees' definitions and understandings of media justice was noted by Catherine Borgman-Arboleda and Al Reynolds of ActKnowledge, who conducted an evaluation of the MJF for the Ford Foundation. "The MJF was the only funder of new, innovative, emerging work, a pipeline for new leadership and new ideas," observed Borgman-Arboleda. "They were able to see media justice in a broader way—not just policy."[44] And relevant policy opportunities do not exist in every community. Where there was no media policy activist group, grantees promoted social justice through training in production, media literacy, media education, and critiques of media policy. Among outcomes noted by Borgman-Arboleda were the strengthening of social justice groups' knowledge of media issues and leadership in their communities and media groups' ability to move from an exclusive focus on media issues to connecting media issues with social justice issues. One source told her, "Getting folks interested in production gets them interested in access and digital and communication rights . . . People progress from 'now I have this skill . . . and I want to share the stories' to understanding that it's really important to think about the communication infrastructure."[45]

ACF declined to participate in the third year of the MJF's distributed funding, which focused on media policy, accountability, and infrastructure.[46] Evans concluded that one-year grants were insufficient for recipients to initiate new projects (although some MJF grantees were able to use their grants to leverage additional support from other sources).[47] ACF's 2007 and 2008 media justice grantees understood the impact of policy and had been able to accommodate the grant requirements within their goals and communities but few were prepared to shift their attention and resources from using media for social justice to media policy, accountability, and infrastructure.[48] The national media reform movement, with its focus on federal policy, is removed from many grassroots activists' experiences and realities. Linking media policy reform to social justice is both reasonable and necessary, but for activists facing daily challenges for survival, media policy reform seems remote.

For these social justice activists toiling in rural communities and small cities on issues like police brutality, environmental devastation, and access to health care, the media reform movement does not match the urgency of getting their stories and perspectives in circulation and representing themselves instead of having to challenge and overcome the distortions of others. These activists and organizers acknowledge the systemic relationship between their struggles over representation and the inequities of federal media policy and ownership, but they have also been successful with strategic and creative use of existing media. For example, the movement to stop mountaintop removal mining now has national recognition, and this was accomplished without significant changes to federal media policy. The continuing importance of creating content (along with media policy reform) was affirmed by Thenmozhi Soundararajan, director of Third World Majority in Oakland, California, in a report evaluating the first few years of the MJF: "Media Justice is different [from media democracy]. We can't separate the fight for a just media from the fight for a just society. It's possible to have a local, highly regulated media and still have content that's racist or homophobic. We need to focus on structural change *as well as* content, and content is a key way for communities to engage with media issues."[49]

Training of spokespeople and new content producers and the development of alternative media communities serve immediate organizing needs and at the same time support the meaning of media justice expressed by Malkia Cyril in a March 2007 blog post about the Southeast Media Justice Conference titled "Deep in My Heart: The South Speaks the Language of Media Justice": "Media justice is more than sexy rhetoric; a powerful re-framing of a centuries-old relationship: the relationship of disenfranchised communities to political power. Media justice houses an analysis of that relationship, a participatory strategy for local to national change, an agenda for relevant policy and structural change, and a broad vision for racial, economic, and gender justice—all of which combine to create a framework for fundamental media and social change that includes the radical redistribution of communication rights and power."[50]

Although the vision of media justice articulated at the 2007 Southeast Media Justice Conference[51] remains unfulfilled and the FEX Media Justice Fund ceased accepting applications in 2009, the movement conceived at Highlander in 2002, bringing together media reform advocates and social justice activists, is likely to continue to rise to the challenge voiced by Cyril: "Media is not the issue. Justice is the issue. Media is the infrastructure for how we communicate about the issue of justice."[52]

Notes

1. *Media Justice or Media Control* (Knoxville, TN: Appalachian Community Fund, 2007), 4, accessed October 1, 2009, http://www.fex.org/assets/262_appalachianfscconvening.pdf.
2. "A key strategic decision was to work on shifting the terms of media organizing from '*Media Democracy*,' to '*Media Justice*' . . . We thought that transforming the concept to Media Justice will put our efforts on the same level as other social justice and human rights organizing." Nan Rubin, *Highlander Media Justice Gathering* (New Market, TN: Ford Foundation, 2002), 9, accessed October 1, 2009, http://www.highlandercenter.org/pdf-files/media_report.pdf.
3. Nicole Davis and the Applied Research Center, *Strategic Grantmaking and Grassroots Organizing for Media Justice* (New York: Applied Research Center, 2006), 11, accessed April 29, 2010, http://www.fex.org/assets/170_media.pdf. The Funding Exchange is a US network of 16 community foundations and a national office that together grant nearly $15 million annually to grassroots organizations working for social, racial, economic and environmental justice; see "FEX," the Funding Exchange, accessed April 29, 2010, http://www.fex.org.
4. The organizations introduced in this chapter and referred to by acronyms include the Funding Exchange (FEX), the Media Justice Fund (MJF), the Appalachian

Community Fund (ACF), the Tennessee Health Care Campaign (THCC), and the Ohio Valley Environmental Coalition (OVEC).

5. "Funding Exchange—Media Justice Fund," Funding Exchange Media Justice Fund, accessed April 29, 2010, http://www.fex.org/content/index.php?pid=51.

6. Davis and Applied Research Center, *Strategic Grantmaking*, 8–9.

7. Nan Rubin described the participants as "planners, project directors, coordinators, campaign organizers, and policy drafters who understand the power of getting content and technology into people's hands, and are willing to take on the unglamorous work of making it so." As the report notes, "There were no people there who were primarily content providers." *Highlander Media Justice Gathering*, 2.

8. Ibid.

9. Ibid., 6–7.

10. Hye-Jung Park, interview with author, July 14, 2009.

11. Suzanne Pharr and Scot Nakagawa of Highlander's staff noted this tension: "The divisions within the group were mainly between the *policy advocates* on one hand, and the *media makers* and *community organizers* on the other." Nan Rubin, *Highlander Media Justice Gathering Final Report prepared for the Ford Foundation*, September 2002, 13.

12. "Funding Exchange—MJF: Grants," Funding Exchange Media Justice Fund, accessed April 29, 2010, http://www.fex.org/content/mjf.php?pid=22.

13. Ibid.

14. "Media Justice Community," Funding Exchange Media Justice Fund, accessed April 25, 2010, http://fexmjf.mayfirst.org; and "Knowledge Exchange Program," Funding Exchange Media Justice Fund, accessed April 25, 2010, http://www.fex .org/assets/320_knowledgeexchangeprogram.doc.

15. Hye-Jung Park, personal communication with author, September 16, 2009.

16. See "About Central Appalachia," Appalachian Community Fund, accessed April 29, 2010, http://www.appalachiancommunityfund.org/html/aboutcentralA.html; Chuck Shuford, "What Happens When You Don't Own the Land," the Daily Yonder blog, July 3, 2009, accessed April 29, 2010, http://www.dailyyonder.com/ what-happens-when-you-dont-own-land/2009/07/03/2205; Richard A. Couto, *Making Democracy Work Better: Mediating Structures, Social Capital, and the Democratic Prospect* (Chapel Hill: University of North Carolina Press, 1999); Stephen L. Fisher, ed., *Fighting Back in Appalachia: Traditions of Resistance and Change* (Philadelphia: Temple University Press, 1993); and Stephen L. Fisher and Barbara Ellen Smith, eds., *Transforming Places: Lessons from Appalachia* (Champaign: University of Illinois Press, forthcoming).

17. "Appalachian Community Fund," Appalachian Community Fund, accessed April 29, 2010, http://www.appalachiancommunityfund.org.

18. Gaye Evans, interview with author, January 14, 2009.

19. "Media Justice Collaboration Draft of Goals and Agenda," Appalachian Community Fund, December 1–2, 2006.

20. Evans, interview with author.

21. Participants quoted in *Media Justice or Media Control*, 24.

22. For one example among many, see Dwight B. Billings, Gurney Norman, and Katherine Ledford, eds., *Back Talk from Appalachia: Confronting Stereotypes* (Lexington, KY: University Press of Kentucky, 1999).

23. Davis and Applied Research Center, *Strategic Grantmaking*, 20. Media Action Grassroots Network (MAG-Net) is a more recent initiative with a similar vision. MAG-Net is a national coalition of regional organizations working together to build a movement for media justice and communications rights. See "About MAG-Net," Media Action Grassroots Network, accessed April 25, 2010, http://www.mediagrassroots.org/about.

24. "Media Justice Project Description for FEX Member Funds," Appalachian Community Fund, n.d.

25. "Media Justice Grantees 2008," Appalachian Community Fund, n.d.

26. "Media Justice Initiative Recommendations," Appalachian Community Fund, June 2007; and "Media Justice Grantees," Appalachian Community Fund, 2008. The aims of the Ohio Valley Environmental Coalition's Mountain Reporter Network—to distribute local citizens' stories and have an impact on policy—will be familiar to many grassroots organizations; Fred Goff, cofounder of the DataCenter in Oakland, California, recently described the DataCenter's "current focus on partnering with low-income communities to help them capture their own story and make it accessible to the media, policymakers, and others working for change." Goff, "Flashbacks," *datacenter update*, Fall/Winter 2008, 6.

27. "Tennessee Health Care Campaign: About Us," Tennessee Health Care Campaign, accessed April 25, 2010, http://www.tenncare.org/AboutUs/home.html.

28. "Final Report to the Appalachian Community Fund from THCC," Tennessee Health Care Campaign, November 7, 2008.

29. Susan McKay, personal communication with author, August 24, 2009.

30. McKay, personal communication; and "Final Report," THCC.

31. "About OVEC," Ohio Valley Environmental Coalition, accessed April 25, 2010, http://www.ohvec.org/about_ovec/index.html.

32. "About Us," Center for Rural Strategies, accessed April 25, 2010, http://www.ruralstrategies.org/about-us.

33. The Mountain Reporter Network also received a grant from FEX's national Media Justice Fund.

34. Vivian Stockman, interview with author, July 22, 2009.

35. "2007–2008 Report to the Appalachian Community Fund," Ohio Valley Environmental Coalition, 2008.

36. "In West Virginia, Big Coal owns interests in the West Virginia MetroNews Radio Network (with newscasts carried over radio stations across the state), West Virginia Media Holdings (four TV stations and the weekly state 'business' newspaper) and several state newspapers. In papers where there is no direct coal-related ownership, the coal industry is a major advertiser that many papers are reluctant to anger. Over the airwaves, there is a virtual black-out of mountaintop-removal-related news." Ohio Valley Environmental Coalition, "Application to the FEX Media Justice Fund, OVEC and the Center for Rural Strategies," n.d.

37. Mimi Pickering, "Mountain Reporter Network Place Stories—Information and Help," April 22, 2009. See also "About Mountain Reporter Network PlaceStories," Mountain Reporter Network, accessed April 25, 2010, www.placestories.com.

38. "2007–2008 Report," OVEC.

39. Stockman, interview with author.

40. Mimi Pickering, interview with author, July 28, 2009.

41. Stockman, interview with author.

42. Pickering, interview with author.

43. Pickering, interview with author; Stockman, interview with author; and "2007–2008 Report," OVEC.

44. Catherine Borgman-Arboleda, interview with author, August 20, 2009.

45. Borgman-Arboleda, interview with author; Borgman-Arboleda and Al Reynolds, "Media Justice Fund: Key Initial Findings for Discussion. Prepared for FEX Skills Workshop 2009," ActKnowledge, 2008.

46. Park, interview with author.

47. In a published evaluation of another Ford Foundation program, the authors observe, "We believe that funders need to commit to specific organizing efforts for a minimum of five years. This period should include time for groups to plan and build relationships for the implementation of activities." Marilyn Gittell, Charles Price, and Barbara Ferman, *Community Collaborations: Promoting Community Organizing* (New York: Ford Foundation, 2009), 46.

48. Evans, interview with author.

49. Davis and Applied Research Center, *Strategic Grantmaking*, 5, emphasis is in the original.

50. Malkia Cyril, "Deep in My Heart: The South Speaks the Language of Media Justice," WIMN's Voices blog, March 28, 2007, accessed April 25, 2010, http://www.wimnonline.org/WIMNsVoicesBlog/2007/03/28/deep-in-my-heart-the-south-speaks-the-language-of-media-justice.

51. "1) Ownership of the means of production is democratized, publicly accountable and directly in our hands, 2) Media content is diverse, fair, informative, culturally relevant, and increases civic engagement, 3) Media rules are in the service of humanity, abide by international standards, and are enforceable protections of collective rights, 4) Movements for justice have the power and resources to use their communication rights to make structural change." *Media Justice or Media Control*, 5–6.

52. Ibid., 4.

CHAPTER 7

Detours through Youth-Driven Media

Backseat Drivers Bear Witness to the Ethical Dilemmas of Youth Media

Lora Taub-Pervizpour and Eirinn Disbrow

Scholarship on youth media in the last decade has done much to identify the social justice dimensions of youth media practices and cultural productions. While youth media production varies in relation to the social, cultural, political, and economic contexts in which it occurs, social justice frames much of this field of activity.[1] There are diverse and clear social justice issues at stake in providing media education and technology resources to young people who are systematically silenced and excluded, and whose stories confront the unjust representations of youth in corporate consumer culture. At the most basic level, the very work of providing access to the technologies and practices of media making to young people who are systematically marginalized and silenced in or by commercial media *is* social justice work. Most youth media programs are local grassroots efforts waged by advocates who aim to redress the exclusion of youth voices from the public sphere.[2] As one practitioner notes, "Those of us who come to this field have done so because we know at our core that working with young people, identifying issues of relevance for them, and guiding their media productions to be powerful tools of change is unmistakably a radical and essential movement in education."[3] Then there are

The voices of many community partners informed this research and the authors acknowledge in particular the Healthy Youth Peer Education (HYPE) teens who share their perspectives through media production, HYPE codirector Jenna Azar, HYPE intern Sylvia Boateng, faculty from the Departments of Media and Communication and Political Science at Muhlenberg College, and HYPE founders Abby Letcher, MD, and Roberta Meek. The authors recognize the generous support for HYPE from Muhlenberg College and the Dorothy Rider Pool Health Care Trust.

the unmistakable questions of social justice at the heart of media content produced by marginalized young people. Across a range of media—radio, video, and Internet—young people are producing stories that document sufferings, losses, and traumas based on class, race, gender, ethnicity, and sexuality that they directly experience or witness within their communities.[4]

This qualitative study is broadly interested in the media practices and productions of Latino and African American youth participating in Healthy Youth Peer Education (HYPE), a summer program for urban, minority high school students in Allentown, Pennsylvania. In their young lives, these teens already have extensive lived experience of everyday injustices—in their schools, their neighborhoods, and their homes. This chapter considers the social relationships between young media producers and the adults who ally with them in their cultural productions and organize the resources and conditions for their making. While a burgeoning scholarship pays close attention to digitally mediated texts produced by at-risk youth and, in particular, to issues of voice, identity, and agency forged through new media tools, the social relationships that support these cultural productions constitute an important and largely overlooked site for analysis in the context of media and social justice. Documentary fieldwork conducted with HYPE over a year underscores the important fact that providing young people access to new technologies and practices will have limited potential or meaning unless participants intentionally construct social relations more just and humane than the inequities that frame adult-youth relations in the community and culture at large. In their cultural productions, HYPE youth have documented those inequities as they play out in their mistreatment by local police, school authorities, neighborhood residents, and commercial mass media. But at another level, HYPE youth remind us of the imperative to build healthier, more just and equitable relationships *within* the activity of youth media production itself.

HYPE: Context and Method of Study

HYPE is a collaboration between a hospital, a college, and other community arts partners. The program offers high school–age youth opportunities to engage in social change and public advocacy through leadership development, digital storytelling, the performing arts, and documentary work. Participants live in the predominantly low-income and racially diverse neighborhoods of center city Allentown.[5] Our study focuses on program activities during summer 2009, when 11 youth—6 Latino and 5 African American—between the ages of 15 and 20 participated in HYPE. The group consisted of three young men and eight young women. We also gathered qualitative data during the yearlong after-school program with a smaller group of continuing HYPE students. One of us (Taub-Pervizpour) is chair of the Media and Communication Department where HYPE is located and has partnered with HYPE for five years; the other author (Disbrow) is a recent college graduate who served HYPE as a media education assistant from June 2009 to May 2010. The study draws on the qualitative methods of participant observation and documentary fieldwork and includes data from field notes written by the researchers and other HYPE staff members, a range of documentary sources, and unstructured interviews conducted by Disbrow with three HYPE students (Alysia, age 16; Jessie, age 16; and Shaniqua, age 18). In-depth interviews were conducted with Jenna Azar, the HYPE program coordinator, and with education scholar Michael Carbone, who, as chair of the education program at Muhlenberg College, has extensive knowledge of the Allentown School District. We also look closely at the documentary video produced by the HYPE teens in summer 2009, *Roots of Change*, which provides important insights for considering the limits and potentials of youth media in Allentown.[6]

Power and Powerlessness behind the Camera

HYPE provides a safe and supportive context for learning and development where young people have possibilities to voice their concerns about the community issues that matter to them most.[7] Disempowering relationships with adults figure prominently in these conversations. HYPE students unanimously view the community as unwelcoming to young people in general and adults as distrusting of youth of color in particular. Person-on-the-street interviews conducted by HYPE on a summer morning confirmed this perception: "What do I thinka teenagers? Buncha hoodlums, that's what I think."[8] No experience better demonstrated how disempowered HYPE students feel in the face of adult authority than their formal interview with the principal of the largest public high school in the Allentown School District.

The interview team—Amanda, Dahlia, Shaniqua, and Sheridan—accompanied by Disbrow and Azar, travelled the eight blocks between HYPE and the high school by car, equipped with a camera, microphone, and a list of carefully worded interview questions. As the interviewers sat in the principal's waiting room, their anxiety was visible. When the principal—a large and gruff-looking man with a thick grey walrus mustache wearing a school jersey—stepped into the room, all the girls sat silently. Doing nothing to put them at ease, he coughed, "Well?" Urged by Disbrow, they mumbled their names without making eye contact and then filed behind him into an office crowded with school spirit paraphernalia. The girls quickly sank into their seats, leaving Disbrow to set up the camera. Amanda held the sheet of interview questions and positioned her chair next to the principal, but out of the camera frame, more reticent and nervous than she had been conducting person-on-the-street interviews earlier in the week. Disbrow asked many of the follow-up questions, hoping to provide a model for the teens to adopt. But they said very little, and the principal made no visible effort to engage them or put them at ease. Close scrutiny of nearly 60 minutes of interview footage reveals to us some of the issues of power and ethics that emerge when young media makers turn their cameras on the adults who have very specific forms of authority over their everyday social lives.

Early in the interview, when asked about the difficulties of his work, the principal reports that his greatest struggle is "getting kids involved" in extracurricular activities. He barely mentions lack of resources before turning to speak at length about the importance of nonacademic after-school activities—band, football, theater, music. This was one of the few times that Amanda veered from her interview script to ask (with evident disbelief and with her own young awareness of larger issues at stake), "Do you think the reason they're not involved is because they choose to be or because the resources aren't there?" The principal replies, "It's a choice thing. These opportunities are there. It's just a matter of kids choosing." Amanda presses on: "Do you think they are motivated [to participate]?" "Well, that's a deeper question. What is motivation?" It is, of course, a rhetorical question that Amanda does not challenge. After an awkward silence, the principal at last acknowledges that "it's tough for our kids. A lot of them have commitments after school, a lot of things beyond their control," but emphasizes that "it's up to each individual student to make the most of the opportunities we provide."

Despite the principal's claim that "fun kids" are the best part of his job, the girls present during the interview experience the school as anything but fun and deeply unwelcoming. What is striking in the footage is the complete absence of any conversation about academics. "He doesn't see these kids as potentiating into anything, as emergent adults," explains Muhlenberg's Carbone, who oversees student teachers placed in the district. "It's disingenuous to talk about the kids' participation. If I were a kid, I'd be thinking, 'this is *my* responsibility?' No, it's the responsibility of the school to be inclusive of all young people and to create a space and activities that are responsive to students' academic needs and interests." This underlying injustice shaped the teens' interview with the principal. Initially eager to conduct the interview, the teens stated after the fact it was really "a waste of time," meaningless, and ultimately disempowering.

In the institutional context of the school, the "principal's office" is, for inner-city students, almost always marked as a space of conflict, punishment, and—above all else—control. Azar recalls the interview experience: "The kids were quiet, they were compliant, they weren't asking any questions that were harder than what they wrote down. They weren't pushing at all, and so in terms of the way that urban institutions are set up to educate youth—that is what you saw. *They were maintaining order.*[9] One of the interviewers, Shaniqua, sat captivated by the principal's power: "I was thinking about while he was talking [how] there are so many kids in that school and it's just him that has the authority over them and that's it."[10] *That's it.* If, as Steven Goodman writes, "urban high schools are taking on the look and feel of prisons," the principal looks and seems like the head security guard.[11] In trying to make sense of the dynamic during the interview, Azar reflects, "What you see when young people come up against power [is that] they only have a few options, and most of the time they chose the power of disengagement, the power of not caring."[12]

Reviewing and editing the interview sequence offered a second opportunity for the teens to critically engage the issues they felt the principal had dismissed and to assert some creative control in how the principal's voice would be included in their video. Back in the editing studio, implicit and explicit struggles over what to include and exclude from this segment began to emerge. Amanda sat to review the footage with Sylvia, a HYPE college intern and former student at the high school presided over by this principal. Sylvia recalls the complexities of that task:

> When I listened to [the principal] talk, I tried to be as objective as possible because we had just talked with Lora [Taub-Pervizpour] about representing someone's voice as true as possible. However, when I heard some of his answers to questions concerning a possible relationship between HYPE and Allen High School or his alleged openness to hearing student opinion, I couldn't help but think it was just a show because there was a camera on him. Having come out of [that high school], only a few students know that it is even possible to start a new club/program in the school and he favors AP/honors and sports teams. If you are not in those two groups, you are pretty much forgotten about. Despite these feelings, I still dragged the clips down and left them as possible ones for the final cut. I knew I probably wasn't going to do the final cut, so I left the clips for others to decide.[13]

Decisions about what to include and exclude are always subjective, and in this case reveal some of the tensions between adult and youth perspectives.[14]

Working from clips identified by Amanda and Sylvia, a small group extracted a sound bite that triggered Azar's concern over representing the principal in the documentary. In her role as program coordinator, she was alert to the potential backlash the young filmmakers faced if they were perceived to be portraying him in a bad or unfair light. Many of the HYPE filmmakers attend the same school as the principal and have to face him in the corridors daily. She also raised the risk of turning the principal against the program, which could potentially undermine wider community support. Azar advocated that the wider context of the clip be restored to the sequence and the teens did so without protest.

Clearly, taking away young people's creative control over their cultural production runs counter to the goals of the youth media movement. Youth media educators share a responsibility to expand young people's right to communicate, not to impose further limitations on that right. But Azar's concerns reflect her awareness of our responsibility to ask the students critical questions that challenge them to think through the implications of their production choices. The teens were disillusioned by the outcome of the interview with the principal, and although they weren't particularly concerned about a negative depiction, they accepted Azar's concern about the bigger picture. Locating conversations about the ethics of representation at the center of our work can empower youth to make production choices that serve the larger social justice objectives at stake.

The Rough Cut: "This Is Our Call to Action"

With just two days until the public screening of the HYPE documentary, the HYPE crew gathered to watch a rough cut. The rough cut was assembled during the weekend by the program's technology assistant from four distinct segments created by four production teams. Prior to that moment, there was but a vague shared sense of how the four segments would come together. All eyes were on the large screen. All watched the 18-minute video intently. When it was over, after a very long silence, the first to speak was one of the program's founders, an educator, who was struck by an overabundance of adults onscreen. "I just don't get the sense of HYPE," she explained and asked with passion, "Where is my HYPE?" Her question is a reminder that documentary is always a partial representation of reality, neither neutral nor objective. It also underscores the multiple and sometimes competing visions and narratives held by adults and teens collaborating in youth media work. This was evident as HYPE teens weighed in: Jessie disappointedly shared that it was not at all what she had envisioned; Jamie called it "boring and unimpressive"; even the ever-optimistic Rashid looked dismayed as he offered his characteristic "thumbs up" and a worried reassurance that "it's going to be OK." With the public screening two days away, things did not feel like they would be OK.

From her location as program coordinator, Azar questioned how the film reflected on HYPE itself and what kind of image would be portrayed to the community. If it were poorly received by the public, would the teens be vulnerable? Concerns about backlash and youth vulnerability are not unique to HYPE.[15] There was reason for Azar's concern. When HYPE media productions were featured at a city event the year before, a short video on unfair treatment by local police angered an assistant police chief who blamed event organizers for not forewarning him of the content.

The rough cut certainly raised the teens' voices and reasserted their role at the center of the media-making process. They spoke passionately about their vision for the documentary and committed themselves to doing the hard work ahead to make it "their own." Those who could stayed after HYPE ended in the afternoon, working until midnight over the next two days. In the fast-paced and high-pressured environment leading up to the public screening, relationships between youth and adults were again renegotiated. As the teens looked to Disbrow for direction, she worried at times that she was assuming the role of director rather than ally or assistant. As she helped the students fill in gaps in the video, she also questioned if we were unwittingly leaving unfulfilled the promise of genuinely youth-led media making. In some ways disappointment over the rough cut was a call to action, compelling the youth to participate more actively. They were now able to sit for long stretches of time at the computers editing in Final Cut Pro, ignoring their vibrating cell phones and the pull of other online pursuits. Disbrow's interactions with the teens during this time were shaped by her awareness of the need to deliver a completed documentary video that would meet the diverse expectations of youth and adult stakeholders alike. Steven Goodman speaks of the responsibilities shared by adults and students in the production process, based on his pioneering work at the Educational Video Center: "Students need to take ownership of their project and create something they will be proud of to show in public. But they can't be expected to move the project through all phases of production unassisted and on schedule. The teacher bears the ultimate responsibility for ensuring the group meets its deadline and the production results in a finished product."[16] As we came closer to the end of the production schedule, assistance and support from the adult educators was vital. Revisiting these last stressful moments of HYPE, Shaniqua recalls, "I think some of us just started giving up because it was just too much. Everybody was stressed, everyone was getting attitude with each other, people were crying. If we didn't have the adults there then I don't know what would've happened."[17] Shaniqua and her peers leaned heavily on Disbrow during these final days, as the students worked at the edges of their digital-editing knowledge. Anyone who has edited in Final Cut Pro appreciates how frustrating and complex the program is, and Disbrow tried hard to maintain the students' role driving the production process. During a short afternoon break, we took the opportunity to refocus and articulate our collective understanding of what was meant by "youth-driven/adult-supported" media production. On the chalkboard, we made a diagram of one circle embedded in another circle. The teens were asked, "What does *youth-driven* look like to you?" Their answers and descriptions filled the inner circle. We then asked, "What does *adult-supported* look like to you?" Their ideas and definitions of the kind of support they were expecting filled the space of the outer circle. This jointly produced artifact became an important guide in the remaining hours of HYPE, particularly in navigating the blurry and shifting boundary between adult participation and adult control. Azar highlights this ambiguity as she considered those final days and hours: "Would we [adults] be doing a disservice to the partnership [with the teens] if we were to sit back and watch and let them be creative but knowing in many senses that they wouldn't be successful . . . or maybe they would be and we've never given them a chance? When are we taking control because we need to and when are we taking control because we don't know how else to respond? Is it simply that we are not comfortable waiting to see what they come up with because it represents us as much as it represents them?"[18] It is clear that as adults we need to take stock of what may be contradictory impulses and responsibilities. We want to encourage youth participants to take ownership of their work, to raise their voices and visions, and *make* media. This goal may at times collide with our obligation to protect the youth who participate in our programs, or at the very least, to do nothing that might make them more vulnerable than they already are within the community.

Youth Cultural Production: Limits and Possibilities

The rough-cut screening was tough on youth and adults alike. HYPE educators left the conversation with conflicted responses: excitement, on the one hand, that the teens were roused to claim ownership of the documentary-making process; and frustration, on the other, that this newfound determination had not surfaced earlier in the five-week program. What responsibility did the teens bear for the disappointments of the rough cut? Some had simply not "shown up" for the documentary work, preferring instead to hang out, or at every opportunity to engage with other online digital media practices—Facebook, MySpace, YouTube, gaming, and texting with cell phones.

Not only does this unsettled tension provide another site for examining the ethical dilemmas that emerge when adult and youth agendas collide, it also raises important issues of class and race embedded in the social conditions of HYPE. For many of the Latino and African American participants, at school and at home, high-speed access to the Internet is limited. While survey data from the Pew Hispanic Center and the Pew Internet & American Life Project suggest the gap in home Internet use between white and Latino households may be shrinking—given the rising percentage of Latino households with broadband connections from 2006 to 2008—disparities in access in households with annual incomes under $30,000 persist.[19] Access to computers in urban public schools is similarly limited by an absence of infrastructure and support and by the current organization of the environment around standardized curricula and testing. Compared to suburban public schools, computers in urban city schools are often older, and Internet access is both slow and heavily restricted. By contrast, at HYPE, youth enter a college environment infused with new digital media tools. The room where most of the collective work takes place is encircled by 16 state-of-the-art Apple computers with high-speed broadband access, two printers, and a scanner. The multimedia production studio is similarly well equipped, with multiple high-definition video cameras, a mobile laptop system, and other production tools—the value of which far exceeds the annual income of a high school teacher in the district. The draw of the technology for the students is undeniable.[20] This social context makes it difficult to dismiss the teens' online activities as mere distraction from the "legitimate" media-making goals at hand and is a reminder of the need to listen closely to the meanings the students make of these disparities.

Cell phones were ubiquitous at HYPE. All 12 students kept their cell phones close by, if not on them physically at all times. Like their peers nationally, HYPE students own and carry with them an array of digital media devices, including cell phones, Nintendo DS and other handheld gaming systems, iPods, and other MP3 players. On these devices they download and share music, text message, participate in Internet social networking sites, play games, and view and share YouTube videos.[21] While the teens mostly observed the rule prohibiting talking on their phones during HYPE, they were almost always connected and online via texting and Internet social networking sites. While at the computer editing in Final Cut Pro or iMovie or doing Internet research, teens had multiple windows open where they would jump between HYPE work and MySpace, Facebook, YouTube, and gaming and fan sites.

For some scholars, these digital media practices signal a new kind of creative production for youth. This perspective unites chapters in the edited volume *Hanging Out, Messing Around and Geeking Out*. In one chapter, "Creative Production," Patricia Lange and Mizuko Ito argue that new online media practices constitute a kind of creative production in the digital age. Writing about MySpace and the particular process of constructing a user profile, the authors suggest that "for most youth, profile creation is a casual activity in defining a personal web page and graphic identity, pieced together with found materials on the internet. This is a form of messing around that can provide some initial introductions to how to manipulate online digital media."[22] At HYPE, we also recognize that beneath the surface of this casual "messing around" is an excitement to connect with new media that can be mobilized to engage youth in other forms of media making. As Lange and Ito point out, "Personal media creation is often a starting point for broadening media production into other forms."[23] New digital opportunities to create personally and socially relevant content may be particularly meaningful for youth of color, in the context of an Internet that is, as Ellen Seiter argues, "so heavily skewed toward white, English-speaking professionals who are interested in making purchases online."[24]

Henry Jenkins and his colleagues at Massachusetts Institute of Technology argue that social networking sites and other online spaces where youth create and share content provide them with possibilities to engage in a "participatory culture."[25] Within this conceptual framework, digital and online media are seen, in Lange and Ito's summary, to open up "new avenues for young people to create and share media" and compose a "new media ecology" that has the potential "to reshape the conditions under which young people engage with media and culture, moving youth from positions as media consumers to more active media producers."[26]

We question some of the exuberance in these calls to focus on Facebook, MySpace, and other online pursuits within youth media education. As a program, HYPE values the knowledge and experiences that youth bring to the table—and this includes, increasingly, their experiences online. But as media educators, we also have a responsibility to provide them with information about the limitations of these practices, situated as they are within a context of commodification that is notoriously relentless in targeting urban Latino and African American youth. It matters that the new avenues for young people to create and share information online are paved by profit motives, and, as Seiter insists, media educators and researchers bear a responsibility to "teach children about the economics of the Internet," including making transparent the "hidden forms of commercialism" implicit in the business of mining and profiling based on user-generated content.[27] There are huge differences between online avenues and the streets one walks down to get to school or to the store, a playground, or work.

In the context of HYPE, cultural production serves larger social justice aims. That is, documentary media making involves a set of practices that help teens from center city Allentown become agents of change within the community. We have witnessed the deep learning and community engagement that opens up when we walk slowly with HYPE teens through center city, mobile Geographic Information System devices and video cameras in their hands—mapping information about public safety, housing, health, and environmental concerns and systematically gathering visible evidence for their documentary productions. Community screenings of *Roots of Change*, at a center city restaurant, a college campus, and a public library, opened up vital avenues for dialogue in which youth who are regularly silenced by community institutions are positioned—position themselves—and recognized by adults as part of the solution, rather than the problem. In other words, youth become agents in transforming their relationships within the community as well as their relationships to media systems, critically exercising their right to communication.

Rather than signaling a new era of possibilities in how young people communicate, online activities like Facebook do not radically transform urban youths' relationship to media in particular and consumer capitalism more broadly. Beneath the hype of transforming them into "producer-consumers" in a "participatory culture," the value of their participation is that Facebook's owners and the advertisers on its site profit from the steady stream of content that users generate in the form of posts, photos, links, friends, and personal profile information.[28] "While these sites can offer participants entertainment and a way to socialize," observes Nicole Cohen, "the social relations present on a site like Facebook can obscure economic relations that reflect larger patterns of capitalist development in the digital age."[29] In the context of digital capitalism, Facebook and other Web 2.0 ventures are best understood as a continuation of the commodification of urban youth. Undeniably, HYPE students, like other youth, find meaning in their online communication. However, a theoretical understanding of the free labor these activities provide and the wider context of capitalist accumulation in which they are situated puts them in direct conflict with youth media's goal to engage young people in forms of meaning making that offer alternatives to the meanings made available within dominant consumer culture.

Facebook, MySpace, and YouTube are very much a part of the institutions of media that form what Goodman describes as a system of authority, one that contributes to the criminalization and commodification of the urban working class and youth of color.[30] Indeed, social networking sites dramatically expand the cultural surveillance of urban youth by market research firms heavily invested in tracking this "taste culture."[31] As Cohen rightly argues, "While there may be an element of agency present as members navigate Facebook, social networking sites created from the Web 2.0 business model should not be misunderstood as open, 'democratic' spaces in which people can act as they please. While there is room within the website to construct an online identity, interact with people in various ways, and generate a sense of empowerment or fulfillment, the structures (in this case, site design, functionality, privacy settings) are set according to the economic imperative of the company, and participation is constrained or enabled by the economic goals of the site."[32] Engaging young people in critical dialogue about these social processes is an important part of supporting their development as media makers. HYPE teens have good reason to look for alternative sites of communication and participation, given the unwelcoming environments they encounter at school and in the community, where they have no voice. "At school, it's like I'm mute," says Jamie, whose experience is echoed by his HYPE peers. But creating social networks online, meaningful as they may be, is no substitute for the daunting work of constructing a more inclusive community for these youth in Allentown. The longing for a more just social world in their community is deeply held by HYPE teens. This longing is articulated by Jessie, a 16-year-old Latina student, who has been in the HYPE program for 3 years.

Jessie's Intro: "In a Short Couple Bars, It's Like Exactly the Point"

The first words uttered in *Roots of Change* are a rap lyric by Jessie.

> Things never stay the same
> They constantly change
> When one looks at the past
> It just rattles your brain
> The way things take form overtime What will it take to form it
> The way we envision it
> In our minds
> Teens are the future
> So trust me enough
> To let me shape the city with a mentor's touch
> With the help of children and adults
> We will work together
> To achieve results
> A beautiful place with so much potential
> If we took a stand
> We'd sell the plans
> And the way it looks states
> That we can create
> A healthy community that we aren't seein'
> That can accommodate
> All Allentonians to be in

Jessie composed these lines two days before HYPE ended. If the hope of "reclaiming their video" was to be realized, this rap, along with an introductory sequence created by the teens, offered a model for "making it their own." The sequence itself featured the students onscreen in ways they were absent elsewhere, and—crucially—the production process that shaped the introductory sequence came as close as anything to HYPE's collectively defined ideal of youth-driven, adult-supported media.

Roots of Change opens with shots of center city Allentown: row homes, storefronts, gas stations, an art museum, and abandoned buildings interspersed with introspective close-up shots of Jessie and Shaniqua gazing at their community from the car window as they drive through center city. Much like a music video, the scene is driven by a rap of Jessie's lyrics performed by Jessie and Rashid. This is the opening they had envisioned.

Jessie was outspoken in assuming responsibility for reshaping the introduction, although she had little experience working with Final Cut Pro. For two days, Disbrow sat with Jessie while she reconstructed the introduction, providing just enough guidance with the program so that Jessie could render visually the ideas about which she was so excited. From a youth media educator's perspective, this was rewarding work, with a student passionate and actively involved in the production. At one point, Jessie beamed, "I could do this forever."

Midway through her rap, Jessie asks, "What will it take to form it / The way we envision it / In our minds?" She is speaking of the community of Allentown, but the question is worth asking in relation to youth media. What does it take, in the context of HYPE and youth media more generally, to create conditions of possibility that empower young people to realize their cultural productions with greater autonomy and agency? A good part of the answer, to be sure, rests with Jessie herself, who demonstrated throughout HYPE a deep engagement and understanding of what it means to be located in this community and to locate oneself, as a Latina, a teenager, and an advocate for social justice. Jessie exhibited a heightened awareness of, and ability to negotiate, the various systems of power pressing down on her life. For example, she articulated the struggle to apply skills learned in HYPE in the classroom, navigating between two learning contexts separated by a wide divide. She was aware of the differing power dynamics at play that shape and constrain the possibilities for action and engagement within these contexts: "It's hard. The way school is set up, it's like a dictatorship. Even teachers say, 'This is not a democracy, it's a dictatorship.' At HYPE, I feel like we learn how to have relationships with adults and we work *with* them and then at school we have to work *for* them."[33]

Jessie managed to locate herself in relationships with HYPE adults as an active participant and partner in creating a community unique to HYPE. We recognize, however, the difficulties HYPE students may encounter when they are challenged to rethink their view of themselves and their relationship to the community beyond HYPE.

Jessie felt these pressures acutely in the context of her home life:

Disbrow: How does HYPE affect other areas of your life?
Jessie: Well, actually, it gets me in trouble a lot with my Dad because we get into arguments and he tells me not to talk back and I'm like, "I don't go to HYPE to learn how to be quiet! I have my own voice!" And then he tells me to shut up [laughter]. But the way we practice stuff [at HYPE], it's really comfortable. It's not like at school where we have to [sit there] and take notes.
Disbrow: What was your favorite memory from HYPE this summer?

Jessie: Filming the intro. I was just really excited and I had a vision. Filming it was really fun because it was like exactly what I had in my head, and then adding the rap—it just made it that much better. That was my favorite part, like every time I watch it I just tell everybody, "This is my part! I did this!" I do love that rap too . . . I feel like in a short couple bars, it's like exactly the point.[34]

Support from Disbrow did not diminish Jessie's sense of ownership over this sequence: "This is my part! I did this!" Disbrow provided just enough technical instruction to enable Jessie to drive the production process.

The trust between collaborators is vital here, but so too is a sociocultural, theoretical understanding of the context shaping this meaning-making encounter between Disbrow and Jessie. Our analysis is informed by a theoretical model developed by the Russian psycholinguist Lev Vygotsky called the *zone of proximal development*. Briefly, the zone of proximal development (or ZOPED) is the distance between the actual developmental level as determined by independent problem solving and the level of potential development as determined through problem solving with guidance from an adult or a more knowledgeable peer. In other words, Disbrow created a situation in which Jessie was able to accomplish complex editing tasks that she could not yet complete independently. But Jessie slowly took over the editing process and could eventually perform the work independently. In Vygotskian terms, Disbrow and Jessie were coconstructing knowledge in the zone of proximal development.[35] The power of this model can be witnessed in the film's concluding sequence. The sequence was edited by Alysia, who mastered the basics of Final Cut Pro through instruction and guidance from Jessie. Jessie's ability to teach the editing software to her peer is evidence of her own degree of mastery over the task.[36]

Years of experience at Educational Video Center have demonstrated to Steven Goodman that media educators must constantly manage and assist the media production work with youth without overstepping their boundaries by "leaving little room for youth decision making or ownership."[37] The collaborative meaning-making process driven by Jessie and supported by Disbrow is a promising response to Jessie's refrain: "What will it take to form it / The way we envision it / In our minds?"

Conclusion

Jessie and her peers completed *Roots of Change* just in time for a community screening attended by family, friends, college professors, public officials, and community leaders. It was received with much praise; one young girl in the audience asked the HYPE filmmakers, "How can I be like you?" The film's message was powerful and the filmmakers' voices were impossible to ignore. As

Azar points out, "These teens are out there challenging stereotypes, challenging assumptions that the community has about them, challenging the assumptions that people have about other people and how people think about their community or what actually happens in their community. I can't tell you how many times I've heard from people, 'Racism doesn't exist.' Challenging those things—challenging the ways that people think—and that's where it becomes absolutely a social justice issue, when these teens are heard, because they are the ones that experience so much of [the stereotyping and racism] on a regular basis."[38] The broad objective of HYPE is to create a space where local youths' voices are not only heard but linked to critical practice. Their desire to shape community change infuses the multivoiced narrative in the documentary's final sequence, edited by Alysia:

> There need to be more opportunities for us to go and advocate and be the mentor that we were trained to be. [Jessie]
>
> It's so when you guys leave—you meaning the audience—you don't just say, "Oh yeah, that documentary was nice," and then go outside and just think about it for two minutes and you're changed for that two minutes you go outside, but to help us because we can't do this alone. Teens too—don't go out and be like, "Yeah, I saw this cool doc and then went home and nothing happened." You can be a part of something like this. Do something you know is going to positively change Allentown—that's why were making this doc. [Clarice]
>
> We wanna go out into the Allentown community and start changing it—start shaping it—start working in it to create a better tomorrow, but we can't do it without the help of the citizens. [Jessie][39]

If youth media is to fulfill its promise as a force for community change, it will require us to constantly reflect on our objectives, methods, and, crucially, the social relationships that shape youth cultural production. Whether we call it youth-driven, youth-made, or youth-created, it is up to media educators and students to collectively articulate what is meant by these terms and how their meaning is instantiated in our media-making practices. And then it is up to us to construct relationships that do justice to the ideal of young people realizing their identities and strengths as cultural producers. This work is hard and it is never finished. As Goodman observes, after more than two decades building the field of youth media, "We have come quite far. But damn, we still have a long way to go."[40]

Notes

1. The diversity among youth media programs globally is mapped by JoEllen Fisherkeller, "Youth Media Around the World: Implications for Communication and Media Studies," *Communication Research Trends* 28 (2009): 21–25.

2. While some high-profile national and even global corporate-driven youth media campaigns have emerged, the complicated relationship of this development to the history of youth media is a subject for another paper. See, for example, Adobe Foundation, "Adobe Youth Voices," accessed April 8, 2010, http://youthvoices .adobe.com.

3. Ingrid Dahl, *State of the Youth Media Field Report* (Chicago: McCormick Foundation, 2009), 8, accessed April 8, 2010, http://www.youthmediareporter.org/SOF -FINAL-Nov24.pdf.

4. Much of this work is represented in the *Youth Media Reporter*, the leading multimedia web journal for practitioners, educators, and academics working in the field of youth media. See the *Youth Media Reporter* website, http://www.youthmedia reporter.org.

5. This area has been the focus of significant community development initiatives and funding efforts, through which it has been designated a "Weed & Seed" area and, more recently, through a collaboration among various philanthropic foundations in the region, the Youth Empowerment Zone.

6. *Roots of Change* (Allentown, PA: Healthy Youth Peer Education, 2009).

7. We conceive of this as a "third space," as theorized by Kris Gutiérrez, Glynda Hull and Katherine Schultz, and others—a site where different activity systems (school, community, family, university, for example) collaborate to create a context that promotes the formation and negotiation of new roles, relationships, learning, and identities. Kris Gutiérrez, "Developing a Sociocritical Literacy in the Third Space," *Reading Research Quarterly* 43, no. 2 (2008): 148–64; and Glynda Hull and Katherine Schultz, *School's Out! Bridging Out-of-School Literacies with Classroom Practice* (New York: Teachers College Press, 2001). A discussion of the genesis and application of this theoretical construct to HYPE is the subject of a larger research study in progress by Taub-Pervizpour.

8. The perspective of this white, middle-aged man was echoed by other residents approached for informal interviews on the main street of Allentown's center city business district.

9. Jenna Azar, interview with Disbrow, September 2009; emphasis added.

10. Shaniqua, interview with Disbrow, September 2009.

11. Steven Goodman, *Teaching Youth Media: A Critical Guide to Literacy, Video Production & Social Change* (New York: Teachers College Press, 2003), 25.

12. Azar, interview with Disbrow.

13. Sylvia Boateng, email message to Disbrow, April 2010.

14. See Robert Coles, *Doing Documentary Work* (New York: Oxford University Press, 1998).

15. A youth media educator in Lynne, Massachusetts, described her responsibilities in "monitoring youth produced content," reflecting on one student's desire to create a documentary about her experiences with cutting and self-mutilation. "As her instructor and mentor, I have the responsibility to make sure that the story that she wants to tell is both appropriate for telling, and that her exploration of the topic can be done in a safe, healthy manner that isn't exploitative or puts her in harm's way." Chris Gaines and Paulina Villarroel, "Art Therapy: A Critical Youth Media

Approach," *Youth Media Reporter*, April 14, 2010, accessed May 3, 2010, http://www.youthmediareporter.org/2010/04/art_therapy_a_critical_youth_m.html.

16. Goodman, *Teaching Youth Media*, 57.

17. Shaniqua, interview with Disbrow.

18. Azar, interview with Disbrow.

19. Gretchen Livingston, Kim Parker, and Susannah Fox, *Latinos Online, 2006–2008: Narrowing the Gap* (Washington, DC: Pew Hispanic Center, 2009), accessed May 3, 2010, http://pewhispanic.org/files/reports/119.pdf.

20. This contrast is not unlike stark divisions documented by Ellen Seiter in her ethnographic study of technology practices in two public elementary schools in Southern California, one urban and one suburban. See Seiter, *The Internet Playground: Children's Access, Entertainment, and Mis-Education* (New York: Peter Lang, 2005).

21. Findings from the Pew Research Center's Internet & American Life Project surveys from 2004–2009 show this pattern among teens nationally and across demographic groups. Although the Pew surveys found no differences by race or ethnicity in phone ownership by teens, ownership rates do vary by socioeconomics, and teens from lower-income families ($30,000 or less) are less likely to own a cell phone. Amanda Lenhart, *Teens and Mobile Phones* (Washington, DC: Pew Internet and American Life Project, 2010), accessed April 27, 2010, http://www.pewinternet.org/Reports/2010/Teens-and-Mobile-Phones.aspx.

22. Patricia Lange and Mizuko Ito, "Creative Production," in *Hanging Out, Messing Around, and Geeking Out*, ed. Mizuko Ito, Sonja Baumer, Matteo Bittanti, danah boyd, Rachel Cody, Becky Herr-Stephenson, Heather A. Horst, Patricia G. Lange, Dilan Mahendran, Katynka Z. Martinez, C. J. Pascoe, Dan Perkel, Laura Robinson, Christo Sims, and Lisa Tripp. (Cambridge, MA: MIT Press, 2009), 243–57.

23. Ibid., 261.

24. Seiter, *The Internet Playground*, 17.

25. Henry Jenkins, Katie Clinton, Ravi Purushotma, Alice J. Robison, and Margaret Weigel, *Confronting the Challenges of Participatory Culture: Media Education for the 21st Century* (Cambridge, MA: MIT Press, 2009), xi.

26. Lange and Ito, "Creative Production," 244.

27. Seiter, *The Internet Playground*, 104. Seiter's study concludes with a compelling list of recommendations that media educators, teachers, and parents can leverage in activities that aim to educate children to be critical thinkers about the Internet. See 103–6.

28. The theory of audience labor developed by Dallas Smythe is essential here, and the business of offloading work onto consumers has a long history traced by Ursula Huws. Dallas Smythe, "On the Audience Commodity and its Work," in *Media and Cultural Studies: Keyworks*, ed. Meenakshi G. Durham and Douglas M. Kellner (Oxford: Blackwell, 2001), 253–79; and Ursula Huws, *The Making of a Cybertariat: Virtual Work in a Real World* (New York: Monthly Review Press, 2003).

29. Nicole S. Cohen, "The Valorization of Surveillance: Towards a Political Economy of Facebook," *Democratic Communiqué* 22, no. 1 (2008): 7.

30. Goodman, *Teaching Youth Media*, 23–24.

31. For example, the recent trend report *Inner City Truth: An Urban Youth Lifestyle Study II* offers marketers a snapshot of the new connected urban teen. "The

overwhelming majority of low-income urban teens are accessing the Internet, buying the latest cell phones and engaging in online social networking. A national survey of more than 1,500 African American and Hispanic teens and young adults, revealed that this group is highly-connected, tech savvy and brand loyal." *Inner City Truth: An Urban Youth Lifestyle Study II* (Motivational Educational Entertainment Productions, Inc., 2009), accessed April 20, 2010, http://www.targetmarketnews .com/storyid02100901.htm.

32. Cohen, "The Valorization of Surveillance," 18.

33. Jessie, interview with Disbrow, September 2009.

34. Ibid.

35. This theoretical model informs the structure of informal learning around media and communication technology in programs designed and researched by Michael Cole (1996) and the University Community Links network, Steven Goodman, Glynda Hull, and others. See Cole, *Cultural Psychology: A Once and Future Discipline* (Boston: Harvard University Press, 1998); Goodman, *Teaching Youth Media*; and Hull and Mira-Lisa Katz, "Crafting an Agentive Self: Case Studies in Digital Storytelling," *Research in the Teaching of English* 41, no.1 (2006): 43–81. On UC Links, see Charles Underwood, Mara Welsh, Mary Gauvain, and Sharon Duffy, "Learning at the Edges: Challenges to the Sustainability of Service-Learning in Higher Education," *Journal of Language and Learning across the Disciplines* 4, no. 3 (2000): 7–26.

36. The same, of course, can be said of the then-undergraduate mentor, Disbrow, this chapter's coauthor. Her ability to effectively communicate the techniques of this complex software to a younger student is meaningful evidence of her own learning in media and communication.

37. Goodman, *Teaching Youth Media*, 104.

38. Azar, interview with Disbrow, September 2009.

39. *Roots of Change.*

40. Goodman, *Teaching Youth Media*, 112.

CHAPTER 8

¡Adelante!

Advancing Social Justice through Latina/o Community Media

Mari Castañeda

Latina/o community media promote social justice not only in Latino communities but also within the broader landscape of US civil society. As global media conglomerates continue to dominate cultural and political spheres with commercially oriented information, community media become critical sites of intervention within and outside American borders. In the context of US Latina/o civil society, Spanish-language and bilingual community media are increasingly important, since the major forms of mass communication are not only commercialized but also owned and operated by corporations that view Latino-oriented media as part of an overall business strategy.

The implications of imagining Latina communities mainly as consumers are not insignificant given the limited information available for political empowerment and the potential for creating a neoliberal orientation to citizenship, which can further marginalize communities of color. As a result, community media are central for developing alternative strategies that challenge the for-profit orientation of mainstream cultural production and for engendering a social justice approach to media production, distribution, and consumption. Community-university partnerships that focus on media and are anchored in social justice have the ability to assemble resources (financial and human) that support the endeavors of community-based cultural workers, and as demonstrated in this chapter, Latina/o community media producers.

In fact, community producers often have a different vision of their audiences and the role that media play in the communities that they serve than the dominant, profit-driven outlets. For instance, in 2002, when NBC acquired Telemundo, the second largest Spanish-language television network in the United States, the CEO of NBC and vice chairman for General Electric declared that the "transaction represent[ed] NBC's strong commitment to growing [its] business strategy and serving the needs of the booming Hispanic market."[1] General Electric's vision of how NBC, and by extension Telemundo, would serve the US Latino population was clearly rooted in money-making and marketing; the company was not interested in transforming Spanish-language television into a venue for social justice and activism. Despite the reference to service, the acquisition was principally a cost-effective endeavor since NBC was following the broader economic trend of corporate consolidation while also attracting the attention of the fastest-growing consumer demographic. In the United States alone, Latinos will constitute 30 percent of the population by 2050. Across the Americas, there will be 900 million Latinos by that same year, thereby producing trillions in consumer dollars.[2] Without a doubt, from a political-economic perspective, there is much at stake in the Spanish-language communications landscape.

Unfortunately, commercial Spanish-language television is not a bastion of social justice nor progressive politics and is comparable to English-language mainstream commercial media as one of the worst offenders in relation to gender, sexuality, class, and race issues. It's not uncommon to witness sexist commentary about women, extreme racial stereotypes, and LGBT-bashing on commercial Spanish-language television and radio programs.[3] Additionally, in an effort to abide by Western ideals of journalistic integrity, despite the deep cleavages of female newscasters, the broadcast stations do not generally participate in social justice struggles.[4] One exception was the 2006 immigrant rights marches in which local and national commercial radio personalities encouraged listeners to participate in the protest.[5] Many of these radio DJs, however, experienced corporate backlash and have since backed down from taking a political stance with regard to immigration policy. Thus even if the workers of commercial Spanish-language television, radio, and print outlets wish to discuss injustices affecting Latina/o communities, corporate owners do not view those mediascapes as community spaces for political, social, and cultural empowerment.[6] In response, Latina/o community media makers have stepped in to fill the void. While this is important, these media are also increasingly at risk of shutting their doors.

This chapter first addresses the role that media has historically played in US Latino communities. It then examines the tensions and opportunities that emerge when Latinos reclaim media spaces for disenfranchised, especially immigrant, communities. Lastly, the chapter describes a community service learning (CSL) project at the University of Massachusetts where I teach, in which the students—largely Caucasian and non-Spanish speaking—in my CSL course work closely with a community-based Latina media producer for the advancement of social justice made possible through such partnerships.

Throughout the chapter, I have also included quotations from four journalists (two based in New England and the other two in Southern California), who I have interviewed three times each over the course of two years. In fear of retribution, especially in an economic climate when media companies are slashing their employee ranks, the interviewees did not feel comfortable disclosing their names or their current sites of employment. Although not ideal, the confidentiality of my informants is critical for advancing this research and, more importantly, as Anna Sandoval has remarked, "the passion for my subject comes not just from a respect and scholarly interest in this body of work, but from my lived experience as a Chicana."[7] Thus my relationship to my informants and subject is itself a social justice issue.

Historicizing the Role of Media in Latino Communities

Latino community media in the United States has a long tradition, dating back to the mid-1800s, of emphasizing community needs and social justice in its coverage of education, politics, culture, and economics. Historically, Spanish-language media, newspapers in particular, aimed to tell a different story about the impact of Latino immigrants in the United States and the ways in which immigration laws concern the future of what it means to be "American" in cultural and linguistic terms. There is a sense within the media industry that Spanish-language and bilingual outlets often take a different approach from mainstream outlets and tend to apply a more "opinionated tone," as is typical in immigrants' home countries.[8] Immigration coverage in this particular media sector has, on some level, attempted to contend with the complexity of immigration and provide a forum for audiences to understand the social realities of immigrants in the United States, especially in the contemporary context. Indeed, Spanish-language media has often tried (not always successfully) to mediate negative views about immigration in ways that are culturally and politically relevant and effective. Despite the dominance of commercialization, the history, success, and continuing growth of the Spanish-language media sector is itself a form of cultural politics whereby its very existence calls into question the melting pot theory as well as the notion that Latin American and Caribbean immigration is a recent phenomenon. While other ethnic and foreign-language media outlets such as German newspapers or Polish radio programs ceased to exist as descendants of those former, white immigrants assimilated into US society, the endurance of Spanish-language media demonstrates the difficulty of nonwhite populations of blending and disappearing "into the pot."

The long history of Spanish-language media in the United States points to a longer history of Latino presence and migration across North America. Journalism historian Félix Gutiérrez affirms that Spanish-language newspapers existed in the West and Southwest since before the 1848 Treaty of Guadalupe Hidalgo.[9] After the new territories were incorporated into the United States, a slew of publications emerged, many of which "exposed atrocities and demanded public services, all the while urging their readers to fight back against European American mistreatment of Mexicans in the United States," according to America Rodríguez.[10] Some Spanish-language newspapers denounced the socially conscious and political stance of their competitors, but these editors and reporters responded with their own denouncements against the exploitation and bigotry hurled at Mexican immigrants and Mexican Americans. Calls to collective action by newspapers became especially common during a decade-long deportation of Mexicans (undocumented and citizens alike), which began in the late 1920s.[11] As a result, many publications were threatened by vigilante Anglo groups and local governments, which investigated the Spanish-language press's possible violation of US neutrality laws. Such laws, which were first developed during the time of the Mexican Revolution, focused on the use of communication outlets—both electronic and print—as weapons of war and propaganda tools that could endanger the country's national security.[12]

In many ways, the great deportation of thousands of Mexicans during this time became a de facto war against immigrants. As a result, a sense of "nationalism and love of *la patria*" within Mexican and Mexican-American communities intensified; and some editors fueled it through their Spanish-language and bilingual publications and radio programs.[13] Since these protests challenged the US status quo, they were in time targeted for their seeming lack of neutrality and later replaced with Latino-oriented newspapers that took a less oppositional approach—and in fact encouraged cultural and political integration. Consequently, the coverage of immigration and Latina/o immigrants in particular within the mainstream English-language and mainstream Spanish-language mass media came to exemplify, as George Yúdice notes, "the asymmetries wrought by the hierarchy of racism [which also functions as] a *normal* and *normalizing* part of U.S. society."[14]

This is evident in the ways in which US mainstream English-language media represents or fails to represent immigrants, immigrant rights, and reform.[15] The coverage has often been negative, inaccurate, and filled with fearful discourse and imagery that evokes a tragic cultural and economic loss for the United States. Mexican immigration has been especially demonized in the US media. In his study of the portrayal of immigration issues in the media, Leo Chávez argues "that public anxiety over immigration and related issues of multiculturalism, race, and national identity did not suddenly burst forth in the 1990s. Rather, these issues received increasing attention and formulation over the last thirty-plus years."[16] Concerns about immigrants' impact on the labor force, their development of separate linguistic and cultural communities, and the challenge they present to "nation building" continue to be reflected in the mass media, public policy, and social interactions. For a country and a continent experiencing widespread economic and demographic change, it is important to examine the verbal and visual discourse of how the media is imagining our transnational community and the implications this may have for creating a more equitable world.

According to Chávez, the media are "sites on which to examine the struggle over the way the nation is to be conceptualized and the place of immigrants in that conceptualization."[17] This means examining not only the cultural politics of mass media in the struggle over social justice for disenfranchised communities but also the ways in which the imbalances of cultural power persist, are challenged, and reconstituted in an era of fractured, transnational migration.

While the mainstream Spanish-language media sector is also affected by the cultural politics of mass media, the difference lies in its appreciation of the Latin American and Caribbean origins of the growing US Latino population. This does not mean, however, that the industry very often challenges the anti-immigration and anti-immigrant rhetoric that is so rampant in the English-language sector. The political economy of US mainstream Spanish-language media is a significant factor. Similar to its English-speaking counterparts, the companies and their subsidiaries are increasingly owned by large multinational conglomerates, such as General Electric, Disney, and the Canadian giant ImpreMedia. Telemundo, as we have seen, is owned by NBC Universal—which General Electric recently sold to Comcast. Disney International–Latin America produces many hours of programming for US Spanish-language television networks; and the largest TV network, Univision, is primarily owned by the private entertainment and communication investment firm Saban Capital Group. Firms like ImpreMedia have in the last several years merged together an array of Spanish-language media products in order to "provide marketers with the most effective [and synergistic] platform to reach the rapidly growing and influential Latino market," with uniform content nationwide.[18] One of my informants, an editor, noted that the recent changes in ownership structure have indeed affected how and which issues get covered at the local and national levels. The reproduction of similar media content does not bode well for the coverage of politically charged issues in Latino communities, such as immigration, education, and urban decline. It is against this political-economic backdrop that we must understand the stakes for local community media, as well as the difficulties of sustaining it.

Media Forums for Latino Communities

Latino community media, much more than commercial outfits, have consistently committed their access to newsprint and the airwaves to addressing pressing issues that affect Latino populations in direct and indirect ways. The immigrant rights debate that peaked in 2006 is an excellent example of how local Latino community media defied the citizenship, ethnic, and racial hierarchization that exists within the broader cultural and political landscape. By participating in "La Gran Marcha de 2006" and instigating the participation of more mainstream Spanish-language outlets, the movement provoked debates within the industry about the media's role in fueling discussions about immigration in the public sphere. At that moment, there was a sense that Spanish-language media may be on the verge of going against "what's normal" for commercial media and, in fact, returning to its roots of community activism.

The cultural politics of mass media became very important during the mobilization period, especially between 2006 and 2007, for its effects on both support for and opposition to the immigrant rights movement. In late 2005, the House Judiciary Committee Chairman James Sensenbrenner had introduced H.R. 4437 ("Border Protection, Antiterrorism, and Illegal Immigration Control Act"), legislation that would virtually criminalize immigrants without documentation and restrict the asylum process. The bill galvanized pro- and anti-immigrant groups, and locally based Spanish-language radio and newspapers became especially vital to the ensuing debate. Not only did these media inform the public about the implications of the Sensenbrenner bill—which ultimately failed to pass in the Senate—but the community media relayed updates about the Department of Homeland Security's Immigration and Customs Enforcement's (ICE) intensification of worker raids in factories suspected of hiring undocumented immigrants.[19] For instance, Spanish-language radio, newspapers, and online outlets such as Radio Campesina, *El Tecolote* community paper, and Justice for Immigrants began sharing more information about immigrant rights, community resources, and worker sites that were raided by ICE. However, other outlets like the nationally syndicated *Hoy* daily in Chicago, Los Angeles, and New York attempted to provide "objective" news and entertainment and thereby avoid the politics of immigration reform.

As debates over immigration policy become more vital than ever for Latino communities, Spanish-language and bilingual media—both mainstream and community-based—are increasingly confronted with an important question: what role will they take in shaping the discursive and visual landscape of what it means to be a Latina/o in the United States today? According to America Rodríguez, Latino news has historically created a symbolic system of representation in which Latinos are both denationalized from their country of origin and renationalized within the US context.[20] Current debates over immigration, however, complicate this process, because to be Latino is to be suspect of cultural and political citizenship in ways that were not manifested in the past. The attempt to delegitimize President Barack Obama's birth in Hawaii is one example of the contemporary US climate.

Community Latino media is at a crossroads as struggles over immigrant rights become increasingly complicated and ruthless. There is tension among media producers between the responsibility of outlets to serve their local communities and national audiences in culturally relevant and political ways, especially with their attempts to counter racist images and discourse while also satisfying advertisers so that they can sustain their outlets economically. In 2004, in a short essay online, Jamie Pehl, an Illinois middle school teacher, argued that the lack of critique by consumers and Latino media makers alike was causing "social and civic damage," especially to non-Latino young people's perceptions of Latinos and Mexicans.[21] Thus it is critical to examine how Spanish-language and bilingual radio, newspapers, and, increasingly, online forums are mediating the cultural and political debates over immigration, the growing anti-Latino immigrant attitudes, and the politicization taking place within Latino communities.

It is important to note, however, the intense market pressures under which commercial Spanish-language media operates. Since the passage of the Telecommunications Act of 1996, the commercial Spanish-language radio and print industries have experienced a good deal of consolidation and corporate concentration. Companies such as ImpreMedia are making the most of the synergy between their corporate holdings and repurposing media content across outlets. In addition, the growing concern over harsh immigration policies at the state level has transformed the issue into a programming staple on media outlets. At the community-based level, newspapers and radio shows are also covering the daily and legal challenges that immigrant audiences are encountering, not just the policies being produced on Capitol Hill or state capitols. One reporter I interviewed stated that her editors were still unclear as to why US-born Latinos cared about immigration—they are citizens, the editors reasoned, so there's nothing for them to worry about. Despite corporate pressure to tone down the political calls for action by Latina media producers, many workers in both the Spanish-language and English-language media landscape are struggling daily with the "obnoxious nativist and racist views" about Latinos in the United States harbored by some of their colleagues, as the journalist I interviewed also noted.

Elena Shore observes that the Spanish-language media are not a unified front in their participation in social and political activism, especially with regards to immigration.[22] Some in the industry consider such activism important since the mainstream English-language media does a poor job of representing the diverse

[margin notes: Reason for no involvement; Not unified Spanish-language media; issues]

voices of the Latina community. One editor stated, "On May 1 we are all immigrants. And with one united voice . . . we have the power to change our world for the advancement of all people."[23] Yet others claimed that such involvement damages Spanish-language media's ability to maintain "objective" journalistic standards and achieve credibility with the advertising world. One radio producer argued, "As media we have no business promoting, either way. I think it's out of line to do that."[24] Consequently, the cultural diversity that Spanish-language and bilingual outlets provide to the broader media landscape is acceptable as long as it does not disrupt the political and ethno-racial status quo. Yet as Shore and others have noted, newspapers, radio, and television for Latino audiences across the Americas have a history of promoting boycotts, mobilizing communities, and speaking out against perceived injustices. This tension over diversity, media activism, and social justice is one that reflects, as Yúdice notes, a more critical issue: it is "an absorption of diversity into a conservative sphere, a necessity if the Republicans are to survive in an increasingly nonwhite world."[25] This means that the absorption of commercial Spanish-language media into the asset holdings of global media corporations minimizes the possibility that they will be used politically and operated more as marketing vehicles.

For this reason, as they come under greater economic and political pressures, Latino community media are increasingly sites of resistance that have the potential to foster social change through media justice. The rising backlash against Latino immigrants, the shifting US demographics, and the inequities that Latinos continue to experience are issues that make coverage by Latina/o community media even more critical, especially since they make visible communities who are voiceless and demonized in mainstream English-language media. Community newspapers such as *El Sol Latino* in western Massachusetts and *La Raza* in southern Texas, and local radio programs like *Tertulia* and *Musica sin Fronteras* offer content that challenge racist educational policies, provide information about community resources, and translate the legal facts of immigrant rights. In these outlets, community members participate in the production of content, and as a result provide a grassroots, on-the-ground examination of issues that affect local Latina/os. For example, community journalists have written articles about the impact of environmental injustice on local children's health, the effects of ICE raids on local families, and the educational differences between neighborhoods. In addition to speaking to the Latino community, these media outlets are also reaching out to non-Latinos as audience members and media makers in hopes that the broader communities will come to a more nuanced understanding of what is at stake for everyone when one particular ethnic or racial group is consistently demonized and negatively targeted in mainstream English-language media. Allies across racial and ethnic lines are vital for social justice to be transformative. With that in mind, the next section describes efforts at the University of Massachusetts Amherst to achieve such a transformation.

Community Service Learning and Social Justice

Aiming to move beyond theory and actively engage students with the issues discussed earlier, I developed a course titled "Spanish-language Media and Latina/o Cultural Production" that includes a critical community service learning (CSL) component.[26] In this course, university students, most of Caucasian descent, work closely with various Latina/o media organizations in western Massachusetts. These service learning partnerships help create a broader context for understanding social inequalities while also encouraging a media justice approach. The partnership with *La Prensa del oeste de Massachusetts* has created an especially positive and productive reciprocity between the class and the community partner. *La Prensa del oeste de Massachusetts* was founded by Natalia Muñoz, a highly respected journalist who had worked at prominent commercial outfits like *Reader's Digest*, *Latina*, and *Disney en Familia*. Muñoz's experiences at these print outlets, however, were often problematic because Latino issues were frequently dismissed or reported in unsophisticated (and, at times, insulting) ways. Since relocating to the Pioneer Valley of Massachusetts, Muñoz has become an important media advocate for the local Latina/o community. Through her work in *La Prensa*, she has also collaborated with other cultural producers and community activists. In 2008, with a group of local community women, she launched the "Nuestras Abuelas" ("Our Grandmothers") traveling photo exhibit, in which local US-born, multiethnic Latinas wrote short essays about their *abuelas'* experiences as immigrants in the United States. The exhibit has since appeared in art galleries at the University of Massachusetts Amherst, Smith College, Mount Holyoke College, and Westfield State College, as well as the Holyoke Public Library and Springfield's Puerto Rican Cultural Center. Responses to the exhibit from Latina/os and non-Latinos alike have been extremely positive since there are very few cultural spaces in western Massachusetts that critically address the role of immigration, migration, and the geopolitics between the United States and Latin America. Through the photos and essays, the exhibit also explores the challenges of being viewed as a foreigner despite holding citizenship, how this has affected the grandmothers and granddaughters, and what it may mean for future generations. Exhibit attendees have mentioned these issues during the public commentary period when the show opens at a new venue and in the feedback *diario* (journal) in which guests are encouraged to record their reactions.

When Muñoz visited my "Spanish-language Media and Latina/o Cultural Production" course, she made it very clear to students that reexamining history is critical for understanding the political, economic, and social conditions of Latinos in the United States. From this perspective, Muñoz challenged the students to approach *La Prensa* as a repository for unheard Latina stories and the critical analysis of Latino issues. Throughout our partnership over the past three years, Muñoz has become a central figure in the course. Several months before the semester begins, I invite Muñoz to lunch so that we may review the syllabus, class readings, academic goals for the semester, and the CSL objectives we wish to achieve. In addition to discussing course logistics—when she will visit the class, organizations with which students will engage, student orientation to local cities—we also spend considerable time discussing the Spanish-language and English-language media landscapes to ensure that the course touches on current topics. The course meets once a week for three hours, allowing for longer and more engaging conversations with Muñoz that would otherwise be difficult to achieve in a 50-minute class. I begin the semester discussing the differences between charity, volunteerism, and social justice-based community engagement; Keith Morton's work has deeply influenced my attempts to include a critically oriented CSL framework, and I use his model to show students how media activism for social justice is possible within and outside of the classroom.[27] I also use these first weeks of class to gain a better sense of how students perceive the issues affecting Latino communities in the United States and Massachusetts more specifically and the role that Latino/a community media can play in empowering people. By the time Muñoz visits the class during the third week of the semester, students are well aware of what the course will entail, what will be expected of them, and the need for constant assessment and reflection in how they engage with community members. This is especially important in the context of course demographics: in any semester, among the 20 enrolled students, there are often only 1 or 2 Latina/o students and 18–19 Caucasian students, many of whom have very little experience with ethnic and racial diversity. The course is challenging for all students because, unlike a traditional college course where students simply interact with the professor, they have to work closely with Muñoz and step off of campus into local communities that struggle with economic and racial inequities and are suspicious of non-Latino/as. The students are also confronted with the discriminatory behavior that Muñoz endures as a Latina, despite her status as a professional journalist, which she discusses during one of her visits.

When the course was offered in 2007, one of the CSL projects centered on interviewing local and regional elected officials to learn how they were working with the growing Latino communities in the area and what they perceived as the major issues affecting those communities. In addition to interviewing the mayor of a large city, a state representative, and a local city councilor, students also interviewed the late Senator Ted Kennedy. Interestingly, Muñoz shared with us that she had tried for months to secure an interview with Kennedy, but as a local Latina/o community outlet, she was not granted access. When Caucasian students from the state's flagship university campus called for an interview (noting that they were working with *La Prensa*), they were granted a phone interview within just a few weeks. This experience was quite jarring, even for the students, since it forced them to recognize that not all media outlets and media producers are the same. More importantly, the experience revealed how the intersections of class privilege, race and ethnicity, and gender affected access to information and how issues are covered.

In 2008, the CSL partnership entailed interviewing local school superintendents. Muñoz explained to the students that as the demographics of the Pioneer Valley of western Massachusetts were changing rapidly, schools were grappling with an increasingly diverse student body for whom English is often a second language. Ironically, the state eliminated bilingual education in 2002, despite projections of a profound population shift led by Latinos. Muñoz wanted readers from *La Prensa* to become conscious of how Latino K–12 students were faring in the postbilingual education environment of Massachusetts. My students interviewed local superintendents, and the wide array of responses (even though school districts were within a 25-mile radius of each other) left the students wondering why this issue was rarely discussed in the state's mainstream news media. In fact, the college students' engagement with local Latino communities consistently raised questions about differences in media coverage and reinforced the importance (but the serious difficulty of sustaining) Latino community media.

Recently, Muñoz announced that the tough economy has forced her to shift *La Prensa* to an online-only format. She questioned whether such a transition removed her from the communities she was serving and covering. This was in fact the focus of our collaborative work during fall 2009. We surveyed local towns and cities to examine whether Internet access was widely available in libraries and schools. We also surveyed *La Prensa* readers in order to find out whether online availability would lessen, increase, or maintain their interest in the community media outlet. We learned that Internet access was available in the local libraries and schools, but with limited hours of availability. Low-income homes, especially in Holyoke and Springfield, had the lowest levels of online access via computers, but they did have some Internet access through their mobile communication devices. Lastly, most readers of *La Prensa* commented that they would continue to access the media outlet even if it was available only online. However, they emphasized the need to continue covering Latino issues in the area, since there are very few Spanish-language and bilingual community media outlets based in the region. Commercial Spanish-language media, after all, pays very little attention to issues local to western

Massachusetts. One aspect readers liked about *La Prensa*'s presence on the web was that it would extend information beyond the region, gather links from other web sources on the *La Prensa* website, and provide a forum for online interactivity that is sorely needed in the Latino Pioneer Valley. In addition to gathering this information, Muñoz encouraged the students to generate their own story ideas based on their research, yielding in turn a wide array of articles to be posted on the *La Prensa* website.

Through this partnership, the students in the course have come to understand the role of Latino community media not only as a form of cultural empowerment but, more importantly, as a critical component for achieving social justice in an era where Latinos are both celebrated as consumers but vilified as citizens. The recent passage of Arizona's especially tough immigration legislation and the media coverage of Latinos, especially Mexicans, in the United States confirm that media activism for social justice is more important than ever. The more college students, particularly those who are non-Latino, can participate in media activism, the better the chances for achieving a critically oriented civic engagement that demands and works toward social justice for all.

Notes

1. National Broadcasting Company, "NBC Completes Acquisition of Telemundo Communications Group, Inc.," news release, April 15, 2002.
2. Comisión Económica para América Latina y el Caribe, "Latin America: Population Projections, 1950–2050," *Boletín Demografico*, no. 59 (January 1997).
3. Maria Elena Cepeda, "Mucho Loco for Ricky Martin or the Politics of Chronology, Crossover, and Language within the Latin(o) Music Boom," *Popular Music and Society* 24, no. 3 (2000): 55–71; and Mari Castañeda Paredes, "The Transformation of Spanish-Language Radio in the United States," *Journal of Radio Studies* 10, no. 1 (2003): 5–16.
4. See Federico A. Subervi-Veléz, ed., *The Mass Media and Latino Politics: Studies of U.S. Media Content, Campaign Strategies and Survey Research, 1984–2004* (New York: Routledge, 2008).
5. Mandalit Del Barco, "Spanish-Language DJ Turns Out the Crowds in L.A.," *Morning Edition*, National Public Radio, April 12, 2006, accessed March 7, 2008, http://www.npr.org/templates/story/story.php?storyId=5337941.
6. Hector Tobar, *Translation Nation: Defining a New American Identity in the Spanish-Speaking United States* (New York: Riverhead Books, 2005).
7. Anna Sandoval, "Building Up Our Resistance: Chicanas in Academia," *Frontiers: A Journal of Women's Studies* 20, no. 1 (1999): 87.
8. Kim Campbell, "Demographics Drive the Latino Media Story," *Christian Science Monitor*, June 21, 2001, 14.
9. Félix Gutiérrez, "Spanish-language Media in America: Background, Resources, and History," *Journalism History* 4, no. 2 (1977): 34–41.

10. America Rodríguez, *Making Latino News: Race, Language, Class.* (Thousand Oaks, CA: Sage, 1999), 21.
11. Rodríguez, *Making Latino News*, 19.
12. Rita Zajácz, "Liberating American Communications: Foreign Ownership Regulations from the Radio Act of 1912 to the Radio Act of 1927," *Journal of Broadcasting and Electronic Media* 48, no. 4 (2004): 157–78.
13. Rodríguez, *Making Latino News*, 17.
14. George Yúdice, *The Expediency of Culture: Uses of Culture in the Global Era* (Durham, NC: Duke University Press, 2003), 66.
15. See Leo Chávez, *Covering Immigration: Popular Images and the Politics of the Nation* (Berkeley: University of California Press, 2001).
16. Chávez, *Covering Immigration*, 12.
17. Ibid., 14.
18. "About ImpreMedia," ImpreMedia, accessed July 22, 2008, http://www.impre media.com/about.
19. Mari Castañeda, "The Importance of Spanish-Language and Latino Media," in *Latina/o Communication Studies Today*, ed. Angharad Valdivia (Lanham, MD: Rowman and Littlefield, 2008), 51–68.
20. Rodríguez, *Making Latino News*.
21. Jamie Pehl, "Latinos in the Media," Teaching Literature, May 12, 2004, accessed March 7, 2008, http://www.teachingliterature.org/teachingliterature/pdf/multi/ latinos_media_pehl.pdf.
22. Elena Shore, "What is the Role of Hispanic Media in Immigrant Activism?," *Social Policy* 36, no. 3 (2006): 8–9.
23. Quoted in Shore, "What is the Role," 8.
24. Quoted in Ibid., 9.
25. Yúdice, *The Expediency of Culture*, 235.
26. See Castañeda, "The Importance of Spanish-Language."
27. Keith Morton, "The Irony of Service: Charity, Project and Social Change in Service-Learning," *Michigan Journal of Community Service Learning* 2 (1995): 19–32.

PART III

Power Struggles

CHAPTER 9

Feminism and Social Justice
Challenging the Media Rhetoric

Margaret Gallagher

Girls [*sic*] today have never had it so good, right? Apart from the fact that you've got more equality than you ever can deal with, the fact of the matter is that you've got real democracy and there really are no glass ceilings, despite the fact that some of you moan about it all the time . . . I mean what else do you want? . . . Women astronauts. Women miners. Women dentists. Women doctors. Women managing directors. What is it you haven't got?

—Sir Stuart Rose[1]

As the twenty-first century celebrated its tenth birthday, to some it may indeed have seemed that women had little to complain about. In 2008 Hillary Clinton got closer than any woman in history to shattering "that highest, hardest glass ceiling"[2]—the presidency of the United States of America. By that same year, a growing number of women—including Angela Merkel in Germany, Michelle Bachelet in Chile, Ellen Johnson-Sirleaf in Liberia, and Gloria Arroyo in the Philippines—had broken through to reach the highest political office. Between 1960 and 1970 only four women were elected as heads of government worldwide. In the decade after 2000, more than 20 female heads of government were elected in countries spanning Africa, Asia, Europe, Latin America, and the Caribbean.[3] This fivefold increase could hardly be interpreted as anything but progress for women.

Yet the claim that women today experience a "surfeit" of equality—"more than you can ever deal with"—does not stand up to even cursory scrutiny. In the United Kingdom, for instance, according to the Fawcett Society, which campaigns for gender equality, women are only 4 percent of executive directors of the country's top 100 companies, less than 20 percent of members of parliament, and earn 17 percent less per hour than men for doing work of equivalent value; less than 7 percent of rape cases reported to the police result in conviction.[4] One in four women in the United Kingdom experiences domestic violence in her lifetime.[5] Only one of Britain's 17 national daily and Sunday newspapers (6 percent) is edited by a woman.

No country in the world has achieved gender equality. The 2010 report of the World Economic Forum, which since 2006 has measured progress on tackling gender gaps in health, education, economic, and political participation, stated that in 16 of the 114 countries for which it has data for the five year period, the overall gender gap has actually widened.[6] Yet media narratives regularly suggest that the struggles launched by the women's movement of the 1970s are no longer relevant, or that women's rights have been achieved at the expense of men, who are the new "victims," or that the pursuit of equality has resulted in women's "unhappiness." In many of these narratives, there is an explicitly negative critique of feminism as a social movement. For instance, in their widely reported study, "The Paradox of Women's Declining Happiness," Betsey Stevenson and Justin Wolfers chart the subjective well-being of women and men in the United States since the early 1970s. While they stop short of "immediately inferring that the women's movement failed to improve the lot of women," they do go on to conclude that "the changes brought about by the women's movement may have decreased women's happiness."[7]

The Stevenson-Wolfers research, and many of the media reports it generated, supports the "backlash" thesis proposed in the early 1990s by Susan Faludi.[8] For Faludi, backlash was integral to a conservative response whose purpose was to deliberately challenge or undermine the achievements of feminism. Over the past two decades, this challenging of feminism has continued in ever-more sophisticated ways. Contemporary responses frequently draw on and invoke feminism itself and feminist vocabulary in a "post-feminist" discourse implying that feminism has been "taken into account."[9] The result is yet another paradox. On the one hand, feminism has ostensibly become part of the cultural field. On the other, modern media narratives frequently present feminism as irrelevant to today's social struggles, and indeed as something to be repudiated—albeit often in a humorous or ironic tone, which of course makes feminist countercritique particularly difficult.[10]

Feminist discourse in the media remains, with few exceptions, conservative. Relying heavily on notions of women's individual choice, empowerment, and personal freedom, media treatments fit perfectly within a vocabulary of neoliberalism. Cultural theorist Angela McRobbie describes this as "disarticulation," a process that, through its insistent focus on female individualism and consumerism, severs the seams of connection between groups of women who might find common cause, and "makes unlikely the forging of alliances, affiliations or connections," whether locally, nationally, or internationally.[11] McRobbie's bleak lament for the displacement of feminism as a political movement is shared by other major feminist theorists such as Nancy Fraser, who distinguishes between feminism as a social movement and feminism as discourse. In the context of neoliberal capitalism, Fraser argues, feminism in the discursive sense has "gone rogue." As a result, today's feminist movement is "increasingly confronted with a strange shadowy version of itself, an uncanny double that it can neither simply embrace nor wholly disavow."[12] These paradoxes and contradictions—in particular, the incorporation of feminist ideas into media discourse that serves to deny the politics of feminism as a movement—makes the pursuit of social justice for women especially challenging in today's world.

Feminism and Social Justice in a Commercial Media World

Feminism is one of the most important social justice movements of modern times. Its broad goal is to make visible and eliminate the subordination, discrimination, and inequalities experienced by women. Marianne Braig and Sonja Wölte argue that we cannot think of the feminist movement as a homogeneous actor. "Rather, we have to conceptualize it as a plurality of social movements of women—and partially men—consisting of and encompassing diversity and differences between class, ethnicity, and other distinctions."[13] Within this plurality, distinctions between feminist activism and feminist scholarship are often difficult to make. While feminist scholars may be engaged in political activism, feminist activists may also do feminist research.

It was a political impetus that first shaped the agenda of feminist media analysis. Much of the Western feminist critique of the 1960s and 1970s was by women outside the academy—women working in the media industries or feminist groups that were organizing in local and national communities. At a global level, the United Nations International Decade for Women (1975–1985) was a catalyst for political debate about the many sites of women's subordination. To some extent influenced by these highly visible polemics, women in the academy began to identify—and to address—the invisibility of "women," as a distinct analytical category, in media and communication studies of the time. As Rosalind Gill has pointed out, one of the most striking things about this early period was the degree of overlap and congruence between the agendas of academics, media workers, and activists.[14] The media were seen to be deeply implicated in the patterns of discrimination operating against women in society—patterns that, through the absence, trivialization, or disparagement of women in media content, were famously said to constitute "symbolic annihilation."[15] This general critique quickly came to be positioned around two central axes: (1) an analysis of the structures of media power from which women were excluded and

(2) a focus on the politics of representation and the production of knowledge in which women were defined as objects rather than active subjects.[16]

The push and pull between theorizing, research, and activism has always been a feature of feminist approaches to the media. For example, feminist critique of advertising—a key site for the production and distribution of sexist media imagery—has built on both scholarly studies of how gender differences are constructed in advertising messages and on activist campaigns that have included boycotting products, petitioning regulatory bodies, posting stickers or graffiti on billboards, giving prizes for "good" and "bad" advertisements, and engaging advertisers in dialogue. Over the years, from one country to another, many of these campaigns have been successful—in the sense that specific advertisements have been dropped or changed, self-regulatory codes of conduct have been introduced, and advertising "observatories" have been established.[17] Certainly the advertising landscape today looks quite different from the world of happy housewives, helpless maidens, and passive sex objects that populated advertisements of the 1960s. Market imperatives demand that contemporary advertising reflects some of the changes in women's position in society. But the industry's claim that it has absorbed a "feminist viewpoint" or that "the history of advertising is deeply entwined with feminism"[18] denotes rhetoric rather than reality. Exposing this rhetoric has been central to the large body of feminist scholarship that has analyzed the specifics of how advertising responds to feminist critique. Essentially, advertising has been given "a gloss for the twenty-first century."[19] In other words, advertising has incorporated feminist ideas, while at the same time depoliticizing them so as to produce more complex representations of the modern woman, whose body and sexuality nevertheless remain vital to the process of selling products.

The Dove "Campaign for Real Beauty," devised by advertising agency Ogilvy & Mather, has been one of the most successful, and perhaps also the most cynical, examples of the advertising industry's eagerness to tap into certain aspects of feminist analysis. A worldwide marketing exercise first launched in 2004, the Dove campaign caused a minor sensation by using "real" women—rather than professional models—in advertisements for the Dove skin-firming lotion (intended to reduce cellulite). The choice of these ordinary-looking women, photographed only in their underwear, was intended to "make more women feel beautiful every day by widening stereotypical views of beauty."[20] The campaign achieved huge media impact, and public reaction was positive. But how "ordinary" were the Dove models? The women selected for the "real beauty" campaigns in both the United States and the United Kingdom were all aged under 30 and were below the body size of the average American or British woman. None showed any sign of cellulite or indeed any other blemish. Following a claim in *The New Yorker* that the photographs had been retouched, Dove placed a statement on its American and British campaign websites: "Colour corrections and other small adjustments are needed in order to meet professional standards . . . These corrections do not mean that people don't see the woman as she really is and do not change Dove brand's commitment to women."[21] The statement reveals the sleight of hand involved in the Dove campaign: even "real" women must meet certain professional standards to feature in the advertisements, whose primary purpose, of course, is to expand the market for the Dove brand. The campaign certainly has been successful. In the year following its launch in the United Kingdom, demand for Dove products rose by 700 percent, making it the fastest-growing beauty products brand in Western Europe.[22]

The power of advertising is immense not only in terms of its influence on consumers but—in an increasingly commercial media world—on the political economy of the media in general. Over the past two decades, as many formerly state-run and public service media enterprises have ceded control to commercial interests, advertising revenue has become ever more central to the production of content in radio and television, newspapers and magazines, and, most recently, the Internet. This gives the advertising industry immense bargaining power in its dealings with regulatory agencies. The entangled relationships between industry and regulatory bodies present an enormous challenge for feminist activists, who in many parts of the world consider the development and enforcement of policy standards and codes of practice to be a key strategy in achieving gender justice.[23] For instance, within the institutions of the European Union, where media and communication have been defined primarily as tradable goods, the commercial principle is immensely influential.

In 2008, the European Parliament approved a resolution on "How Marketing and Advertising Affect Equality between Women and Men." A nonlegislative resolution, it was a much watered-down version of a draft text adopted several months earlier by the parliament's Committee for Women's Rights and Gender Equality. For example, clauses in the original that sought the establishment of national media monitoring bodies and of ethical codes or legal rules covering the creators and distributors of advertising were dropped in the final version. This merely calls for adherence to existing guidelines and for training, dialogue, and awareness-raising among advertisers. Yet the response of the European Commission to this rather weak document could be read as an apologia for the advertising industry, the effect of whose lobbying seems obvious.[24] Citing (unspecified) "strong evidence" that the depiction of women in advertising has kept up with social change and that existing industry advertising codes deal "effectively" with the objectionable stereotyping to be found in a "small minority" of advertising campaigns, the Commission suggests that "freedom of expression arguably provides a basis for tolerance of stereotyping in advertising given its limitations" (i.e., advertising's "short-form, ephemeral nature"). Importantly, the Commission continues,

> one should take into account the positive role that advertising plays in reducing the cover price of print media and in funding free online media, together with commercial television channels . . . Heavy-handed interventions to limit stereotyping could be counter-productive in terms of overall media policy priorities, since they would divert promotional expenditure outside the media.[25]

The response illustrates how market-oriented considerations take precedence over social justice arguments in determining policy. Gender stereotyping in advertising is not denied. Indeed it is acknowledged. However, in the logic of the commercial world, attempts to limit it—that are a priori presumed to be "heavy-handed"—would undermine media financing and profit, and are therefore rejected. Also noteworthy is the way in which the concept of "freedom of expression" is used not just to argue for "tolerance of stereotyping" but to support adherence to "overall media policy priorities"—priorities that are of course rooted in another "freedom" discourse, the freedom of the market.

Freedom, Empowerment, and Choice

As one of the paramount values used to define democratic media systems, "freedom"—of expression, the press, the media—is conventionally argued to be at risk in the face of feminist advocacy for equal rights. This tension is regularly expressed in debates about the media and social justice, whether at the local, national, or international level. For example, the Beijing Platform for Action (BPfA), adopted unanimously by 189 member states of the United Nations at the Fourth World Conference on Women in 1995, acknowledged the media as one of twelve "critical areas of concern" that must be addressed if equality between women and men is to become a reality. The BPfA identified two overall strategic objectives: (1) to "increase the participation and access of women to expression and decision-making in and through the media and new technologies of communication"; and (2) to "promote a balanced and non-stereotyped portrayal of women in the media."[26] Yet negotiations during the Beijing conference led to the introduction of the phrase "consistent with freedom of expression" in relation to many of the media proposals in the BPfA—a reminder of the highly contested nature of this particular "critical area of concern." Resistance to actions perceived as threatening media freedoms intensified in the years after Beijing, with the widespread adoption of a neoliberal economic model and market-driven policies propelled by the World Trade Organization (WTO), which was formally established in the same year as the Beijing conference. For instance, in 2000, during the Beijing +5 review and appraisal, the US delegation stipulated in its reservation statement that nothing in the outcome documents could be considered binding on the media.[27]

The apparent impregnability of "freedom of expression" discourse in the domain of media and social justice gives rise to an inevitable question: whose freedom, defined by whom? Clearly, rights and freedoms are not gender-neutral. To illustrate this, feminists have focused on the concept of freedom to highlight gender inequities and to argue that women's right to freedom of expression and information is severely limited by layers of structural, economic, and cultural constraints. This means shifting conventional understanding of freedom of expression away from "freedom from government control" toward a conception that acknowledges the right of women, as well as men, to be informed and to have their voices heard. For example, starting with the question, "Can free media be only a male domain?" Patricia Made has pointed to the shortcomings of the influential 1991 Windhoek Declaration on Promoting an Independent and Pluralistic African Press. By ignoring internal gender biases within media systems—biases which mean that "the media do not provide access to expression to more than half of the region's population: women"—policies like this, she argues, have failed to link "democracy, freedom of expression, governance and issues of gender justice to the editorial content of the media."[28]

Such arguments have yet to find much resonance within either media organizations or media policy-making institutions. For instance, in its 2010 review of implementation of the BPfA in the European Union, the European Women's Lobby concluded that "women and the media remains one of the objectives of the BPfA which is most neglected by the EU and its Member States."[29] Nevertheless, the BPfA is still considered by many to be the comprehensive blueprint for women's human rights and social justice in relation to media and communication. The Beijing conference was indeed a breakthrough in that it moved beyond the concept of women's "advancement" (within taken-for-granted, existing structures) to that of women's "empowerment" (implying the potential to transform those structures). The empowerment of women, as advocated in the BPfA itself, is a radical demand. It depends on "the full realization of all human rights and fundamental freedoms of all women."[30] Yet in the years since Beijing, the concept has been emptied of its radical essence. Empowerment has become "the word of the moment" not just for development actors but also for the media.

In the field of development communication, Susanna George argues that allusion to "women's empowerment" has become indispensable to a vocabulary that has been institutionalized so as "to accessorise and make 'nice' documents that are essentially treatises to the neoliberal, market-based globalisation agenda of the world's elite."[31] The World Summit on the Information Society (WSIS), held in Geneva in 2003 and Tunis in 2005, is a case in point. The final outcome document affirms a "commitment to women's empowerment" in the Information Society.[32] In reality, the overarching technology-driven and market-led paradigm that framed the WSIS debate provided no space for substantive discussion of gender inequality or women's human rights. The empty rhetoric of the WSIS "commitment to women's empowerment" is demonstrated by its main follow-up mechanism, the Internet Governance Forum, which has consistently and conspicuously failed to engage with women's rights issues.

Women's access to new information and communication technologies (ICTs) is obviously a matter of social justice. However, the supposition that this will "empower" women often fails to acknowledge the contexts of gender inequality in which most women live. As Ineke Buskens and Ann Webb have pointed out in their review of women's use of ICTs in 12 African countries, for there to be "real" empowerment, "women have to be the agents of their own processes, in charge of and in control of their environment."[33] This is far from being the material reality of many women—perhaps the majority—in today's world. The review by Busens and Webb shows how very slim is the margin for empowerment among all but a tiny minority of women. Yet the empowerment mantra is seductive. Stripped of its association with a radical, transformative agenda, it has been reduced to "empowerment-lite"[34]—perceived as a simple act of personal advancement that can occur through a specific circumstance, such as access to information or income. In this conceptualization, transformation of the social norms, institutions, and relationships that are part of gendered realities are not understood as fundamental to women's empowerment.

It is this stripped-out, neutered version of "women's empowerment" that we find in a great deal of modern media discourse, which explicitly equates empowerment with sexual assertiveness, buying power, and individual control. Thus, for instance, later stages of the Dove Campaign for Real Beauty involved online contests that promised women "empowerment" and "creative control" by contributing their own advertisements to promote the Dove Supreme Cream Oil Body Wash.[35] In this highly conservative version of empowerment, which chimes fully with the neoliberal economic model, gender equality becomes confused with individual "lifestyle" choices. Told that "you have the power to be what you want to be," the woman of the commercial media world responds logically: "Today, I decided to stop being fat. My decision. My weight loss."[36] The false-feminist rhetoric in these exhortations to exercise "choice" gives the illusion of progress, while merely recreating age-old anxieties. Choice, in this lexicon, functions as a new form of constraint.

Gender Justice, Social Transformation, and Media Reform

Women's experience of inequality has changed worldwide since the 1970s. However, it remains unequivocal and substantial. Media and communication systems have been transformed over the same period. Yet here too, much remains depressingly familiar. More women than ever before are working in the media but few have reached the most senior positions. In any case, the relationship between media practitioners and media output has proven to be infinitely more complex than was assumed in feminism's early campaigns to get more women working in the media as a way of ensuring "better" media content. One of the most striking aspects of today's mainstream media culture is its privileging of personal, identity politics—in talk shows, reality television, even news and current affairs—at the expense of political or structural critique. This offers scant hope to social justice movements such as feminism, whose agenda of radical social change depends to some extent on striking a chord with citizens who access their information through the media.

Other strategies are necessary, and women have not been content merely to criticize biases and inequities in the established media. In their study of women's media activism in 20 countries, Carolyn Byerly and Karen Ross identify a number of "pathways" through which women's agency has opened up spaces for both media and social reform. This, they argue, is part of a broader political process in which women media activists envisage a world in which "women's influence shapes everything from culture to social policy, advancing women in the process."[37] For instance, "women's movement media" have certainly played a crucial role in women's struggle around the world. Part of a global networking, consciousness-raising, and knowledge creation project, they have enabled women to communicate through their own words and images. Women's radio has been immensely important in this project; with the possibilities opened up by Internet radio, radio can make new connections between local and global feminist struggles.[38] Women's news services on the web, as well as blogs, e-zines, and social networking sites have introduced content and opinions different from those found in traditional media. There has been a steady growth of women's media networks and activist groups too. Many of these—for example, Cotidiano Mujer in Uruguay, Women's Media Watch in Jamaica, Women's Media Centre in Cambodia, Gender Links in South Africa, to name just a few—use research and media monitoring data to develop dialogue with media professionals so as to stimulate thinking about gender as a factor in the choices that are made in producing media content.

Drawing on the concept of democratic accountability inherent in social justice arguments, this effort has built on the influential Global Media Monitoring Project (GMMP), established in 1995. The GMMP provides a snapshot of gender patterns in the world's news on a single day, every five years. In 1995 women were only 17 percent of news subjects (newsmakers or interviewees). By 2010 this figure had increased, but only to 24 percent across the 108 countries monitored. The GMMP depends on the labor of volunteers, many of whom have no prior experience of research or monitoring. Indeed, an important aim of the project is to build monitoring and advocacy expertise among grassroots groups.[39] It is thus much more than a data collection exercise. By putting simple but reliable monitoring tools in the hands of activists and developing media literacy and advocacy skills through the monitoring process, the GMMP aims to be genuinely transformational.

The lesson of several decades of feminist activism and scholarship is that gender justice in the media will not be achieved by increasing the number of women journalists or by getting rid of the worst excesses of sexism in advertising. What is actually required is a wide-scale social transformation in which women's rights—and women's right to communicate—are respected and implemented. Social transformation is fundamental to twenty-first-century media reform. The struggle of social movements and campaigning groups around the future direction of the media—including the Internet—has reopened what had become somewhat defunct debates about the ownership and control of media and communication systems. Concepts such as the media as "public goods," the right to communicate, and the airwaves and cyberspace as part of a "global commons," have reentered international discussion. Creating alliances with such groups can be an important strategy for feminists, for at least two reasons. First, alliance building with other public interest groups may provide more leverage in achieving gender justice in media systems. The second reason is even more pragmatic. Despite the good intentions of those who work for media democracy, many of them operate within an implicitly masculinist paradigm.[40] To the extent that such groups are successful in making their voices heard, those voices may—yet again—exclude women.

"What Is It You Haven't Got?"

In the spring of 2010, the United Kingdom was preparing for a general election. The Conservative Party—with only 18 women among its 195 members of parliament (9 percent)—circulated a glossy photograph of a group of 13 female candidates whom party leader David Cameron had backed to contest winnable seats in the new parliament. Media reports labeled them "Cameron Cuties" or "Dave's Dolls." Labour Party leader Gordon Brown's "new generation" of female candidates became known as "Brown Sugars." The party leaders' spouses were said to be engaged in a "war of the wives" and a "fashion-off."[41]

New century, same old media clichés. Now, just what *is* it that women haven't got?

Notes

1. Sir Stuart Rose, interview by Amelia Hill, "Women Have Never Had it So Good at Work, Says M & S Chief," *The Observer*, May 31, 2009, accessed March 6, 2011, http://www.guardian.co.uk/business/2009/may/31/sir-stuart-rose-marksspencer. At the time of the interview Rose was chairman of Marks & Spencer, one of the largest retailers in the United Kingdom.
2. As referred to in Hillary Rodham Clinton's concession speech, June 7, 2008.
3. Inter-Parliamentary Union, April 2010, accessed April 11, 2010, http://www.ipu.org/wmn-e/world.htm.
4. Fawcett Society, "The Facts," April 2010, accessed April 11, 2010, http://www.fawcettsociety.org.uk/index.asp?PageID=981.
5. Government Equalities Office, *Domestic Violence Fact Sheet* (London: Government Equalities Office, 2008).
6. Ricardo Hausmann, Laura D. Tyson, and Saadia Zahidi, *The Global Gender Gap Report 2010* (Geneva: World Economic Forum, 2010).
7. Betsey Stevenson and Justin Wolfers, "The Paradox of Women's Declining Happiness," *American Economic Journal: Economic Policy* 1, no. 2 (2009): 222–23. For a feminist rebuttal of Stevenson and Wolfers, see Barbara Ehrenreich, "Are Women Getting Sadder? Or Are We All Just Getting a Lot More Gullible?" *Guernica*, October 13, 2009, accessed April 11, 2010, http://www.guernicamag.com/blog/1354/barbara_ehrenreich_are_women_g.
8. Susan Faludi, *Backlash: The Undeclared War Against Women* (London: Chatto and Windus, 1992).
9. Angela McRobbie, *The Aftermath of Feminism: Gender, Culture and Social Change* (London: Sage, 2009), 12.
10. Rosalind Gill, *Gender and the Media* (Cambridge: Polity Press, 2007), 268.
11. McRobbie, *The Aftermath of Feminism*, 26.
12. Nancy Fraser, "Feminism, Capitalism and the Cunning of History," *New Left Review* 56 (March–April 2009): 114.
13. Marianne Braig and Sonja Wölte, "Introduction," in *Common Ground or Mutual Exclusion? Women's Movements in International Relations*, ed. Marianne Braig and Sonja Wölte (London: Zed Books, 2002), 3.
14. Gill, *Gender and the Media*, 10
15. Gaye Tuchman, "The Symbolic Annihilation of Women by the Mass Media," in *Hearth and Home: Images of Women in the Media*, ed. Gaye Tuchman, Arlene Kaplan Daniels, and James Benét (New York: Oxford University Press, 1978), 3.
16. The range and complexity of feminist media scholarship today bears little resemblance to the small body of work that emerged in the 1970s. For a historical analysis of the development of feminist media studies, see Margaret Gallagher, "Feminist Media Perspectives," *A Companion to Media Studies*, ed. Angharad Valdivia (Malden: Blackwell Publishing, 2003): 19–39; and Gill, *Gender and the Media*, 9–32.

17. Examples from many countries can be found in Margaret Gallagher, *Gender Setting: New Agendas for Media Monitoring and Advocacy* (London: Zed Books, 2001), 60–79.

18. Juliann Sivulka, *Ad Women: How They Impact What We Need, Want and Buy* (Amherst, MA: Prometheus Books, 2009), 16.

19. Gill, *Gender and the Media*, 112.

20. Dove Canada, "Campaign for Real Beauty Mission," September 3, 2008, accessed April 11, 2010, http://www.dove.ca/en/#/cfrb/mission_statement.aspx.

21. Dove, "A Word On Our Images," November 3, 2008, accessed April 11, 2010, http://www.campaignforrealbeauty.co.uk/#/cfrb/arti_cfrb.aspx[cp-documentid =10639068. The claim that the photographs had been retouched appeared in Lauren Collins, "Pixel Perfect: Pascal Dangin's Virtual Reality," *The New Yorker*, May 12, 2008. Pascal Dangin later stated that he had worked only on the Dove Pro-Age campaign.

22. Liz Hoggard, "Why We're All Beautiful Now," *The Observer*, January 9, 2005, accessed March 6, 2011, http://www.guardian.co.uk/media/2005/jan/09/advertising.comment.

23. Gallagher, *Gender Setting*, 35–45.

24. As the executive body of the 27 member states of the European Union, the European Commission is responsible for proposing legislation and implementing decisions. It is accountable to the European Parliament, whose elected members represent the citizens of the European Union. The Parliament cannot initiate legislation, which it must request the Commission to draft.

25. European Commission, "European Parliament Resolution on How Marketing and Advertising Affect Equality between Women and Men," September 3, 2008, accessed April 11, 2010, http://www.europarl.europa.eu/oeil/DownloadSP .do?id=15132&num_rep=7576&language=en.

26. *Beijing Declaration and Platform for Action* (New York: United Nations, 1995), paragraphs 234–45, accessed April 11, 2010, http://www.un.org/womenwatch/ daw/beijing/pdf/BDPfA%20E.pdf.

27. Sally Burch and Irene Leon, "Directions for Women's Advocacy on ICT," in *Networking for Change: The APCWNSP's First 8 Years*, ed. Pi Villanueva (Philippines: APC Women's Networking Support Programme, 2000), 37.

28. Patricia Made, "Can Free Media Be Only a Male Domain?," *Media Development* 51, no. 4 (2004): 48, 49.

29. European Women's Lobby, *From Brussels to Beijing: An Unfinished Journey* (Brussels: European Women's Lobby, 2010), 11.

30. *Beijing Declaration and Platform for Action*, paragraph 9.

31. Susanna George, "Mainstreaming Gender as Strategy: A Critique from a Reluctant Gender Advocate," *Women in Action*, August 2004, accessed March 5, 2011, http://www.isiswomen.org/index.php?option=com_content&task=view&id=515 &Itemid=207.

32. World Summit on the Information Society, *Tunis Commitment*, Document WSIS -05/Tunis/Doc/7-E (Tunis: WSIS, 2005), paragraph 23.

33. Ineke Buskens and Anne Webb, "Epilogue," in *African Women and ICTs: Investigating Technology, Gender and Empowerment*, ed. Ineke Buskens and Anne Webb

(London: Zed Books, 2009), 207. See also Radhika Gajjala, Yahui Zhang, and Phyllis Dako-Gyeke, "Lexicons of Women's Empowerment Online: Appropriating the Other," *Feminist Media Studies* 10, no. 1 (2010): 69–86.

34. Wendy Harcourt, *Body Politics in Development* (London: Zed Books, 2009), 34.
35. Brooke Erin Duffy, "Empowerment Through Endorsement? Polysemic Meaning in Dove's User-Generated Advertising," *Communication, Culture & Critique* 3, no. 1 (2010): 26–43.
36. See Michelle M. Lazar, "'Discover the Power of Femininity': Analyzing Global 'Power Femininity' in Local Advertising," *Feminist Media Studies* 6, no. 4 (2006): 510.
37. Carolyn M. Byerly and Karen Ross, *Women & Media: A Critical Introduction* (Malden, MA: Blackwell Publishing, 2006), 232.
38. Caroline Mitchell, "'Dangerously Feminine?' Theory and Praxis of Women's Alternative Radio," in *Women and Media: International Perspectives*, ed. Karen Ross and Carolyn Byerly (Malden, MA: Blackwell Publishing, 2004), 178.
39. For further information about the GMMP and all the project reports, accessed March 5, 2011, http://www.whomakesthenews.org.
40. Mojca Pajnik and John D. H. Downing, "Introduction: The Challenges of 'Nanomedia,'" in *Alternative Media and the Politics of Resistance: Perspectives and Challenges*, ed. Mojca Pajnik and John D. H. Downing (Ljubljana, Slovenia: Peace Institute, 2008), 11.
41. Amanda Platell, "Have Cameron's Cuties Really Got What it Takes to Transform Politics?" *Daily Mail*, April 8, 2010, accessed April 11, 2010, http://www.dailymail .co.uk/femail/article-1264330/Have-Camerons-Cuties-really-got-takes-transform -politics.html; Eleanor Harding, "New 'Brown Sugars' Set to Take on 'Cameron Cuties,'" *Daily Telegraph*, March 1, 2010, accessed April 11, 2010, http://www .telegraph.co.uk/news/politics/gordon-brown/7341395/New-Brown-sugars -set-to-take-on-Camerons-cuties.html; Jan Moir, "War of the Wives: Saintly but Sinister Sarah vs Outspoken Miriam," *Daily Mail*, April 8, 2010, accessed April 11, 2010, http://www.dailymail.co.uk/debate/article-1264337/JAN-MOIR-War -wives-Saintly-sinister-Sarah-vs-outspoken-Miriam.html; and Julia White, "General Election 2010 Wife Watch: Sarah Brown and Sam Cam's Fashion-off Gets Underway," *Daily Express*, April 7, 2010, accessed April 11, 2010, http://www.express .co.uk/posts/view/167751/General-Election-2010-Wife-Watch:-Sarah-Brown -and-Sam-Cam's-fashion-off-gets-underway.

CHAPTER 10

Defending Dissent

Brian Martin

My first brush with defamation law was in 1980. The biggest environmental issue at the time was nuclear power. I was a member of Friends of the Earth and involved in writing leaflets, organizing rallies, and giving speeches. At the time I worked as a research assistant in applied mathematics at the Australian National University in Canberra. The two most prestigious advocates of nuclear power in Australia at the time were Ernest Titterton, professor of nuclear physics at the Australian National University—just across campus from me—and Philip Baxter, former head of the Australian Atomic Energy Commission. They were active in giving speeches and writing articles and had sway with government.

To show the inconsistencies and absurdities in their positions, I decided to write an analysis of their viewpoints about nuclear power, nuclear weapons, and the nuclear debate. The result was an 80-page booklet that I titled *Nuclear Knights.*[1] Titterton and Baxter had been knighted for their contributions to Australian society—a knighthood is the highest government honor—and were known as Sir Ernest Titterton and Sir Philip Baxter, or Sir Ernest and Sir Philip for short. I thought the whole idea of knighthoods was absurd and was happy to make fun of them through the title.

I found a publisher: Rupert Public Interest Movement. A small lobby and activist group based in Canberra, Rupert was pushing for freedom of information laws; I knew two key members, Kate Pitt and John Wood. They were happy to lend Rupert's name to a challenge to the establishment. John drew some wonderful graphics, including the cover showing Sir Ernest and Sir Philip as Don Quixote and Sancho Panza tilting at windmills.

There was one final barrier to overcome: defamation.

Defamation

Defamation law is designed to deter and penalize unfair comment that damages a person's reputation. If I write a letter to the newspaper saying you are corrupt and nasty, you might well be upset about damage to your reputation—imagine all those people believing you are corrupt and nasty too! Defamation law allows you to sue me—and the newspaper—for damages.

Defamation by publication—a newspaper story or any other written or broadcast form—is called libel. Verbal defamation, for example a comment at a public meeting or a party, is called slander.

Defamation law sounds reasonable in principle but it has a number of serious shortcomings. It costs a lot to go to court. To bring a case might require $10,000, and if there is a vigorous defense then expenses escalate into hundreds of thousands or more. That means protecting your reputation is expensive indeed. Only the rich can afford it.

Even if you win a case for defamation, the main thing you get is usually money. You may or may not obtain a public apology or retraction, and even if you do, it may not restore your reputation.

However, my main concern was the effect on targets of defamation suits—especially me. The effect of defamation law is to inhibit free speech. If Baxter or Titterton sued me or Rupert, the consequences could be disastrous. Legal costs could be stiff, the case could drag on for years, and we might lose and be forced to pay even more.

One of the other shortcomings of defamation law is its incredible complexity. It is possible to lose on a technicality.

My experiences and examples here are Australian, but many of the points apply elsewhere. Defamation laws are found in nearly every country and are based on the same general principles. However, the details of the laws and their implementation can vary quite a bit, so it is valuable to understand the local scene.

For me, the scene was Australia, where the history of defamation law was not pretty, at least from the point of view of free speech. There are lots of cases ending with enormous payouts for what seems like a trivial offense. One case that astounded me involved Alan Roberts, a physicist who I knew through the movement against nuclear power. In 1980, Alan wrote a book review for *The National Times*, a weekly newspaper, of a book by Lennard Bickel, *The Deadly Element: The Men and Women Behind the Story of Uranium*.[2] Bickel was especially upset by Roberts's comment that "I object to the author's lack of moral concern." Bickel sued the publisher. After a trial, an appeal, another trial, another appeal, the two parties reached a settlement. The publishers paid somewhat less than the amount awarded in the second trial: $180,000.[3] That was in 1980 dollars—it is more like half a million today.

That was one expensive comment to make in a book review. Apparently, according to the law, the cost to Bickel's reputation was greater than the cost of literally losing an arm and a leg, for which compensation under the law would be considerably less.

Alan didn't have to pay anything himself; luckily, the publisher covered his legal costs. But you can imagine the effect on his future writing. And then there is the effect on others who see what happened. This is a prime example of what is called the chilling effect of defamation law on free speech.[4]

My publishers, Rupert Public Interest Movement, were committed to free speech but nonetheless had no desire to open themselves to massive costs in a lawsuit. So they asked me to post the final draft of *Nuclear Knights* to Titterton and Baxter. If the knights threatened to sue, this would be a good signal to be more careful; if they didn't, this would weaken their claims if later they did sue because they hadn't used a timely opportunity to prevent publication. I have used this method repeatedly ever since.

Tittterton and Baxter didn't reply. Safe enough? No, because they might claim they had never received or read the draft. Two key figures in Rupert Public Interest Movement, Kate Pitt and John Wood, assisted. Kate called each of the knights, with John listening in on the telephone line. Kate and John then wrote a statement vouching that the two knights had received the manuscript.

First, Titterton commented that the manuscript was "rubbish." Abuse, but no threat to sue: little danger there. Next, Baxter said he would sue. This was bad news. That meant further checking.

It is OK to say defamatory things as long as you have a legal defense. The most common defense is truth. That can be tough to prove. Not only does every statement have to be true, you have to be able to prove it is true, which often means having some document to back it up. You might have seen your neighbor dumping hazardous chemicals down the drain, but in a court you would be asked, "How did you know he was pouring cyanide?" You might answer, "He was pouring it from a cyanide container, and other cyanide containers were found in his garage." You might then be asked, "Yes, but how do you know he wasn't pouring dirty water from an empty cyanide container?" Every statement with a defamatory imputation had to be checked.

There are some other defenses too. If you have made a statement in a professional capacity—for example, as a teacher making a statement about a student in a report card—you are protected by qualified privilege. A statement made in court or parliament is protected by absolute privilege. If all else failed, perhaps we could have *Nuclear Knights* read out in parliament!

Back to reality: Kate and John knew a barrister in Western Australia who would read the manuscript yet again. He suggested a few small changes. Then it was off to the printers.

Baxter didn't sue. Probably he never intended to. His threat was a bluff. This happens all the time and can be remarkably effective in deterring publication. People are afraid of being sued. Defamation law does indeed have a chilling effect.

In *Nuclear Knights*, I included a list of prominent advocates of nuclear power in Australia. One of them was Don Higson. He worked for the Australian Atomic Energy Commission and wrote pronuclear letters to newspapers. After *Nuclear Knights* was published, he wrote to me fairly amicably to discuss our differences—amicably except for one thing: he claimed he wasn't an advocate of nuclear power but instead was just presenting the facts. I thought this was absurd but persisted with the correspondence until Higson suggested he might sue because of this alleged misrepresentation.

A couple of years later, I continued with my critiques of pronuclear experts by writing an article about Leslie Kemeny, a nuclear engineering academic at the University of New South Wales. After my article, "The Naked Experts," appeared in the British magazine *The Ecologist*,[5] Kemeny wrote several people threatening to sue: me, the editor of *The Ecologist*, and two friends of mine who had commented on a draft of the article and who I listed in the acknowledgments. Kemeny even drafted an apology letter for us that made all sorts of sweeping rejections of our views. This didn't seem a very credible threat; for example, it didn't come via lawyers. Nevertheless, the editor of *The Ecologist* was sufficiently alarmed to ask me to send copies of all the material about Kemeny I had relied on in writing the article. Kemeny never sued.

These experiences sensitized me to defamation threats, both to me and to others. I sought out what I could find to learn about the practical aspects of defamation, such as how to write in ways that reduced the risk of defamation actions. A general rule was to present just the facts and let the reader draw conclusions. For example, instead of saying "Jackson Bragidan is a liar," it is safer to say, "Jackson Bragidan said he has a Harvard PhD; Harvard does not record any PhD graduate with his name."

I came across more and more cases in which defamation threats and actions were used to suppress free speech. When individuals asked me to advise them about defamation threats, I knew enough to say something helpful. These experiences helped me learn more.

Whistleblowers

In 1991, a group called Whistleblowers Australia was formed. I knew about it from the beginning through correspondence with the founder John McNicol. In 1993 I joined the national committee of the organization. At that time the president was Jean Lennane, a psychiatrist who had worked for a government hospital, spoken out about cuts to health services, and been dismissed. The secretary, Lesley Pinson, had been a whistleblower in the railways and lost her job. The treasurer, Vince Neary, an engineer, was also a railways whistleblower.

In fact, most members of Whistleblowers Australia were whistleblowers. Hearing their stories, I learned an enormous amount about the dangers of speaking out and about the predictable patterns of attacks on whistleblowers. The same methods and outcomes were found in government departments, schools, churches, police departments, and private companies.

Typical whistleblowers are conscientious employees who see something wrong—corruption, abuse, hazards to workers or the environment—and report it to their bosses or others up the chain of command. Instead of the problem being investigated, they come under attack themselves. This is often a total shock to their self-understanding: their sense of how the world works is undermined, causing bewilderment and self-doubt.[6]

Most whistleblowers are ostracized—this cold-shoulder treatment seems almost universal and very hard to handle. They are subject to petty harassment. Rumors are spread about them. The serious reprisals include reprimands, demotions, referral to psychiatrists, punitive transfers, dismissal, and blacklisting. As well as losing jobs and sometimes having their entire career derailed, with drastic financial consequences, whistleblowers also suffer terribly in their personal lives, with ill health and damage to relationships commonly reported.

Whistleblowers speak out because they believe the system—or some part of it—works. In fact, a lot of them didn't think of themselves as whistleblowers at all. They were just doing their jobs, reporting a problem to the boss—a financial discrepancy, a hazard at work—and suddenly found they had become the target.

When whistleblowers understand what is happening, they often seek justice by going to higher authorities, for example reporting the problem to their boss's boss or the chief executive officer or making a formal complaint to a grievance body internal to the organization or going outside to an ombudsman, auditor-general, professional body, anticorruption agency, court, politician, or some other official body. The trouble is that this hardly ever works.

Vince Neary, the railways whistleblower, went to his boss, the chief executive officer, the auditor-general, the ombudsman, his local member of parliament, and the Independent Commission Against Corruption, among others.

None gave much satisfaction in addressing his concerns, namely unsafe signaling processes and unaccounted expenses—and the higher up he reported the problem, the worse the reprisals: he was ignored, ostracized, reprimanded, demoted, and eventually dismissed.

Bill De Maria carried out a large survey of Australian whistleblowers; they reported being helped in less than one out of ten approaches to official bodies and sometimes they were worse off.[7] What is going on? Essentially a whistleblower is a single person who is speaking truth to power. If every worker who spoke out about abuses at work—payoffs, special deals, unsafe operations, bullying, hiring of cronies—was vindicated, the entire system would come under threat. There are way too many dodgy operations for any agency to vindicate more than a tiny minority of complaints. Energetic official bodies are typically starved of funds, burdened with onerous bureaucratic reporting duties or—if they start tackling corruption too high in the system—have their powers taken away.

Jean Lennane, Whistleblowers Australia's first president, said that only two things reliably aided whistleblowers: meeting other whistleblowers, which helped them stop blaming themselves and realize why they were being attacked, and media coverage.

Yes, media. Of course the media are themselves subject to defamation threats and actions. Indeed, they are juicy targets because they have so much money. Quite a few Australian politicians have built holiday homes with payouts obtained after suing the media for some derogatory comment. Some, it is said, have paid staff members to scour the media looking for pretexts to sue.

This use of defamation law is one of the reasons why Australian media are so cautious about breaking stories. From 1965 to 1975, Robert Askin was premier of New South Wales, Australia's most populous state. He was officially lauded, indeed awarded a knighthood. Yet Askin was widely known in media circles as being corrupt, receiving brown paper bags filled with cash to allow gambling and prostitution to thrive. But there were no news stories about this during his time in office. Shortly after Askin died, *The National Times* ran a front-page story titled, "Askin: Friend to Organised Crime."[8] Australian defamation laws do not allow the dead to sue.

So Australian media are quite cautious about what they publish. Nevertheless, they are receptive to whistleblower stories, which often score high on news values: personalities and powerful organizations are involved and the tale of a courageous employee being victimized resonates with audiences.

Good journalists will present both sides to a whistleblower story, but the impact is usually very damaging to the organization. For this reason, organizational elites do whatever they can to limit media coverage. They encourage whistleblowers to use official channels, and they offer generous settlements with legal conditions that no further public comment be made.

In the stories from whistleblowers, I noticed another recurring theme: defamation threats. Whistleblowers seek to speak out in the public interest. What better way to shut them up than to threaten to sue them? That led me to say that if Australian governments were really serious about assisting whistleblowers, they would reform defamation laws and get rid of laws preventing government employees from speaking out about anything to do with their jobs. Instead, governments are quick to pass whistleblowing laws that don't work.

Law reform commissions in Australia have been recommending changes to defamation laws for decades, but governments have repeatedly ignored them. I realized that defamation law reform was not a productive way to help whistleblowers, at least not in the short term. So what is? My answer is knowledge and skills.

Jean Lennane urged me to take over from her as president of Whistleblowers Australia, and in 1996 I did. Defamation was high on my priority list and now I felt more commitment to a constituency, the two hundred or so members of the organization plus numerous others who contacted us each year. I decided to write a leaflet on defamation.

It was a hefty leaflet: eight large pages with plenty of text. I included a description of what defamation law is, listed the problems with it along with examples—such as the Alan Roberts case—and described some responses.

I then went to considerable lengths to get everything in the leaflet exactly right. To make a single mistake in describing the law would undermine the leaflet's credibility. I sent drafts to lots of people, including whistleblowers—the sort of people the leaflet was aimed at—and legal experts. Judith Gibson, a barrister specializing in defamation who also edited the magazine *Defamed*, was very helpful; her check of the legal details gave me confidence.

Having produced the leaflet, titled "Defamation Law and Free Speech," I circulated it to anyone who might be interested, such as whistleblowers who contacted me for assistance. As president of Whistleblowers Australia, suddenly lots of people wanted to talk to me. I had thought I had a good grasp of the issues before, but soon I was overwhelmed with case after case.

The Web: Defamation Havens

This was the time when the World Wide Web burst on the scene, with a rapidly expanding audience. I obtained a manual, learned how to write in HTML (the standard web language), obtained software to convert word-processed documents to HTML, and set up a website. One of the first things I put on my site was the defamation leaflet.[9] Years later, I discovered that it had become the most-read item on my site, out of hundreds of articles.

On my website I included a section called "Suppression of Dissent."[10] Well, it was more than a section, closer to half the site, filled with all sorts of documents about dissent, whistleblowing, analysis, and responses. Before the web, people who wanted to publicize their case had to rely on the media—which often were not interested or only covered it briefly—or they had to laboriously send out copies of documents by post. And that is exactly what people did. The web made direct distribution far easier.

In 1997, I was contacted by Dudley Pinnock, an entomologist at the University of Adelaide. Although he was a senior academic who was bringing in lots of money through research grants, he had been declared redundant. Furthermore, he alleged that senior figures in his department were inappropriately accessing his research funds.

I advised him that official channels were unlikely to help him retain his job, but he preferred to follow the advice of the academics' union and go through an appeal process. It was unsuccessful. At that point Pinnock authorized me to put an account of his story on my website. It was basically the chronology he had used for his appeal.

Having posted the Pinnock file, I alerted a couple of higher education journalists and within a matter of days I was instructed by University of Wollongong management to remove the file from my site. Why? One of the journalists had contacted the University of Adelaide for a comment about the Pinnock file. Finding out about the file, Mary O'Kane, vice-chancellor of the University of Adelaide—equivalent to president of an American university—telephoned Gerard Sutton, vice-chancellor of my university, threatening defamation actions unless the file was removed.

From my perspective, this would have been a great opportunity to take a stand for free speech. Imagine the publicity: "University of Adelaide threatens to sue to restrict free speech!" But no, instead the University of Wollongong management took a cautious route, minimizing risk by acquiescing rather than resisting.

At this point, I could have taken a stand and refused to remove the file. This might have resulted in disciplinary action or, more likely, simply an administrative takeover of my site and forced removal of the file. This could have been newsworthy in its own right, but my concern was with the Pinnock case, not making a scene at Wollongong. So I removed the Pinnock file, replacing it with a statement that it had been removed due to a defamation threat.

Next I contacted a friend in Electronic Frontiers Australia—an Internet freedom lobby and activist group—and asked for assistance in posting the Pinnock file on other sites. Before long, four different sites posted it. I made links to each of these sites. Mary O'Kane's attempted censorship was thwarted. Even better, the Pinnock file received additional publicity through this enterprise.

The Pinnock experience led me to the idea of "defamation havens," analogous to tax havens.[11] A tax haven is a country with low taxes; running some operations there allows tax in the home country to be reduced. A defamation haven could be a country where there is no law against defamation, or laws that are less draconian than the home country. To get around the risk of defamation, just post a document on a website in the haven country.

For example, if Australian Internet service providers (ISPs) are threatened with defamation actions over a document, then use an American ISP, because US defamation laws do more to protect free speech and anyway, it is a lot of extra expense for an Australian to launch a legal action in the United States. Of course, the ISP is only one target: anyone involved in disseminating defamatory material can be sued—most obviously the author. But the author in such cases is not the target—Pinnock was not threatened with a defamation suit—because the purpose is censorship.

Defamation havens can be physical places, namely countries with low penalties for defamation, but in practice the most important haven is virtual: by putting a document on several websites, it becomes nearly impossible to eradicate. The University of Adelaide approached the ISPs hosting a couple of the copies of the Pinnock file, but to no avail: the ISPs didn't take the threats seriously. Even if they had acquiesced and removed the file, the next step was straightforward: find yet more sites to host the file, generating ever more publicity along the way. The Internet in this way becomes a censor's nightmare: every attempt to squash undesirable information only spreads it further.

With these experiences, I now have a fairly standard approach when proposing to publish potentially defamatory material. The first step is to apply my own understanding of what is defamatory and see whether statements can be defended. The most important part of this is to state facts and be careful in expressing judgments.

The next step is to consider sending the material to the person potentially defamed—just as Rupert and I did decades ago with Titterton and Baxter. This is a good way to flush out risk.

Then I post the material on my website and wait. If there is no response, then it is fine and good. If someone threatens to sue, I can either remove it, modify it, or send it to others for posting.

Michael Wynne is a retired medical academic who collects material about corruption and abuse by corporate medicine, especially hospital corporations and especially ones in the United States. He has produced a vast amount of material, much of it taken from media reports. I host his files on my suppression-of-dissent website.[12]

Four different health care companies have threatened to sue for defamation because of Michael's material. Do they contact Michael first? No. Do they contact me as the site manager? No. They instruct lawyers who send a letter of demand direct to the University of Wollongong administration, which runs the website. This is a typical sign of an attempt at suppression of dissent: no negotiation, just threats to one's superiors. The university's managers then ask me to remove the offending webpage.

The sequence is becoming routine. I remove the webpage, replacing it with a statement that it has been removed because of a defamation threat. I inform Michael and he prepares a modified page, omitting what seems to be opinion and relying more on quotes from media stories. Sometimes he ends up with a lot more material. I then write to the health care company lawyers asking for an opinion on the revised page. If the lawyers respond with a letter with continued complaints about the content but no threat to sue, this means it is safe to post the revised page. If there is no response at all, I wait a few months and put up the new page.

In one case after I sent Michael's modified page to a company's lawyers, the company head wrote a letter to the chancellor of the university—a ceremonial position—making accusations about my status as an academic for having such material on my website. This was a sign that a legal action wasn't feasible. Luckily, the administration is concerned mainly about possible costs and is able to stand up to abuse.

Backfire

In 2001 I came up with the idea of backfire and tactics against injustice. Gene Sharp, the world's leading researcher into nonviolent action, developed the idea of political jiujitsu: if peaceful protesters are brutally assaulted, lots of people will see this as terrible and turn against the attackers.[13] This occurred in Russia in 1905, when hundreds of people, protesting to the czar, were slaughtered by government troops. The result was a dramatic loss of support for the czar, undermining the credibility of the entire system and laying the foundation for the 1917 revolution. In 1960, white South African police opened fire on peaceful black protesters in Sharpeville, killing perhaps one hundred of them. News of the massacre punctured the South African government's reputation, at that time, as a legitimate democracy. Sharp also had examples from Gandhi's campaigns in India, especially the 1930 salt march, during which police beatings of nonviolent protesters undermined the credibility of British rule over India. I knew of a later example, the shooting of peaceful protesters in Dili, East Timor, by Indonesian troops. Photos and video of the massacre catalyzed the international movement for East Timor's independence. In cases like this, the violent assaults rebounded against the attackers, analogous to the sport of jiujitsu in which the attacker's energy and momentum can be used against them—hence Sharp's expression "political jiujitsu."

In every one of these examples, a key to the process was communication: people had to find out about the atrocity. For example, there had been other massacres in East Timor but because there were no Western journalists present, no photos, and no videos, news leaked out slowly and had little impact because of Indonesian government denials and censorship.

My brainwave went like this: just like massacres in East Timor, lots of terrible things happen in the world, but only a very few of them generate outrage. So what about all the rest? Perhaps the attacker is doing something to reduce outrage. I eventually came up with five main methods: (1) cover-up, (2) devaluation of the target, (3) reinterpretation of the events, (4) official channels that give an appearance of justice, and (5) intimidation and bribery.

How to apply this model of tactics? It would help to have lots of case material, so I thought of collaborating, finding someone who knew a lot about an area involving an injustice and who was interested in the theory and practice of challenging this injustice.

I thought of Steve Wright, one of the world's leading researchers on technology used for repression—for example, the manufacture and trade in shackles, thumb screws, electroshock batons and many other horrible tools used in torture and control. I had met Steve just once, in Manchester in 1990, but had kept in regular touch. Steve was receptive to my approach and before long we had completed an article titled "Countershock: Mobilizing Resistance to Electroshock Weapons."[14]

I also thought of Sue Curry Jansen, whose book *Censorship: The Knot that Binds Power and Knowledge* I had read and with whom I had exchanged a couple of letters over a decade earlier.[15] Sue was also interested in collaborating and we soon produced a paper, "Making Censorship Backfire."[16] I met Sue for the first time after we had finished the paper.

One of our censorship case studies was the so-called McLibel case, in which McDonald's sued two London anarchists, Helen Steel and Dave Morris, who had helped produce a leaflet titled "What's Wrong with McDonald's?" The legal action ended up being the longest court case in British history and was a public relations disaster for McDonald's, triggering a massive grassroots campaign in defense of Steel and Morris and disseminating the offending leaflet to millions of people. Sue and I treated this as a case of censorship backfire: the attempt by McDonald's to censor the leaflet using a legal action was seen as unfair and ended up being counterproductive for McDonald's even though the corporation used all the five methods for inhibiting outrage.

The McLibel case can also be seen as a defamation backfire because McDonald's sued on the grounds of defamation. Later I collaborated with Truda Gray on studies of defamation backfire, using the McLibel case and several others to illustrate the tactics typically used by those who sued and what tactics in response were most likely to deter actions or make them counterproductive.[17]

So what should you do if you are threatened with a defamation suit? My advice goes along these lines: don't panic—don't be intimidated. Consider your options. Sometimes it is best to make an apology or to withdraw your statement and, like Michael Wynne with his health care documents, prepare a stronger, more documented version. Other times you may want to make a stand, like Helen Steel and Dave Morris. If so, don't rely on the courts for defense; instead, go public. Let people know about the defamation threat and about the important issue that is threatened with silencing.

For most people, defamation actions are frightening. The backfire model offers a different perspective: being attacked is an opportunity to generate greater attention to your concerns. You may or may not want to take up the opportunity, but it is there.

Conclusion

If you do decide to resist, and publicize your efforts, you can help others through your example. The McLibel campaign sent a powerful message to large corporations: sue at the risk of extreme damage to your reputations. That is indeed a powerful message considering that defending reputation is what suing is supposed to achieve.

My attention from the beginning was on the use of defamation law as a form of censorship, as spelled out in the leaflet "Defamation Law and Free Speech." The visibility of the leaflet on the web has generated a continuing stream of correspondence, much of it from people asking what to do. Roughly two-thirds are about dealing with defamation attacks, anything from an ex-husband threatening legal action over comments made to a friend to someone wanting to set up a website about bad debts asking about avoiding suits.

But then, unexpectedly, there is the other one-third: people who have been defamed asking me what to do about it. One woman was disturbed by hostile rumors being spread around her neighborhood; another had her business disparaged on television and wanted to respond. So regular were the requests that I wrote a little article, using the backfire model but in the opposite direction, looking at the tactics of defamers and how to counter them.[18]

I usually spell out a series of options rather than giving a specific recommendation. One option is to just ignore the slurs, as most people will forget about them and challenging them will simply make people remember. Another option is to make a prompt, succinct, factual, and nonemotional response. This is easiest on the Internet; it is easy to send a quick reply on an email list. Then there is the option of suing. That is usually why people who have been defamed contact me. Some of them ask me to recommend a lawyer. I always say this is probably the worst option. Suing is very expensive, not guaranteed to win, slow, and procedural. And it won't help your reputation. In fact, it might make the damage to your reputation far worse—especially if the other side knows how to make defamation actions backfire.

Notes

1. Brian Martin, *Nuclear Knights* (Canberra, Australia: Rupert Public Interest Movement, 1980).
2. Lennard Bickel, *The Deadly Element: The Story of Uranium* (New York: Stein and Day, 1979).
3. David Bowman, "The Story of a Review and its $180,000 Consequence," *Australian Society* 2, no. 6 (1983): 28–30.
4. Eric Barendt, Laurence Lustgarten, Kenneth Norrie, and Hugh Stephenson, *Libel and the Media: The Chilling Effect* (Oxford: Clarendon Press, 1997).
5. Brian Martin, "The Naked Experts," *The Ecologist*, July/August 1982, 149–57.
6. C. Fred Alford, *Whistleblowers: Broken Lives and Organizational Power* (Ithaca, NY: Cornell University Press, 2001).
7. William De Maria, *Deadly Disclosures: Whistleblowing and the Ethical Meltdown of Australia* (Adelaide: Wakefield Press, 1999).
8. David Hickie, "Askin: Friend to Organised Crime," *National Times*, September 13–19, 1981, 1, 8.
9. Brian Martin, "Defamation Law and Free Speech," 1996, http://www.bmartin.cc/dissent/documents/defamation.html.
10. Brian Martin, ed., "Suppression of Dissent," accessed March 8, 2011, http://www.bmartin.cc/dissent.
11. Brian Martin, "Defamation Havens," *First Monday: Peer-Reviewed Journal on the Internet* 5, no. 3 (2000), accessed March 8, 2011, http://firstmonday.org/htbin/cgiwrap/bin/ojs/index.php/fm/article/view/734/643.
12. Michael Wynne, "Corporate Healthcare Web Site," accessed March 8, 2011, http://www.bmartin.cc/dissent/documents/health.
13. Gene Sharp, *The Politics of Nonviolent Action* (Boston: Porter Sargent, 1973), 657–703.
14. Brian Martin and Steve Wright, "Countershock: Mobilizing Resistance to Electroshock Weapons," *Medicine, Conflict and Survival* 19, no. 3 (2003): 205–22.
15. Sue Curry Jansen, *Censorship: The Knot that Binds Power and Knowledge* (New York: Oxford University Press, 1988).
16. Sue Curry Jansen and Brian Martin, "Making Censorship Backfire," *Counterpoise* 7, no. 3 (2003): 5–15.

17. Truda Gray and Brian Martin, "Defamation and the Art of Backfire," *Deakin Law Review* 11, no. 2 (2006): 115–36; Brian Martin and Truda Gray, "How to Make Defamation Threats and Actions Backfire," *Australian Journalism Review* 27, no. 1 (2005): 157–66.

18. Brian Martin, "What to Do When You've Been Defamed," *The Whistle*, newsletter of Whistleblowers Australia, no. 45, February 2006, 11–12.

CHAPTER 11

Software Freedom as Social Justice
The Open Source Software Movement and Information Control

John L. Sullivan

The Internet Age has brought with it unprecedented access to textual, audio, and audiovisual information via networked computers. While computer software manufacturers and traditional media corporations profited tremendously from these new technologies, they almost immediately began forms of legal pushback against rearguard actions by consumers who attempted to expand the availability of information in ways that threatened copyright and other forms of intellectual property. The initial rise of distribution software such as Napster and Gnutella in the late 1990s, for instance, allowed consumers to freely distribute copyrighted music and posed a major threat to the recorded music industry before these sites were ultimately disbanded or transformed into legitimate music sellers as a result of court action. These early battles between computer or audiovisual media companies and consumers were symptomatic of the challenges to traditional notions of intellectual property in an era of digitalization and media convergence.

In the shadow of these high-profile battles over information distribution via computer networks, a small group of dedicated computer programmers and technology enthusiasts have been bypassing the limitations of proprietary information systems by rewriting those systems to fit their own needs. Beneath the radar of the mainstream media, in the pages of technology-oriented periodicals, online blogs, and Internet chat rooms, a group of libertarian-minded programmers have joined a debate about how to short-circuit the rising tide of closed, proprietary computer code that administers the functions of computers and their interactions in cyberspace.[1] The free, open source software (FOSS) movement has countered the market dominance of corporations like Microsoft and Apple by developing and encouraging the distribution of alternatives to these closed systems. Some of the most successful efforts of this movement have been a rival computer operating system (Linux) and other open source software alternatives that are distributed freely over the Internet.

This chapter provides a brief overview of the FOSS movement, focusing specially on the development of the Linux operating system in the 1990s and the creation of a new copyright regime to prevent the privatization and corporatization of this new operating system. I argue that the freedom to access, manipulate, and distribute information is, at its core, a social justice issue. While posing a direct challenge to existing copyright regimes through its emphasis on the commons, open source software development also marks a profound shift away from the dominant mode of capital accumulation toward new modes of cultural production that emphasize collaboration and communal property ownership. The production of this software by "hackers"—individuals who write computer programs and other code and who are outsiders to institutionalized and corporatized forms of software production—also offers a glimpse into a new form of cultural production that exists outside of the boundaries of the wage labor system. Finally, this push for software freedom is beginning to dovetail with larger movements for free culture and electronic privacy, suggesting the emergence of a larger umbrella movement for cultural and software freedom on the horizon.

The Problem: Proprietary Software, Bundling, and Vendor Lock-In

Most computer users today regularly use proprietary software to help operate their computers and perform a myriad number of useful tasks. Most of the world's computers run some version of the Windows operating system, with a much smaller percentage running Apple's Mac OS X operating system. Linux, the open source alternative to these operating systems, makes up only a tiny fraction of the overall total. Microsoft's dominant position in the industry is not necessarily a sign of the popularity of its information products—in fact, Microsoft's Windows Vista operating system has been much maligned in the popular press, becoming a kind of corporate albatross that the company hoped to remedy with the release of Windows 7 in 2009. The factors most responsible for the ubiquity of proprietary software have to do with the outsized influence the companies that manufacture this software enjoy and their close ties with other market players to effectively "bind" the software together in packages for sale to consumers. For instance, the Windows operating system is often the default operating system included on new computers that are sold to consumers because of preexisting business relationships between Microsoft and computer hardware manufacturers like Hewlett-Packard and Dell. Along with this operating system bundling, Microsoft bundles its own Internet browser (called Internet Explorer) in the operating system itself, thereby encouraging end users to utilize this browser by default when they start up the computer for the first time.

This practice is potentially harmful to consumers because it denies them the opportunity to decide whether or not to purchase a specific operating system or software package, and it makes the potential cost of changing to another software application more difficult because of potential incompatibilities with other types of software. Moreover, deals between companies to bundle materials for the customer can thwart market competition because the choice of which product to purchase is taken out of the hands of the consumer and placed in the hands of the companies making cooperative arrangements in advance of manufacturing and distribution to the market. Since so few end users actually modify the default settings of their computers, these actions by technology firms may constitute a de facto form of regulation.[2] This last problem was one of the major anticompetitive practices that resulted in the US Department of Justice's investigation of Microsoft in the late 1990s.[3]

The proprietary model of bundling software and hardware applications together for sale to consumers has begun to extend into other media industries as well. Faced with dwindling audience share for mainstream media outlets like broadcast and cable television, as well as broadcast radio, media corporations have turned increasingly to the Internet to try to reconnect with past audiences and to colonize new ones. The problem faced by these companies is that they have had to compete with the sheer enormity of offerings available on the web, many of which have been created by other Internet users. Easy distribution of copyrighted content via peer-to-peer file sharing also makes the Internet a somewhat unlikely partner for traditional media firms. The solution media conglomerates have found for the convergence and digitalization of copyrighted content is to slowly absorb important distribution channels on the Internet and then begin to exert control over the kinds of information that are found there. This has already happened with the popular video-sharing website YouTube, for instance, which was purchased by new media giant Google, and MySpace, which was purchased by Rupert Murdoch's News Corporation. The consequence of these moves is the artificial fencing off of separate, proprietary realms on the Internet and through software programs that are increasingly necessary to productively interface with the Internet.

The creation of these artificial barriers by media companies has been likened to a "second enclosure movement," a reference to the practice of taking public lands and handing them to private interests for commercial exploitation.[4] This first "enclosure" movement occurred during the emergence of capitalism in feudal Europe, resulting in "the transformation of the European agricultural system from production for use to production for exchange . . . Throughout Europe, the mercantilist states enacted laws privatizing the village commons and depriving the peasantry of its means of subsistence, forcing many into wage labor. The enclosure movement, therefore, involved tendencies that brought both land and labor into the realm of commodity production."[5] The goal of restricting access to hitherto public lands was twofold: (1) to amass surplus production for the purposes of exchange and (2) to create incentives for wealthy landowners to invest in new aqueducts and irrigation systems in order to maximize the productive potential of these lands. The artificial creation of private property was intended to ward off the so-called tragedy of the commons, in which lands left to the common interest would lie fallow and underutilized (thereby endangering the full economic potential of such lands).[6]

The "second" enclosure of information materials is a trend with deep historical roots, dating back to the invention of the printing press, when monarchs began granting exclusive licenses to printers for specific types of documents, often appropriating as proprietary certain plays, poems, and songs that had been popularly available.[7] This shift—defining information and intellectual products as property akin to land—became the core of English copyright law, which was transferred to the American colonies in the 1800s. More recently, the reach of copyright was extended to computer software in the Computer Software Act of 1980, which characterized computer source code as "a form of writing" and thereby subject to intellectual property protections.[8] This law opened the floodgates for the enclosure of computer programming during the deregulatory zeal of the 1980s. Writing in his 1981 book *Who Knows?*, critical scholar Herbert Schiller expressed alarm at the enormous sums of taxpayer funds that were poured into research and development in areas such as microcomputing and nuclear power, only to see the outcomes of those project immediately transferred to the private sphere. These public investments, spurred by Cold War fears, became the private intellectual property of Fortune 500 corporations and deprived the public of the benefits of these government-funded programs. In Schiller's words, "The private attack is characterized by an insistence that information is a commodity and that those who wish to use it should pay for it."[9] In the 1990s, the equation of computer software with intellectual property had become so ingrained in the legal and political discourse that protecting copyrighted material over the Internet emerged as one of the major cornerstones of efforts such as the Clinton administration's National Information Infrastructure (NII).[10]

While the rigorous protection of intellectual property may have spurred new innovations in technology, there are numerous potential dangers here for democratic citizenship, the most glaring of which is freedom of speech: "As culture increasingly becomes fenced off and privatized, it becomes all the more important for us to be able to comment on the images, ideas, and words that saturate us on a daily basis—without worrying about an expensive, though meritless, lawsuit. The right to express one's views is what makes these "copy fights" first and foremost a free-speech issue. Unfortunately, many intellectual-property owners and lawyers see copyright only as an economic issue."[11]

There are numerous recent examples in which the types of "copy fights" that Kembrew McLeod mentions have boiled over onto the pages of the mainstream media. For instance, users of the Amazon.com's ebook reader, the Kindle, were outraged in July 2009 when the company surreptitiously deleted copies of books that users had already purchased due to a disputed licensing agreement with the estate of the author.[12] In this case, digital content that end users believed that they owned was reclaimed and deleted by Amazon. This copyright tussle was fraught with ironic overtones because the titles that were deleted from users' Kindles were books by George Orwell such as *1984* and *Animal Farm*. Although the company subsequently apologized and agreed to restore the books to readers' Kindle devices, the incident vividly demonstrated the pitfalls of vendor lock-in for the digital distribution of media content. Apple's iTunes software and proprietary audio encoding codec (AAC) also exemplifies an attempt to lock users into a particular content delivery system: Apple's iTunes store. Even though other hardware manufacturers such as Palm have attempted to link their hardware devices (such as the Palm Pre smartphone) to Apple's iTunes, Apple has continually modified its software through updates to prevent this linkage, thereby protecting the locked-in nature of the software and hardware ecosystem that is a key profit center for the company.[13] These are but a few examples of issues of information control and copyright protection that proprietary software is designed to support. What alternatives, if any, exist to these closed information ecosystems?

What Is Free, Open Source Software?

Despite the growing popularity of free, open source software in the last 15 years as viable alternatives to proprietary programs, the concept of open source is unfamiliar to most. What I mean by "free, open source software" is software that reveals its source code to the user. Software source code is computer programming language that any experienced user can read and understand and therefore also manipulate and change. Much of the computer software on the market today, including widely used productivity software such as the Microsoft Office suite and operating systems such as Windows and Mac OS X are closed or proprietary software; they do not allow end users to modify the programs to improve them or personalize their uses. (Indeed, this is also strictly forbidden in the software's "End User License Agreement," or EULA.) The notion of free software originated with a Massachusetts Institute of Technology (MIT) computer programmer Richard Stallman (or RMS, the initials of his name that formed his login password to the MIT computer systems). Stallman had been working at MIT during the formative 1970s, when other computer programmers or "hackers" were experimenting heavily with Unix-based systems and developing software tools that were passed around among users, who admired the skill in writing the code and suggested further improvements.[14] Although the term "hacker" has become something of a pejorative, referring to dangerous individuals who break into secure computer systems in order to steal valuable data, its "old" meaning from the 1970s and 1980s was quite a positive one, referring to a technologically savvy, intelligent individual who worked against a centralized authority and the rigid enforcement of property boundaries.[15] As Helen Nissenbaum explains about the early hacker movement, "If there is something political that ties together these descendents of early hackers, it is protest—protest against encroaching systems of total order where control is complete, and dissent is dangerous. These hackers defy the tendencies of established powers to overreach and exploit without accountability. With their specialized skills, they resist private enclosure and work to preserve open and popular access to online resources, which they consider a boon to humanity. Ornery and irreverent, they represent a degree of freedom, an escape hatch from a system that threatens to become overbearing."[16]

Stallman and other programmers at MIT embodied these antiauthoritarian and communitarian ideals in the work that they performed on the university's computer systems. Each time one programmer came up with a useful program (or "hack"), it was quickly distributed to others who would read and admire the code, and then promptly alter it to create new software programs that fulfilled some other utilitarian need.

The camaraderie and communitarian ethos at the MIT lab began to unravel, however, when the US Department of Defense became interested in utilizing these projects to develop its own applications, insisting that these software projects become closed to outsiders to protect national security. Additionally, private companies became less interested in sharing their source code with university programmers and computer science students since new business models for software were emerging, and many of the best minds at these universities were being hired by these firms (one of which was Bill Gates's fledgling start-up company called Microsoft).

Stallman worked to preserve the "hacker ethic" he had once experienced at MIT by resigning his position there in 1984 and devoting himself to the advocacy of what he called "free software." Stallman founded the Free Software Foundation (FSF) as a nonprofit organization that would be able to support the development of free software projects. Free software, according to Stallman's vision and the tenets of the Free Software Foundation, comprises four essential freedoms:

1. The freedom to run the program, for any purpose (freedom 0).
2. The freedom to study how the program works, and change it to make it do what you wish (freedom 1). Access to the source code is a precondition for this.
3. The freedom to redistribute copies so you can help your neighbor (freedom 2).
4. The freedom to improve the program, and release your improvements (and modified versions in general) to the public, so that the whole community benefits (freedom 3). Access to the source code is a precondition for this.[17]

In essence, then, free software allows users to run, copy, distribute, and change or improve existing software without being prevented from doing so by the originator of the software. This does not mean, however, that financial transactions are anathema to the free software movement: in Stallman's words, "free" simply meant free as in "free speech," not as in "free beer." In fact, some of the earliest businesses created around open source software offered technical support for these tools—something that Stallman himself strongly supported. While software companies sometimes charge users money to download and install open source software, most free software projects today are distributed on the Internet without cost to users, which makes them particularly attractive to computer users in developing countries with few financial resources to spend on computer software.

The primary distinction between proprietary software development and that of volunteer, networked hackers has been beautifully explained by hacker activist Eric S. Raymond as the distinction between "cathedrals" and "bazaars."[18] Raymond argued that proprietary software is designed from the top down to meet a specific set of goals identified by a few senior managers or organizational figureheads, with the only involvement from the public or market emerging when the information product has been fully completed. This is the cathedral model. In contrast, open source hacker communities offer an organizational model more akin to a bazaar, where individual programmers work simultaneously on different and sometimes interrelated projects with little or no supervision or input from any centralized authority. Often, programmers are motivated to write pieces of software code to satisfy a particular need of the moment, such as allowing a specific peripheral device such as a printer or scanner to work with another type of operating software. The quality of the finished product is then judged collectively by the hackers who download and use the software, who then may in turn offer suggestions, file bug reports, or even improve on the code themselves and upload the results of their efforts for other hackers to see. Raymond's notion of the bazaar suggests that the more programmers choose to work on software code and improve it, the better the ultimate quality of the code will be (and the quicker it will be debugged).

Participation in open source software projects, therefore, is voluntary. In his overview of the sociology of the open source movement, Steven Weber notes that "the key element of the open source process, as an ideal type, is voluntary participation and voluntary selection of tasks. Anyone can join an open source project, and anyone can leave at any time . . . There is no consciously organized or enforced division of labor."[19] Voluntary participation, however, does not mean that open source projects are anarchic and aimless. Instead, many open source projects work continuously and often swiftly toward a common set of goals and purposes that are mutually agreed upon by the project participants.[20]

Stallman's orientation to free software was about more than preserving the collaborative atmosphere among computer scientists at MIT. Instead, his definition of free software outlined the philosophical underpinnings of a larger social movement to transform the tools that were to become vital conduits of commerce, information, and artistic expression. As Weber describes, "Software for [Stallman] was not just a tool to run computers. It ultimately was a manifestation of human creativity and expression . . . Traditional, exclusionary property rights do not incentivize people to write good software, as mainstream intellectual property rights law would have it. Rather, imposing traditional property rights on software makes 'pirates' out of neighbors who want to help each other."[21] Stallman's notion here is that digitized information and computer software is not simply utilitarian but is instead an outgrowth of the creative capacities of human beings. Additionally, as social creatures, it is part of our inherent nature to form collectives and to cooperate. These fundamental aspects of the human experience, however, have been artificially curtailed by the restrictive code that is inserted into proprietary software, making "pirates" out of "neighbors."

Stallman's emphasis on reinvigorating a sense of common good via artistic and other cultural expression has become the philosophical foundation for the larger "free culture" movement. Indeed, Lawrence Lessig, one of the most visible proponents of the free culture movement, credits Stallman as the primary inspiration for his concept of free culture.[22] In a passage that directly channels Stallman's thinking, he writes, "The opposite of a free culture is a permission culture—a culture in which creators get to create only with the permission of the powerful, or of creators from the past."[23] Likewise, some scholars have associated Stallman's exhortation to retain access to computer source code as a fundamental push to protect freedom of speech from government and corporate control. As anthropologist Chris Kelty argues, "Coding, hacking, patching, sharing, compiling, and modifying of software are forms of political action that now routinely accompany familiar political forms of expression like free speech, assembly, petition, and a free press. Such activities are expressive in ways that conventional political theory and social science do not recognize: they can both express and 'implement' ideas about the social and moral order of society."[24] The FSF argues, therefore, that FOSS movements encompass a much broader range of social and political issues such as information access and control.

GNU and Linux

Stallman's goal, through the FSF, was to develop an entirely free computer operating system that could be downloaded, utilized, and changed by anyone. Stallman's training was in the Unix operating system, one of the most widely used operating systems for large mainframe computers at universities and government laboratories at the time. The problem, however, was that Unix was a proprietary operating system (owned at the time by AT&T) and could not be distributed to other users without the threat of copyright infringement. Stallman and a group of programmers therefore took it upon themselves to begin rewriting the Unix operating system from scratch, one application at a time. Between the 1985–1992 period, they succeeded in replacing almost every Unix application that programmers relied on. Stallman playfully referred to this new collection of programs as "GNU," which stood for "GNU's Not Unix"—a recursive acronym. Despite the usefulness and popularity of some of these reconfigured programs among computer hackers and enthusiasts, they remained a loose collection of applications that did not cohere together as a full operating system. It was a young Finnish computer science student named Linus Torvalds who in 1991 actually finished the GNU operating system by creating the kernel for a version of Unix called Minix.[25] Armed with his new operating system, which he dubbed "Linux," along with Stallman's GNU tools, he began to distribute an entirely free operating system that would develop throughout the 1990s and 2000s into a viable alternative to Windows and other proprietary operating systems.

Legal Foundations for Open Source: The GPL and Free Speech

Many FOSS projects, including GNU/Linux, have progressed beyond simple "adhocrasies" and bazaar-style organizations to create sophisticated institutional structures of their own. These infrastructures not only have regularized the development of open source software but also have provided an organizing structure for nascent FOSS social and political movements. A critical aspect of new organizational self-awareness is the self-definition of Linux hackers, FOSS developers, and open source software users as free speech advocates in opposition to the closed, proprietary software that is in widespread use on personal computers today. The legal cornerstone of free speech in open source software communities is the GPL, or GNU General Public License. Stallman's vision for new technologies free from the confines of proprietary software would have been only an idealistic fantasy if it attempted to survive under existing copyright regimes. Consequently, Stallman initiated a substitute system for copyrighting software. Rather than protect the property rights of the individual creator, Stallman's version turns the notion of copyright (which links specific lines of computer code with individual property) on its head by keeping software in the public domain in perpetuity, something that he playfully refers to as "copyleft." In essence, the GPL ensured that the four essential software freedoms would remain intact whenever free software was modified and redistributed by other users. If the end user decides to change GPL-protected software and distribute that new software code to others, then another provision of the open source definition comes into play: the modified software must be distributed under the same terms as the original software—that is, with the source code revealed and the opportunity for those new users to modify and redistribute the software.[26] The license also prevented users from adding proprietary software to GPL'd software and then obtaining a restrictive license for the newly created program, making it impossible to "combine a free program with a non free program *unless* the entire combination is then released as free software under the GPL."[27] The GPL was a major innovation in Stallman's battle with multinational corporations like AT&T (which owned the rights to the Unix operating system) since it turned "copyright law against itself, limiting its reach and carving out a legally protected zone to build and protect the public domain."[28]

The GPL was the first step in expanding the boundaries of free speech beyond the specific interests of computer hackers to encompass much broader concerns about the restriction of culture in a networked society. By creating a legal alternative to copyright, Stallman "provided the rudiments of a rival liberal legal vocabulary of freedom, which hackers would eventually appropriate and transform to include a more specific language of free speech."[29] Increasingly, open source communities are also getting more sophisticated in their facility with the legalities of copyright law, becoming ersatz copyright lawyers in their use of various software licensing schemes in order to challenge the existing intellectual property regimes. As Gabriella Coleman explains in her overview of legal and political activism among FOSS developers, "developers construct new legal meanings by challenging the idea of software as property and by crafting new free speech theories to defend this idea of software as speech."[30] In particular, Coleman describes how new developers for Debian, a version of the Linux operating system and the largest open source software project in the world, must complete an extensive application that asks them detailed questions about different sorts of software licenses under the GPL, including how to "correct" some existing software licenses to bring them into compliance with the Debian Free Software Guidelines (DFSG) or the GPL. These practices not only maintain the integrity of the Debian operating system, but they also help to form a coherent social movement by "transforming technologists into informal legal scholars who are experts in the legal technicalities of FOSS as well as proficient in the current workings of intellectual property law."[31]

Along with these activities among hacker communities, a number of key nonprofit organizations have taken shape in the last 15 years that have bolstered the legal power of open source software licenses, including the GPL. Richard Stallman's decision to resign from the artificial intelligence laboratory at MIT and to start the Free Software Foundation, for instance, gave a public face to the movement and allowed him to begin soliciting donations to support the development of free software tools. The FSF has continued to support the cause of free software both by channeling donations and by bringing attention to some of the perils of proprietary software. Their "Bad Vista" campaign from 2006 to 2009, for example, helped to focus media attention on the fact that Microsoft no longer sold their operating system to end users; instead, the software was only "licensed" to these users, which gave Microsoft the ability to potentially remotely disable a user's computer through the use of a so-called kill switch.[32] More recently, the Software Freedom Law Center (SFLC), a nonprofit organization founded in 2005 to support FOSS developers with legal advice on software licensing and "license defense and litigation support," is in some ways analogous to the American Civil Liberties Union (ACLU) in that it serves as a watchdog for GPL-licensed software and will file injunctions and engage in other court actions to prevent the "contamination" of open source software with proprietary code.[33] In December 2009, the SFLC filed suit against major consumer electronic companies and retailers such as Samsung, Westinghouse, JVC, and Best Buy for releasing proprietary products that utilized GPL-protected software called BusyBox.[34] This action is only the most recent in a string of incidents in which proprietary software developers (one of them was Microsoft) have been informed by the SFLC that they have violated the terms of the GPL. The existence of visible organizations such as the SFLC and the FSF, then, has given the FOSS movement a centralized public identity and has protected the digital commons from incursions by profit-driven electronics and software companies.

Creative Commons and the Notion of Socially Created Value

The efforts of software hackers and open source advocates to emphasize the collective, communitarian ethos of the Internet has also inspired activists to expand the notion of the public domain to include all information and creative works. The rallying cry of free software advocates for openness in both the code and the content of new media on the Internet has also dovetailed with the broader free culture movement, which has worked to circumvent the restrictions of copyright law in order to reserve the rights of individuals to use, modify, and redistribute cultural materials. The aims of the free culture movement read like a social justice manifesto. As Lawrence Lessig, one of the key figures in the free culture movement, writes, "So uncritically do we accept the idea of property in culture that we don't even question when the control of that property removes our ability, as a people, to develop our culture democratically."[35] Modeled on Stallman's GPL, Lessig and two colleagues created an alternative copyright regime for cultural materials in 2002, the Creative Commons.[36] In essence, Creative Commons was conceived as a private "hack" to produce a more fine-tuned copyright structure, to replace "all rights reserved" with "some rights reserved" for those who wished to do so. It tried to do for culture what the General Public License had done for software."[37]

The ultimate goal of alternative copyright systems such as Creative Commons and the GPL is to preserve the ability of individuals to both share and build on each other's knowledge, artistic creativity, and expertise. This not only reduces barriers for individuals to participate with one another in communal projects but also works to equalize access to information for all members of society, which is a core aim of classic redistribution theories of social justice. New forms of value and innovation are created through this new form of networked creativity, which have been collectively dubbed "the commons." The commons is "a vehicle by which new sorts of self-organized publics can gather together and exercise new types of citizenship. The commons can even serve as a viable alternative to markets that have grown stodgy, manipulative, and coercive. A commons arises whenever a given community decides that it wishes to manage a resource in a collective manner, with special regard for equitable access, use, and sustainability. The commons is a means by which individuals can band together with like-minded souls and express a sovereignty of their own."[38]

New means of modular, collective cultural production thrive on a vibrant public domain. Since this is increasingly under threat, FOSS projects that release their software under the GPL are advancing a critical twenty-first-century goal toward collectivism that is at the forefront of the social justice purpose. One simply has to look at the motivations behind most forms of cultural production to realize the historical shift in perspective. Under the traditional systems of copyright, the end goal of artistic and intellectual creation is to generate private property that—while it may be experienced by others—ultimately serves to benefit the creator. Under "copyleft" regimes like Creative Commons and the GPL, the goal of cultural production is to add value and creativity to a set of resources to which everyone has free access. This not only encourages more creativity that can then be fed back into the collective commons, but it creates new incentives for intellectual production that go beyond the accumulation of capital.

As a result of the possibilities for innovation offered by the collective commons, new forms of cultural production are also being created, many of which challenge the existing wage-labor system of postindustrial capitalism. Like software engineers in general, as well as teachers, artists, and others who work in the cultural industries, open source hackers are knowledge workers. What is less obvious about hackers is the fact that their efforts lie outside the traditional realm of the capitalist economy since the goal of the software is to be freely available to computer users around the world. Absent the profit incentive, there are a number of other motivations that typify hacker involvement in FOSS. Instead of a work environment structured by institutional or market-based demands, free software communities are often loosely organized and centered around the contributions of lines of code in order to solve specific problems. Since the computer code written by hackers is an abundant resource, writes hacker anthropologist and spokesperson Eric Raymond, the social and economic model of open source communities most closely resembles a *gift culture*.[39] Raymond writes that "abundance makes command relationships difficult to sustain and exchange relationships an almost pointless game. In gift cultures, social status is determined not by what you control but by *what you give away*."[40] Giving or uploading useful code to the community not only provides others with a gift but also establishes one's reputation as a successful hacker through positive recognition from the community of other hackers. For Manuel Castells, this suggests a "techno-meritocratic" culture that develops among online hacker communities.[41] He writes, "Naturally, money, formal proprietary rights, or institutional power are excluded as sources of authority and reputation. Authority based upon technological excellence, or on an early contribution to the code, is respected only if it is not seen as predominantly self-serving. In other words, the community accepts the hierarchy of excellence and seniority only as long as this authority is exercised for the well-being of the community as a whole, which means that, often, new tribes emerge and face each other. But the fundamental cleavages are not personal or ideological: they are technological."[42] In this utopian vein, Castells and other scholars of the postindustrial transition suggest that technological prowess creates new possibilities for autonomy, individuation, and freedom from wage capitalism that emerges from the networked interfaces of the postindustrial economy.[43] FOSS movements fit somewhat naturally into this vision because the tools to rewrite the basic operating code of networked computers are readily available on the web for anyone with access and the patience to master. The power to change the technological course of society, therefore, is effectively taken out of the hands of industrial elites and reclaimed by individual hackers who choose to work on open source projects to fulfill their own goals and desires.

Open source software advocates often point to the Mozilla Firefox web browser as the project that most clearly demonstrates the power and value of collective labor in a networked information economy. The Netscape browser, released in 1995 and based on Mosaic, the first graphical browser for the Internet, was a favorite with end users (because it gave away its product for free) and was a much faster Internet interface than Microsoft's Internet Explorer (IE). To counter this growing threat during the boom times of the late 1990s, Microsoft began bundling IE into new version of its operating system, making the browser the default upon installation and integrating its functions into Windows. Although Microsoft was eventually sued by the Justice Department for these actions, the Netscape Corporation began to falter in the late 1990s until it made a fateful decision for the future of the free software world in January of 1998: Netscape decided to release the source code for the browser and established a nonprofit organization (called the Mozilla Foundation) to look after the development of the browser.[44] To make the notion of free software more palatable to business interests, a number of hacker advocates led by Eric Raymond adopted the term "open source" to avoid the misleading term "free" (as in no cost). Along with convincing Netscape to reveal the source code for its browser, Raymond urged his compatriots to standardize their terminology around the open source moniker, as well as to co-opt the business media such as *The Wall Street Journal*, *The Economist*, and *Forbes Magazine*, which predominantly reflected the interests of the Fortune 500.[45] The new Mozilla browser, nicknamed Firefox, thereafter began a new phase in its development—one that took place in the open and that allowed hackers and end users to understand how the software worked in order to write additional "add-ons" to extend the functionality of the browser, all under the terms of a license that kept the browser in the public domain. Today, Mozilla Firefox is one of the most popular applications for browsing the web and has demonstrated the staying power of an open source project in an environment that has hitherto privileged proprietary, closed systems. Although the advocacy community began to debate the relative merits of "free software" versus Raymond's "open source" terminology, the catalyzing event of Netscape's rebirth as an open source project crystallized Stallman's early vision into a larger social movement. As Chris Kelty notes, "the practice of creating a movement is the practice of talking about a movement . . . It was in 1998–99 that geeks came to recognize that they were all doing the same thing and, almost immediately, to argue about why."[46]

Conclusion

The development of the GNU/Linux operating system and other open source software projects in the 1990s points to some important trends in the networked economy of the twenty-first century. First, FOSS projects like GNU/Linux and Firefox are mounting serious technological and economic challenges to proprietary software such as Microsoft Windows and Internet Explorer. As a byproduct of their collective efforts, open source computer programmers and users are increasingly connecting their own activities to larger philosophical issues of free speech and greater access to information. Indeed, FOSS movements have catalyzed interest in issues of excessive copyright protections enjoyed by corporations, which has expanded the reach of these movement beyond computer programmers and technology geeks. The FOSS movement has made significant inroads in the last 20 years because of the creation of some core institutions (such as the FSF and SFLC) that serve to further the interests of free software and because of new "copyleft" regimes such as the GPL and the Creative Commons. Finally, the free software movement has also spearheaded the development of an alternative form of cultural labor, one that harnesses the power of collective labor via the Internet, which exists parallel to, and often in opposition to, the wage labor system of postindustrial capitalism. Although the goals of these movements have yet to be fully realized, the coordinated efforts of these loosely organized volunteers and hackers have already begun to change the ways that we think about information and computers in a networked society.

Notes

1. Lawrence Lessig, *Code: And Other Laws of Cyberspace* (New York: Basic Books, 2000).
2. Rajiv C. Shah and Christian Sandvig, "Software Defaults as de facto Regulation: The Case of the Wireless Internet," *Information, Communication & Society* 11, no. 1 (2008): 25–46.
3. David McGowan, "Between Logic and Experience: Error Costs and *United States v. Microsoft Corp.*," *Berkeley Technology Law Journal* 20, no. 2 (2005): 1185–1245.
4. James Boyle, *The Public Domain: Enclosing the Commons of the Mind* (New Haven, CT: Yale University Press, 2008), 45.
5. Ronald V. Bettig, "The Enclosure of Cyberspace," *Critical Studies in Mass Communication* 14, no. 2 (1997): 138.
6. James Boyle, "The Second Enclosure Movement and the Construction of the Public Domain," *Law and Contemporary Problems* 66, no. 1/2 (2003): 33–74.
7. Ronald V. Bettig, "Critical Perspectives on the History and Philosophy of Copyright," *Critical Studies in Mass Communication* 9, no. 2 (1992): 131–55; Elizabeth L. Eisenstein, *The Printing Press as an Agent of Change: Communications and Cultural Transformations in Early Modern Europe* (Cambridge: Cambridge University Press, 1979).

8. Michael E. Johnson, "The Uncertain Future of Computer Software Users' Rights in the Aftermath of MAI Systems," *Duke Law Journal* 44, no. 2 (1994): 327–56.
9. Herbert I. Schiller, *Who Knows: Information in the Age of the Fortune 500* (Norwood, NJ: Ablex Publishing Corporation, 1981), 56.
10. Bettig, "The Enclosure of Cyberspace," 138.
11. Kembrew McLeod, *Freedom of Expression®: Overzealous Copyright Bozos and Other Enemies of Creativity* (New York: Doubleday, 2005), 8.
12. Bobbie Johnson, "Amazon Kindle Users Surprised by 'Big Brother' Move," *The Guardian*, July 17, 2009, Technology section, accessed January 8, 2010, http://www.guardian.co.uk/technology/2009/jul/17/amazon-kindle-1984; Brad Stone, "Amazon Erases Orwell Books from Kindle," *The New York Times*, July 18, 2009, Technology/Companies section, accessed January 8, 2010, http://www.nytimes.com/2009/07/18/technology/companies/18amazon.html.
13. Priya Ganapati, "Apple Blocks Palm Pre iTunes Syncing Again," *Wired.com*, October 30, 2009, accessed January 8, 2010, http://www.wired.com/gadgetlab/2009/10/palm-pre-itunes.
14. Steven Levy, *Hackers: Heroes of the Computer Revolution* (Garden City, NY: Anchor Press/Doubleday, 1984).
15. E. Gabriella Coleman and Alex Golub, "Hacker Practice: Moral Genres and the Cultural Articulation of Liberalism," *Anthropological Theory* 8, no. 3 (2008): 255–78.
16. Helen Nissenbaum, "Hackers and the Contested Ontology of Cyberspace," *New Media & Society* 6, no. 2 (April 2004): 195–217, 212.
17. Free Software Foundation, "The Free Software Definition," 2009, accessed January 8, 2010, http://www.gnu.org/philosophy/free-sw.html.
18. Eric S. Raymond, *The Cathedral and the Bazaar: Musings on Linux and Open Source by an Accidental Revolutionary*, rev. ed. (Sebastapol, CA: O'Reilly, 2001).
19. Steven Weber, *The Success of Open Source* (Harvard, MA: Harvard University Press, 2004), 62.
20. The exact nature of collaboration among open source software developers is the subject of a good deal of sociological work. The form of these collaborations range widely from loose "adhocrasies" to sophisticated democratic projects (such as Debian) with mutually agreed-upon rules for development of software. Finally, some open source projects, like the development of the Linux kernel, are essentially benign dictatorships in that they are controlled centrally by a single developer (in this case, Linux founder Linus Torvalds), who personally selects each and every individual who contributes to the development of the project.
21. Weber, *The Success of Open Source*, 47.
22. Lawrence Lessig, *Free Culture: How Big Media Uses Technology and the Law to Lock Down Culture and Control Creativity* (New York: Penguin Press, 2004).
23. Ibid., xiv.
24. Chris Kelty, *Two Bits: The Cultural Significance of Free Software* (Durham, NC: Duke University Press, 2008), 8.
25. Weber, *The Success of Open Source*, 54–55.
26. Open Source Initiative, "The Open Source Definition," accessed December 30, 2009, http://www.opensource.org/docs/osd.

27. Free Software Foundation, "The GNU General Public License," accessed December 30, 2009, http://www.gnu.org/copyleft/gpl.html; Weber, *The Success of Open Source*, 48–49.
28. David Bollier, *Viral Spiral: How the Commoners Built a Digital Republic of Their Own* (New York: New Press, 2008), 30.
29. Gabriella Coleman, "Code is Speech: Legal Tinkering, Expertise, and Protest among Free and Open Source Software Developers," *Cultural Anthropology* 24, no. 3 (2009): 420–454, 424.
30. Ibid., 421.
31. Ibid., 422.
32. Free Software Foundation, "BadVista," 2006, accessed January 8, 2010, http://badvista.fsf.org.
33. Software Freedom Law Center, "What We Do," January 8, 2009, accessed January 8, 2010, http://www.softwarefreedom.org/services.
34. Software Freedom Law Center, "Best Buy, Samsung, Westinghouse, and Eleven Other Brands Named in SFLC Lawsuit," December 14, 2009, accessed January 8, 2010, http://www.softwarefreedom.org/news/2009/dec/14/busybox-gpl-lawsuit.
35. Lessig, *Free Culture*, 261.
36. Creative Commons, "History—Creative Commons," 2009, accessed January 8, 2010, http://creativecommons.org/about/history.
37. Boyle, *The Public Domain*, 182.
38. Bollier, *Viral Spiral*, 4.
39. Raymond, *The Cathedral and the Bazaar*.
40. Ibid., 81.
41. Manuel Castells, *The Internet Galaxy: Reflections on the Internet, Business, and Society* (Oxford: Oxford University Press, 2002).
42. Ibid., 48.
43. Daniel Bell, *The Coming of Post-Industrial Society: A Venture in Social Forecasting* (New York: Basic Books, 1973); Michael Hardt and Antonio Negri, *Empire* (Cambridge, MA: Harvard University Press, 2001).
44. The Netscape Corporation was purchased by America Online (AOL) in November 1998, but not before they had released the source code to their browser under the newly created Mozilla Public License (which had a structure very similar to the GNU Public License).
45. Raymond, *The Cathedral and the Bazaar*, 178–79.
46. Kelty, *Two Bits*, 98.

CHAPTER 12

Watching Back
Surveillance as Activism

Mark Andrejevic

As a freelance reporter in 1992 covering police preparation for street riots in Ann Arbor during the NCAA basketball championship, I remember the officer in charge briefing his forces to remember that they could be videotaped at any time, and to behave accordingly. "Remember Rodney King," he told them, referring to the internationally publicized evidence of police brutality that, at the time, was only a year old. It was an interesting moment—an instance of what Ming Kuok Lim has described as "inverted-panopticism": the police were having to behave not only as if they might be watched at any time but, perhaps more importantly, as if their activities could be *recorded* (for broadcast) at any time.[1] Long accustomed to having the last word in "our-word-against-theirs" exchanges about police behavior, the example of Rodney King demonstrated the power of the amateur video in holding authorities publicly and (potentially) legally accountable for their behavior.

Since that time, other high profile examples of amateur video documenting abuse by authorities have surfaced, from a police officer tackling a bike rider in New York City's Critical Mass ride in 2008 to a 2005 incident in Malaysia in which concerns about abuse were raised by a cell-phone video of police forcing a detainee to do naked "ear-squats" (squatting repeatedly while holding one's ears) as part of a strip search. Perhaps one of the most highly publicized international examples of amateur documentation of abuse is the case of the torture of prisoners by American troops at the Abu Ghraib prison in Iraq, documented by digital images that were taken by soldiers and eventually leaked to the media.

The systematic use of video cameras to hold police accountable has led to the creation of "cop watch" groups across the country (and internationally) and predates the Rodney King incident. The Berkeley Copwatch group, for example, was formed in March 1990 "in response to escalating abuse of people in the

Telegraph Avenue area of Berkeley," and similar groups have emerged in several other cities, thanks in part to the increasing availability of relatively inexpensive video recording and editing equipment and the emergence of new platforms for distributing video content.[2] In many cases, without the video and photographic evidence, it is unlikely that acts of abuse would have received public notice or that investigations into misconduct would have occurred.

What made these such high profile examples of abuse (or allegations thereof) was the fact that there was a video record that could be circulated by the mainstream media, and, in more recent examples, on the World Wide Web. The recorded evidence carried with it both the affective charge of the image (as in the case of the Abu Ghraib photos) and the evidentiary clout of a mechanically generated record. As John Durham Peters observes in his work on witnessing, the mechanical act of recording endows the evidence with an impersonal (albeit vexed) sense of objectivity: "Such mechanical 'dumb' media seem to present images and sounds as they happened, without the embellishments and blind-spots that human perception and memory routinely impose."[3]

Lurking in the background of these various examples of amateur monitoring of police and state activity is the familiar claim of subversion or empowerment—that the widespread availability of relatively inexpensive digital cameras combined with the Internet as a medium for distributing amateur content represents a shift in power relations. Even as forms of state and commercial monitoring proliferate, the means of monitoring are becoming increasingly available to the public as a tool for holding authorities accountable. As Stephen Green observes, "New media technologies make possible the surveillance, however non-systematic and sometimes manipulated, of concentrations of social power."[4] We might add the prospect of *inverse surveillance*—watching the watchers—to the list of forms of empowerment associated with increased access to the means of media production and distribution associated with digital media. Richard Kahn and Douglas Kellner, for example, elaborate the ways in which "internet developments themselves have furthered oppositional politics generally."[5] But Kahn and Kellner omit the tactic of turning the cameras back on the authorities in their list of revolutionary developments: "Whether by using the Internet to take part in a worldwide expression of dissent and disgust, to divert corporate agendas and militarism through the construction of freenets and new oppositional spaces and movements, or simply to encourage critical media analysis, debate, and new forms of journalistic community, the new information and communication technologies are indeed revolutionary."[6] Copwatching, as a form of inverse surveillance—or monitoring the activities of authorities—might also be added to the list of such (potentially) revolutionary developments.

In this chapter, I explore some of the ways in which authorities respond to the challenge posed by "copwatchers," highlighting the relationship between access to the means of surveillance and the power of those they challenge. The chapter's intent is to take seriously the political potential of inverse surveillance as a tool for holding authorities accountable, while at the same time qualifying the claims of empowerment made on its behalf. It is not clear that access to monitoring technologies necessarily shifts the overall balance of power relations in the direction of the people, not least because of the ways in which civilian monitoring relies on the legal protection provided by the authorities being monitored. It is best, in other words, to interrogate all-too-ready claims of empowerment.

Alternative journalism and blogging, especially of the investigative variety, might also be described as ways of holding authorities accountable, but in this chapter I focus on a particular subspecies of media activism devoted to the use of video monitoring for progressive ends: preventing police infringement of civil liberties at public demonstrations and protests. Drawing on Steve Mann's formulation, Mann and his coauthors have described the practice of turning the cameras back on the watchers as a form of *sousveillance* (watchful monitoring from below) as opposed to *sur*veillance (monitoring from above, or literally, to watch *over*). Facilitated by portable digital technology, they claim that "the social aspect of self-empowerment suggests that sousveillance is an act of liberation, of staking our public territory, and a leveling of the surveillance playing field."[7] Picking up on such claims, this chapter is the result of my ongoing engagement with theories of surveillance and its practice in the digital era. In it, I consider what happens when a surveillance strategy typically associated with oppressive regimes of state control is appropriated by the public in an attempt to hold state power accountable.

Surveillance is understood here as a practice conducted against the background of existing power relations. Even the model of the panopticon relies on the power to enclose, to sanction, and to punish: disarticulated from these powers, it becomes a very different mechanism. As David Lyon defines it, surveillance typically refers not just to the collection of information about particular individuals or groups but also to a context in which information is collected "for the purposes of influencing or managing those whose data have been gathered."[8] The very notion of surveillance invokes a force field of power relations. The necessary background to a politics of sousveillance or inverse surveillance is one in which there is both a public expectation of accountability and some mechanism, legal or otherwise, for the public to exert control back on authorities. For example, the Los Angeles riots in response to the verdict in the trial of the officers who beat Rodney King might be described as the result of a combination of an expectation of accountability (police officers should behave appropriately and be sanctioned if they do not) with the perceived failure of existing legal mechanisms to hold authorities accountable. Without expectations and mechanisms of accountability, sousveillance or inverse surveillance would be rendered ineffective as a political tool. If, indeed, there were no penalty for police abuse, attempts to record it would have no deterrent power.

However, expectations of accountability on their own are insufficient to explain the potential political efficacy of inverse surveillance. Monitoring, in this context, is not merely about gathering data; it is also about the narrative that makes sense of the information collected. That is, inverse surveillance relies on the ability to offer a convincing counternarrative to that promulgated by authorities, who may have better access to mainstream media or public relations strategies. In this regard, the success of inverse surveillance depends on the efficacy of such counternarratives—or, similarly, on the ability to subvert a particular dominant narrative. The forms of media production described by Kellner and Kahn—blogging, independent online journalism, and so on—complement the process of inverse surveillance: they help provide narratives that make sense of the video record. Consequently, the political struggle over inverse surveillance often has to do with control over the narrative explanation of this record.

Finally, one of the potential dangers of sousveillance is that associated with other forms of monitoring: function creep. Archives collected by activists, like any database, may become tempting "honeypots" for authorities including police investigators and intelligence organizations. To the extent that authorities have an interest in accumulating as much information as possible, it is questionable whether it is possible to imagine such a thing as a subversive database. The following sections explore the concrete examples of both the victories and setbacks of countersurveillance in examples of the activities of video activist groups I-Witness Video and the Glass Bead Collective, both based in New York City.

I-Witness: Government Response to Inverse Surveillance

The I-Witness Video collective was formed in 2000 by citizens concerned over what they believed to be more aggressive forms of policing at public demonstrations, according to founding member, community activist, and self-described forensic video analyst Eileen Clancy: "Basically individuals started to see police attacks at demonstrations, a lot of arrests, seemingly without cause, and we knew that there were a lot of video cameras out on the streets. But it seemed that the video never got to the lawyers."[9] The group's goal was to find ways to collect video about police actions and ensure that these made it to lawyers defending those arrested under false pretenses. The distributed monitoring of public demonstrations was already taking place, thanks to the proliferation of relatively inexpensive video cameras—but there was no system for assembling or coordinating the monitoring to hold authorities accountable. The group not only recruited amateur videographers and coordinated their activity but also served as a clearinghouse for anyone with video evidence relevant to charges of police misconduct or abuse. The group's philosophy is to defend public space for public dissent and expression by ensuring that authorities are held accountable for violations of civil rights. As the group's website puts it, "I-Witness Video uses video to protect civil liberties. We probe police actions at First Amendment events."[10] Members of the collective devote their energies to filming police activity at public events and demonstrations where protest activity is anticipated.

I-Witness Video played an important role in defending people arrested at the 2000 Republican National Convention in Philadelphia. In one instance, a man who was being held on bail of a half-million dollars was released and charges dismissed after a video supplied by I-Witness revealed that the officer who had claimed to observe his activity was in a completely different location from the accused at the time when he was arrested. The case demonstrated the power of the technology as an electronic witness: "The most important thing, in case anybody wants to do any of this, is to have the clock on your camera set at the right time, because if there's a police misstatement or there is confusion about when something happened, that's very potent evidence."[11]

Through its partnership with the National Lawyers Guild, the group works with defense lawyers to search for video relevant to the cases of individual defendants. This means hours spent poring over video in order to find footage of defendants and police involved in pending trials. It also means that the sworn statements of police officers can be matched to the video record more systematically than ever before: a form of accountability to which police officers are perhaps not yet accustomed. Even members of I-Witness were surprised by the results, according to Clancy: "What we learned was, it turned out, that much more than we would have imagined, the police were lying in their sworn affidavits about the charges."[12]

One of the results of I-Witness's activism has been to shine a light on what seem to be a relatively routine practice, at least with mass arrests at public demonstrations: police officers filling out false reports as they process arrests. After the 2004 Republican National Convention in Manhattan, during which the New York City Police Department proved particularly aggressive in arresting and detaining protestors and bystanders, I-Witness video records were responsible for acquittals or the dismissal of charges in cases involving about 400 of the 1,800 people arrested.[13] In almost one in four cases, in other words, it turned out that there were inconsistencies or falsehoods in the police statements. And those were just the cases for which I-Witness was able to discover video related to the arrests. In one case, I-Witness's Clancy discovered that a police videotape had been altered before being submitted as evidence. The edited tape omitted scenes that contradicted the police report, which accused the defendant of ramming police with a bicycle and resisting arrest. As *The New York Times* reported, the "police videotape had been altered to remove sections showing Mr. Dunlop's [the defendant's] pre-arrest behavior, which did not include the violence a police officer had described under oath. After Ms. Clancy found an unedited videotape that showed Mr. Dunlop strolling calmly and then being arrested without a struggle, the district attorney's office dropped the case against him."[14] In another case, charges against a group of demonstrators holding a banner in front of the New York Public Library were dropped after video evidence contradicted a police report accusing demonstrators of blocking traffic. The video showed that they weren't even in the street.[15] Yet another false police report accused one defendant of resisting arrest and having to be carried away by four officers when the video clearly showed him walking "down the steps under his own power, and that the officer who testified against him had no role in his arrest."[16] The officer in question provided detailed testimony about the arrest— "We picked him up and we carried him while he squirmed and screamed . . . I had one of his legs because he was kicking and refusing to walk on his own"— even though he was nowhere to be seen in the videotape of the arrest.[17]

What emerged in the aftermath of I-Witness's activities was a pattern: a division of labor in which officers who weren't involved in arrests were routinely filling out false complaints. The process amounted to the production of false reports to provide after-the-fact justification for aggressive policing and intimidation. As *The New York Times* put it, "Dozens of complaints were sworn by police officers who said they had witnessed people violating the law . . . but later admitted under oath that their only involvement was to process the arrests, and that they had not actually seen the disorderly conduct that was charged."[18] Perhaps unsurprisingly, there were no prosecutions of police officers who filled out false statements or perjured themselves when they lied under oath. The only response to a clear pattern of police abuse was a letter written by an assistant district attorney to the New York City Police Department "to stress the importance of officers' not swearing to things they had not seen themselves. The prosecutors said the confusion surrounding mass arrests made it hard to bring perjury charges."[19]

More recent evidence circulated—at least originally—by the Glass Bead Collective, a New York–based group of video artists and activists that has collaborated with I-Witness, indicates that the NYPD may not have taken the district attorney's message to heart.[20] During one of the regular and heavily policed Critical Mass group bike rides in downtown Manhattan, a police officer arrested one of the riders for allegedly attacking him with a bike by riding directly into him. A mobile phone video taken by a tourist and circulated by activists at Time's Up and the Glass Bead Collective, however, revealed the officer's account to be fabricated: the video clearly shows the rider veering to avoid the officer who first gets in his path and then violently pushes him off the bike. *The New York Times*, once again, noted the inconsistencies in the officer's account: "The officer said he was knocked to the ground by Mr. Long. Throughout the tape, though, he remains on his feet, even after banging into Mr. Long. The police officer wrote that Mr. Long had been 'weaving' in and out of traffic, 'thereby forcing multiple vehicles to stop abruptly or change their direction in order to avoid hitting' Mr. Long. However, in the videotape, it appears that there are no cars on the street."[21] The amateur video went viral on YouTube, receiving more than 400,000 views only days after the incident and leading to public criticism of the arrest by both the mayor and the police commissioner. The officer ended up resigning from the police force.

The result of these acts of inverse surveillance by both I-Witness Video and the Glass Bead Collective was to reveal a clear pattern of abuse of power facilitated by what authorities perceived as their monopoly over the official story. As *The New York Times* put it, with perhaps a sense of premature triumph, "The availability of cheap digital technology—video cameras, digital cameras, cellphone cameras—has ended a monopoly on the history of public gatherings that was limited to the official narratives, like the sworn documents created by police officers and prosecutors."[22] Beyond some relatively brief media coverage and the letter from the district attorney's office amid revelations about what seemed to be the standard practice of concocting reports to legitimize mass arrest, however, there was little in the way of response or reform. But police made it clear that they were not going to succumb to a new regime of citizen monitoring without a fight, as the events of the 2008 Republican National Convention in St. Paul demonstrated. Apparently forewarned about the activities of I-Witness and the Glass Bead Collective, the St. Paul police took preemptive action prior to the convention, detaining members of the Glass Bead Collective, searching them, and confiscating their equipment after they passed near a railroad track bordering the street on their way home late one evening. The police used the fact that members of the collective were near the track late at night to detain them on "homeland security"–related matters—questioning them about what they would be reporting on and refusing to provide them with a receipt for confiscated items.[23] Police held the items and returned them after 24 hours, perhaps in response to mainstream media coverage of the detention and the group's accusations of police harassment.

Despite the harassment, members of the Glass Bead Collective were able to get some footage of aggressive treatment of video activists, including the forced entry into a home where members of I-Witness were meeting. Police surrounded the house, claiming they had a warrant to search the house for, among other things, "packages and contents, firearms and ammunition, holsters, cleaning equipment for firearms, [and] weapons devices."[24] When members refused to allow the police entry because the warrant was for a different address, police entered forcibly, detained and searched members of I-Witness and their equipment. Four days later, police surrounded an office building where I-Witness had rented space, claiming they had received a report from an undercover officer that anarchists were holding hostages in the office. A lawyer from the National Lawyers Guild was able to convince police that they were mistaken, but it was a charge that could have allowed forcible entry and violent response by police.[25]

The incidents in St. Paul revealed two things: first, that police were monitoring video activists—many of whom were videotaped by police during detentions, presumably to facilitate identification in the future—and second, that police were developing strategies for harassing those who monitor them by detaining them and confiscating their equipment preemptively. Monitoring, in other words, is not necessarily a *counterforce* to state authority—even in social contacts in which public accountability is a civic expectation. The harassment of video activists received minimal mainstream media coverage—largely in the local press, although reports were circulated widely by independent and alternative media. Perhaps not surprisingly, the apparent antidote to police harassment of video monitors was more monitoring: the videotaping of police detaining members of I-Witness by other video activists and reporting on the detention and search by the alternative news outlet *Democracy Now!*

Police harassment was not the only challenge posed to inverse surveillance as a form of political activism. In 2007, New York City proposed changes to city rules that "would have required any group of two or more people using a camera in a public location for more than half an hour, and any group of five or more people using a tripod for more than 10 minutes, to get a permit and [$1 million in liability] insurance."[26] Although the changes were prompted by the actions of a documentary filmmaker, the rule had obvious implications for groups like I-Witness Video and the Glass Bead Collective, which may have been barred from documenting public demonstrations without permits or costly insurance. After public protest from a number of quarters, the city backed away from the proposed changes—but they are suggestive insofar as they reveal the type of controls deemed desirable by authorities in an era of increased public access to relatively inexpensive video equipment.

Finally, it is worth noting one more response by New York City to the success of I-Witness in holding police accountable for arrests during the 2004 Republican National Convention: ongoing attempts to gain access to the group's video archive. After previous, unsuccessful attempts, the city argued in 2008 that it needed to access I-Witness's videos in order to determine whether it may contain any tapes that the city had lost. The attempt pitted city lawyers interested in gaining access to the video record compiled by I-Witness—perhaps because it might help them to determine which cases to prosecute or to identify activists or other possible targets for police investigation—against a district attorney's office that did not want to admit to misplacing evidence. As an account in *The New York Times* put it, "Such statements would seem to cast the district attorney's office in an unenviable light. Few prosecutors would relish the idea that they might have lost track of videotapes or displayed a cavalier attitude toward maintaining the integrity of evidence."[27]

Nevertheless, city lawyers pressed their case, claiming that they needed access to the archive in order to defend themselves against six hundred claims of unjust arrest and detention during the convention. But lawyers for the city have said that the tapes they possess provide only a glimpse of the turbulent events surrounding the convention. As the city law department put it, "These undisclosed tapes are of critical importance to many disputed issues in these case . . . We need to verify the source of those tapes and want to ensure that all videos are available to all parties in this complex litigation."[28] To date, the requests to gain access to the archives of I-Witness, which is not party to any lawsuits against the city, have been unsuccessful, but they highlight another response of authorities to inverse surveillance: the attempt to access activist archives for the purposes of law enforcement and intelligence gathering. The logic at work is a familiar one to neoliberal regimes reliant on outsourcing of government functions—in this case, what might be described as the crowd-sourcing of public surveillance. Just as intelligence agencies are interested in exploiting databases gathered for other purposes (market research, library records, or video rentals), they are also interested in tapping into activist data, which, to the extent they are centralized and searchable, become a double-edged sword.

Countering Inverse Surveillance: The Borrowed Kettle Alibi

A too-narrow focus on surveillance runs the danger of isolating it from the broader context of power and social relations on which it relies. This decontextualization is misleading because it can treat surveillance itself as a form of power—a tool that, in and of itself, can empower the bearer of the monitoring gaze. Hence the attribution of subversive power to inverse surveillance. As Steve Mann, Jason Nolan, and Barry Wellman put it, before adding their own qualifications, "The social aspect of self-empowerment suggests that sousveillance is an act of liberation, of staking our public territory, and a leveling of the surveillance playing field."[29] Similarly, Laura Huey, Kevin Walby, and Aaron Doyle note that "when the activities of Cop Watch groups are conceptualized as sousveillance, counter-monitoring from below using video recording equipment appears to be progressive and leveling of surveillance hierarchies."[30] But absent expectations of and mechanisms for accountability, the ability to watch—to merely watch— can also be a form of helplessness. Thus any account of the political potential of inverse surveillance must take into account at least two sets of counterstrategies on the part of authorities. The first undermines mechanisms of accountability and the second thwarts expectations of accountability. Attempts to preempt organized forms of countersurveillance might be considered to fall into the for- mer category insofar as they bypass laws and expectations regarding the right of citizens to monitor activities that take place in public spaces. In this regard, the ability of authorities to devise pretexts (homeland security, invented accusations of barricaded hostages) for preemptively detaining activists and confiscating their equipment circumvents established legal regimes of public accountability. These pretexts are legitimated, at least in the United States, by right-leaning, post-9/11 rhetoric that assumes a tradeoff between security and civil liberties. According to such accounts, protecting the "homeland" means submitting to increasingly aggressive forms of policing and security measures—the type that were used to detain members of the Glass Bead Collective and confiscate their equipment. In this regard, we might invert the activist slogan: power preempts the ability to speak truth to it. To the extent that it is the very authorities who are being monitored that have the discretion to enforce or thwart the rules that guarantee the right to monitor, power and monitoring are not symmetrical or coequal forces.

A second counter-countersurveillance strategy entails undermining *expecta- tions* of accountability. Consider examples of Bush-era legislation such as the USA Patriot Act, which exempts measures taken in its name from the Freedom of Information Act—that is, from public accountability. In this instance, it is the threat of terrorism that is used to gain acceptance for diminished expectations of accountability—a trend that was an integral part of the Bush administration's style of corporate executive governance. The threat of terror is mobilized to reduce expectations of accountability, which in turn helps legitimate changes to existing accountability mechanisms. The attempt to get the public to view the threat of terror as one that justifies a tradeoff between security and civil liberties licenses more aggressive forms of preemptive policing.

But there is another, equally insidious aspect to the challenge of *expectations* of accountability: the undermining of what might be called the evidence-based form of argument on which narratives of inverse surveillance rely. This is a strategy abetted by the multiplication and amplification of narratives facilitated by the Internet and is perhaps epitomized by the public relations tactics of the postmodern Right: flood the zone with counternarratives of all kinds, heighten- ing cynicism and denying the possibility of rationally discriminating between them. As one example of how this strategy works, Bruno Latour points to a press account of the Republican response in the United States to the threat of global warming: "Most scientists believe that [global] warming is caused largely by manmade pollutants that require strict regulation. Mr. Luntz [a Republican strategist] seems to acknowledge as much when he says that 'the scientific debate is closing against us.' His advice, however, is to emphasize that the evidence is not complete. 'Should the public come to believe that the scientific issues are settled,' he writes, 'their views about global warming will change accordingly. Therefore, you need to continue to make the *lack of scientific certainty* a primary issue.'"[31] This is a generalizable strategy for dealing with counternarratives and critique: challenge the critique and respond not with attempts to reinforce the dominant narrative but rather with a flood of information that demobilizes the ability to choose. By multiplying the narratives—and in particular those narratives that cast uncertainty on one another—the goal is to highlight the absence of any "objective" standard for arbitrating between them. The signature move is the conflation of the insight that all knowledge is characterized by bias with the assertion that such knowledge is wholly reducible to bias. As Joshua Micah Marshall puts it, in a description of the tactics of the political Right, at the heart of such a strategy "is the belief that . . . ideology isn't just the prism through which we see the world, or a pervasive tilt in the way a person understands a given set of facts. Ideology is really all there is."[32]

Thus for example, while the Abu Ghraib photographs gave the lie to the claim that the United States does not torture, the struggle continues over the narrative of responsibility: was this the act of a few undisciplined soldiers run amok or the direct result of policy promulgated at the highest level of government? It is telling that the contemporary response of Republican authorities to evidence that appears to contradict their dominant narratives is not to dispute the facts but to multiply the accounts of their significance to the point of uncertainty and confusion. This might be described, following Slavoj Žižek's invocation of Sigmund Freud, as the "borrowed kettle" alibi of power. The term refers to the multiplication of contradictory narratives refuting apparent facts: confronted with the fact that the kettle he borrowed was returned with a hole in it, the person accused of breaking it responds with several mutually contradictory excuses: "There was already a hole when I borrowed it; the hole wasn't there when I returned it; I didn't even borrow the kettle."[33]

Such is the familiar response of the Right to evidence of global warming: "Global warming is a hoax trumped up by those who hate industry; global warming does exist, but it is an inevitable part of a natural cycle independent of human activity; global warming is taking place, for whatever reason, but it may be actually be good for us: extending growing seasons, creating new shipping routes, and so on." The strategy here is to sow sufficient confusion to neutralize a challenge to the dominant narrative. It is a strategy predicated on the notion that the existence of counternarratives is not in itself a threat to the authority of the dominant narrative. At the same time, sowing confusion can have the politically demobilizing effect of fostering a generalized skepticism that undermines recourse to narrative itself, thereby undermining attempts to challenge power with counternarratives of truth.

The borrowed kettle strategy relates to inverse surveillance insofar as it calls into question the context of seemingly straightforward video evidence, pointing out that every account is perspectival: every shot necessarily leaves something out of the frame. Thus the response to video evidence of police abuse is to argue that something left out by the camera justified violent action or to call into question the motives of those collecting the video as a means of distracting attention from its content. The conservative goal of what might be described as the postmodern Right is to undermine the efficacy of an oppositional strategy that relies on crafting a clear counternarrative to power. This is a strategy directly addressed to (undermining) the potential of interactive media technologies and one that turns them to its own ends.

All of which is not to discount the potential of inverse surveillance or sousveillance but rather to highlight the ways it is caught up in existing power relations, triggering the various responses available to authorities who retain control over the legitimate use of force. At the same time, it is worth noting the advantages afforded to activists by practices of distributed or crowd-sourced monitoring and the availability of the Internet as a means of circulating the results of this monitoring. As Vlad Teichberg, a member of the Glass Bead Collective, observed, the Internet not only serves as an alternative news and information source but also, critically, provides a way of attracting the attention of the mainstream media: "In our experience, mainstream media is an integral part of the process, and in fact the only way to reach mass appeal is to somehow co-opt the mainstream media to report the information that we are trying to get out. Internet and viral stuff becomes very important because it creates cultural objects the media just can't ignore—if one succeeds in making something go truly viral."[34]

Neither the mainstream media nor the authorities have the resources to provide the kind of collective documentation that can be assembled not only from video activists but, increasingly, from the hundreds or thousands of citizens with digital cameras and mobile phones at public events. It is precisely this glut of monitoring resources that Teichberg sees as a defense against police counterstrategies: "What's working against the ability of the state to control this is the spread of availability of cameras . . . So in the end this becomes a situation of whack-a-mole for them."[35] There aren't enough cops to confiscate all the cameras. Because documentation of the action is both decentralized and synoptic (the many watching the few) in a sense invoked by Thomas Mathiesen, it achieves the amplification effect associated with the panopticon, but through different means.[36] To the extent that police understand they are the targets of surveillance, they find themselves among the few at the center of the action to which the cameras of the many may turn *at any time*. As there is no central location from which such monitoring occurs, it cannot be shut down, blocked, or evaded in advance. At the same time, there is no guarantee that individual acts of abuse will be caught on tape—escape from the monitoring gaze is possible. But any act might be captured and promptly distributed to millions online. As Teichberg points out, preempting activist monitoring does not eliminate countersurveillance. Some of the most high-profile examples of police abuse caught on video—such as the 2009 New Year's Day shooting of a 22-year-old man by a transit policeman in Berkeley, California—have been the result of bystanders with mobile phones. Moreover, attempts to interfere with the coverage of police action by journalists and activists may only attract the lenses of the public.

The default antidote to strategies of preemption, then, becomes more monitoring. Mann, Nolan, and Wellman warn of a spiral of surveillance that, in the end, leaves power relations unchanged: "Universal surveillance/sousveillance may, in the end, only serve the ends of the existing dominant power structure . . . by fostering broad accessibility of monitoring and ubiquitous data collection."[37] This warning should be read, I think, not so much as an argument against the monitoring of authorities—a bedrock principle of democratic governance—as a concern about the disappearance of inframonitored spaces—spaces that fall below the threshold of monitoring—altogether. The concern is not over the disappearance of those spaces that allow the police to bend or break the rules but rather with those that allow activists to challenge and subvert them. It is hard not to read such a warning as a call to leave the monitoring in the hands of authorities. Perhaps the more salient concern, in an era of "monitoring glut," is access to and control over the resources for making sense of distributed information collection: sorting through it, discerning patterns, and putting these to use. The question of control over such resources reintroduces the issue of asymmetry in the monitoring relationship: on the one hand, distributed forms of monitoring for holding targeted authorities up for scrutiny; on the other, comprehensive forms of data mining monopolized by state and commercial authorities to discern patterns, target suspects, and preempt dissent. The progressive potential of monitoring as a political tool may hang in the balance between these two strategies.

Notes

1. Ming Kuok Lim, "Inverted-Panopticism: The Use of Mobile Technologies in Surveillance" (paper, International Communication Association meeting, San

Francisco, CA, May 23, 2007), accessed July 10, 2009, http://www.allacademic.com/meta/p172572_index.html.

2. The founding date of Berkeley Copwatch is taken from the group's *Copwatch Handbook: An Introduction to Citizen Monitoring of the Police* (Berkeley, CA: Berkeley Copwatch, n.d.), accessed August 2, 2009, http://www.berkeleycopwatch.org/resources/Handbook_06.pdf. Laura Huey, Kevin Walby, and Aaron Doyle include a list of cities with Copwatch groups: "Cop Watching in the Downtown Eastside," in *Surveillance and Security: Technological Politics and Power in Everyday Life*, ed. Torin Monahan (New York: Routledge, 2006), 149.

3. John Durham Peters, "Witnessing," *Media, Culture & Society* 23, no. 6 (2001), 708.

4. Stephen Green, "A Plague on the Pantopticon: Surveillance and Power in the Global Information Economy," *Information, Communication & Society* 2, no. 1 (1999), 29.

5. Richard Kahn and Douglas Kellner, "New Media and Internet Activism: From the 'Battle of Seattle' to Blogging," *New Media & Society* 6, no. 1 (2004), 93.

6. Ibid., 93.

7. Steve Mann, Jason Nolan, and Barry Wellman, "Sousveillance: Inventing and Using Wearable Computing Devices for Data Collection in Surveillance Environments," *Surveillance & Society* 1, no. 3 (2003), 335.

8. David Lyon, *Surveillance Society: Monitoring in Everyday Life* (Buckingham, UK: Open University Press, 2001), 2.

9. "NYPD Officer Caught on Tape Body-Slamming Cyclist During Critical Mass Ride," *DemocracyNow.org*, August 1, 2008, accessed August 2, 2010, http://www.democracynow.org/2008/8/1/i_witness_video_nypd_officer_caught.

10. "About," I-Witness Video, accessed August 2, 2010, http://iwitnessvideo.info/about/index.html.

11. Eileen Clancy, quoted in "NYPD Officer," *DemocracyNow.org*.

12. Ibid.

13. Colin Moynihan, "City Subpoenas for Access to Tapes of 2004 Protests," *The New York Times*, June 20, 2002, accessed August 2, 2010, http://www.nytimes.com/2008/06/20/nyregion/20convention.html.

14. Colin Moynihan, "To Get '04 Tapes, City Cites Lost Evidence," *The New York Times*, July 26, 2008, accessed August 4, 2010, http://www.nytimes.com/2008/07/26/nyregion/26video.html.

15. Jim Dwyer, "When Official Truth Collides With Cheap Digital Technology," *The New York Times*, July 30, 2008, accessed August 4, 2010, http://www.nytimes.com/2008/07/30/nyregion/30about.html.

16. Ibid.

17. Dwyer, "Videos Challenge Accounts of Convention Unrest," *The New York Times*, July 30, 2008, accessed August 4, 2010, http://www.nytimes.com/2005/04/12/nyregion/12video.html.

18. Dwyer, "When Official Truth Collides."

19. Ibid.

20. Founded in 2002, the Glass Bead Collective has a somewhat broader focus than I-Witness: it circulates videos of police abuse and documented police mistreatment

of activists, as during the 2004 and 2008 Republican National Conventions in videos called *Watch This!* and *Terrorizing Dissent*. The collective also stages multimedia artworks and lends its video expertise to other activist and performance groups.

21. Dwyer, "When Official Truth Collides."
22. Ibid.
23. Mary Turck, "Homeland Insecurity in the Twin Cities," *The Twin Cities Daily Planet*, August 26, 2008, accessed August 4, 2010, http://www.tcdailyplanet.net/article/2008/08/26/homeland-insecurity-twin-cities.html.
24. Liliana Seguro, "RNC Raids Have Been Targeting Video Activists," *AlterNet. org*, September 1, 2008, accessed August 4, 2010, http://www.alternet.org/rights/97110/rnc_raids_have_been_targeting_video_activists_.
25. For an account of the events on the I-Witness Video Blog, see http://iwitnessvideo.info/blog/110.html.
26. Diane Cardwell, "After Protests, City Agrees to Rewrite Proposed Rules on Photography Permits," *The New York Times*, August 4, 2007, accessed August 2, 2010, http://www.nytimes.com/2007/08/04/nyregion/04filmmakers.html.
27. Moynihan, "To Get '04 Tapes."
28. Ibid.
29. Mann, Nolan, and Wellman, "Sousveillance," 335.
30. Huey, Walby, and Doyle, "Cop Watching in the Downtown Eastside," 160.
31. Bruno Latour, "Why has Critique Run Out of Steam? From Matters of Fact to Matters of Concern," *Critical Inquiry* 30 (2004), 226.
32. Joshua Micah Marhsall, "The Post-Modern President," *Washington Monthly*, September 2003, accessed August 2, 2010, http://www.washingtonmonthly.com/features/2003/0309.marshall.html.
33. Slavoj Žižek, *Iraq: The Borrowed Kettle* (London: Verso, 2004), 25.
34. Vlad Teichberg, personal communication, September 8, 2009.
35. Ibid.
36. Thomas Mathiesen, "The Viewer Society," *Theoretical Criminology* 1, no. 2 (1997), 215.
37. Mann, Nolan, and Wellman, "Sousveillance," 342.

PART IV

Media Justice

CHAPTER 13

Drawing and Effacing Boundaries in Contemporary Media Democracy Work

Christina Dunbar-Hester

In recent years, particularly in the wake of the Telecommunications Act of 1996, a movement has emerged whose goal is to change the media system in the United States. This movement developed out of a regulatory environment favoring national broadcasting networks and corporate media consolidation, embedded practices of community media production and pirate radio, Indymedia and the transnational "antiglobalization" movement, and the emergence of "new media" including the Internet.[1] However, due to the heterogeneity of its constituents and the way in which it overlays other, related social justice agendas, the "media democracy movement" represents a "variegated, even chaotic field of collective action."[2] Based on ethnographic research at sites where these constituents of the media democracy movement interact, this chapter sketches out key loci of intervention, including radical activist, "reform," and scholarly agendas.[3]

This chapter focuses on the relational positioning of these different groups that each envision their actions to be in support of media democracy. Media activists and other kinds of advocates, including scholars, consider their work to be in service of wider, movement-level goals and a general notion of the public good; however, the various movement actors frequently find themselves experiencing difficulty collaborating with other groups who nominally share their goals for social change through critique of the media system. In examining the attempts of groups—including social scientists, media activists, and policy advocates—to collaborate, the chapter will explore resources on which actors draw: "boundary work" to establish differences between groups and an opposite impulse, which I call "boundary effacement," to reconcile them.[4] These complementary practices of asserting difference between groups on the one hand,

and assigning coherence to their projects on the other, constitute a key dynamic of the movement for media democracy.

The Background

The observations in this chapter are drawn from ethnographic fieldwork mainly conducted from 2004 to 2008. That fieldwork was primarily oriented to the activities of the Philadelphia-based Prometheus Radio Project, an organization working to promote low-power FM (LPFM) community radio, both legislatively and by building new radio stations in partnership with community groups. This chapter aims to address the wider phenomena of media democracy activism and advocacy, not merely radio activism. Yet the ethnographic vignettes presented here must be understood as constitutively related to my research on radio activism; often, my observations of other groups occurred at points of interaction with the radio activists. While the points I make about the relational positioning of groups vis-à-vis one another are meant to shed light on the dynamics of media democracy activism generally, the radio activists are perhaps somewhat overrepresented in this account due to their centrality in my fieldwork. Nonetheless, the chapter is meant to offer a representative, if not exhaustive or wholly symmetrical, account of the shifting alignments and points of rupture between different constituents of the media democracy movement. This illustrates the overlapping and conflicting articulations of media democracy and media change that underpin the movement.

Positions: Tensions and Complements

During my fieldwork, a recurring theme was the radio activists' awareness of disharmonies between their own understanding of politics and goals for media justice and social justice more generally and those of other groups with whom they interacted. While it was understandable that the activists would routinely disagree with groups such as the corporate broadcast lobby, an adversarial relationship with this group did not present particular difficulties for the activists as they went about their work and formulated their goals as an organization. More vexing was the fractiousness of constituents working in the terrain of media reform and media activism who desired to collaborate strategically in order to attain wider goals; disagreements between nominal allies were potentially much more frustrating. This chapter represents an opportunity to reflect on those differences, illustrating how positionality differences among constituents are negotiated in practice. An effect of this reflection is the location and interrogation of my specific position throughout the course of my own research process as well as more general thoughts about the consequences of ethnography and the politics of scholarly engagement.

Media activism may be a special sort of social movement, as it is characteristically embedded in other forms of activism, incorporating diverse and autonomous movements who share the goal of media reform but may also have independent concerns.[5] Communications historian and Free Press cofounder Robert McChesney acknowledges this in his claim that "whatever your first issue of concern, media had better be your second, because without change in the media, the chances of progress in your primary area are far less likely."[6] Also, media democratization efforts must be understood as split between groups who wish to use the media instrumentally to draw attention to their political efforts versus those who wish to change the media system itself.[7] In other words, some groups hope to gain access to the media in order to have a platform for specific views, while others view structural change in the media as an end goal in itself; of course, it is difficult to fully separate structure from content because it is assumed by many that structural change will lead to content change.[8] And of course movement actors pursue diverse tactics and ends. William Carroll and Robert Hackett distinguish between different modes of action among people working to change media systems, including: "(1) influencing content and practices of mainstream media—for example, finding openings for oppositional voices, media monitoring, campaigns to change specific aspects of representation; (2) advocating reform of government policy/regulation of media in order to change the structure and policies of media themselves—for example, media reform coalitions; (3) building independent, democratic and participatory media."[9] The first mode is represented, for example, by Media Matters for America, a nonprofit organization that monitors media content in order to correct conservative bias and misinformation in US news and media commentary, while the radio activists' efforts fall along the latter two lines.

As Carroll and Hackett indicate, even among groups whose primary interest is media democratization, differences emerge. Examples of this abounded during my fieldwork; both radio activists and members of other groups would at times critique the goals or worldviews of other groups or individuals, calling into question any notion of univocality within the movement. Indeed, it is with no little hesitation that I write of "a" movement; while many actors believed themselves to be part of "a" movement, it was not necessarily apparent that they were all referring to the same thing. Even the terms used by groups who are putatively members of the same movement indicate their differing goals and differing degrees of radicalization (compare "media reform" to "media justice," for example).

Anthropologist and Philadelphia-based Media Mobilizing Project cofounder Todd Wolfson argues that Indymedia is "in its essence an anti-capitalist resistance,"[10] whereas an advocacy group like New York–based Fairness & Accuracy In Reporting (FAIR) frames itself as a "watchdog" of mainstream media that uncovers bias and censorship. Both view change in media systems as necessary to uphold democratic ideals, but as Wolfson writes, Indymedia's scope is incredibly wide reaching: "The indymedia movement is working, *in its ideal*, as the backbone of a [newly cohering, spatially distributed] class formation."[11] Consider the mission statement of the Philadelphia Independent Media Center: "PhillyIMC seeks to play a major role in social, economic, and environmental justice movements by creating alternatives to the profit-driven agenda of the corporate media and providing an open forum for the 'passionate and accurate tellings of truth.'"[12] By contrast, Free Press (a Washington, DC–based advocacy group) offers this description of itself: "Free Press is a national nonpartisan organization working to increase informed public participation in crucial media policy debates, and to generate policies that will produce a more competitive and public interest–oriented media system with a strong nonprofit and noncommercial sector."[13] It should be evident from these descriptions that the scope and degree of explicit engagement with other social justice struggles may vary between different strands of groups working to promote media democracy.

Anthropologists Hugh Gusterson and Faye Ginsburg have both studied how people may come to have strong beliefs about polarizing topics.[14] While Ginsburg studied pro- and antichoice activists and Gusterson examined nuclear weapons scientists and antinuclear activists, both found that people's deeply held beliefs were often accompanied by what Ginsburg calls "collective narrative forms for interpreting" facts or events that they encountered in their lives; this was true for people on both sides of these polarizing issues. Something I noted in the course of fieldwork was that while the activists tended to deploy these narrative forms, policy advocates did not. An example is one Philadelphia-based activist who said, "A big problem [for] a lot of activists is that the more you get involved [in social justice work], the more you see how fucked up everything is, and how you really have to change everything in order to change one thing . . . A big problem of oppressed groups and activists is that they don't have any access to the media, and I thought that building [a radio station so that] they could have their own show[s] would be a way to help everybody that I wanted to without focusing on one thing."[15]

Conversely, I observed that in Washington, when I asked people how they had come to the area of telecommunications policy, they might typically reply that they had gone to law school, become a law clerk, and been assigned to research an issue in telecommunications.[16] Compared to the grassroots activists, these members of Washington policy circles displayed a much more dispassionate and agnostic attitude toward the area in which they worked. Even a former Federal Communications Commission (FCC) commissioner who was hailed by activists and advocates as a strong supporter of LPFM characterized her interest in promoting LPFM as derived from her obligation to correctly interpret the statute governing radio and the public interest.[17] Rather strikingly, the activists imputed a "conversion narrative" to William Kennard, the FCC chairman who oversaw the introduction of LPFM; in telling the narrative of how LPFM became legalized, they routinely said that he became passionate about LPFM partly due to learning about the role of unlicensed community radio in combating the apartheid regime in South Africa. (Kennard is African American.) When I asked his former chief of staff whether this was true, she would not speak for him nor confirm the claim;[18] whether or not the conversion story is true, it seems significant that the activists wish to claim Kennard as "one of them" in terms of experiencing a profound and fervent commitment to media democracy. Whether or not policy advocates privately express more passion about these issues, the activists' reliance on these "life scripts"[19] and policy insiders' aversion to them points to a difference in style. This distinction may present obstacles to collaboration even when policy goals are similar.

The 2005 National Conference for Media Reform (NCMR), sponsored by Free Press, provided a useful site to examine the internal politics of media democracy work. During and after the conference, the second of its kind, groups on the more radical-activist end of the spectrum voiced a number of critiques. First, a major concern for Indymedia participants was that the conference venue provided no dedicated space for media production and was not Wi-Fi enabled. This not only presented a practical obstacle to people who expected to report and blog from the conference but also represented to many a symbolic fissure between their goals and those of the conference organizers (perceived by many as a moderate, Beltway, "reform" group without grassroots engagement). After the conference, some participants posted their objections online: "NCMR suckiness/concerns included: lack of any focus on Indymedia & access to answers to questions people had about Indymedia; banging of heads between Indymedia & Free Press—because Indymedia is subversive and Free Press is reform-oriented . . . lack of an open media lab; framing of actionable items (in caucuses) as 'how can you amplify Free Press's message'; . . . lack of discussion about how capitalism is intertwined with the issues of the NCMR; and the lack of centering of media justice issues at the conference."[20] Another attendee registered a somewhat complementary viewpoint but drew different conclusions, in that she was less bothered by what she perceived as the differences between Indymedia's and Free Press's goals for engagement:

> It's interesting to see the continued tension between the small professional-
> ized media reform ngo's [nongovernmental organizations] and participatory
> social movements like indymedia. On some level i agree with what [another

commenter] said, "I refuse to get upset with the reform conversations because it was a reform conference." She's right, it's a reformist conference by reform minded organizations with fundamentally reformist goals. That's ok, they don't want to tear down the system. It's good that indymedia and other radicals are engaging and participating in that process while acknowledging that it's a process lead by free press and the other ngo's.[21]

Though these participants were to greater and lesser degrees dismissive of Free Press (and other "NGOs"), they agreed that the concerns of Indymedia were fundamentally different from those of "media reformers" who were perceived as more institutionalized and less radicalized. And Indymedia itself is not immune from radical critique. One person who had been active in Indymedia commented to me that "'Let 1000 flowers bloom' is not a fucking politics—this is totally naïve!"[22] by which he meant that more structured efforts were needed to put media production into the hands of people without power; he was extremely critical of the race and class backgrounds of the people he saw having self-organized to form Independent Media Centers (IMCs), at least in the United States.

Interestingly, not everyone was attuned to the critiques of the NCMR emanating from more radical groups. In 2005–6, Free Press handed over responsibility to administer a database and other program areas it had been planning about media research to the Social Science Research Council (SSRC) in New York City. That fall I met with an administrator at the SSRC, who was generally concerned about fractiousness between the media advocacy and activist groups with whom he was going to be working and their potential inability to collaborate with academics to produce research. He, however, viewed the NCMR as a success and was dismayed when he learned how unsatisfactory some of the Indymedia and radical groups had found it. He was explicitly worried about the potential for infighting between groups to present difficulties for the SSRC, which hoped to provide a clearinghouse for useful research but not mediate between the concerns of different groups.[23] The SSRC initiated a grant-giving program area ("Necessary Knowledge for a Democratic Public Sphere: Bridging Media Research, Media Reform, and Media Justice," funded by the Ford Foundation), providing grants to advocacy groups and academics working in collaboration to produce policy-relevant research.[24] In spite of its concerns, the SSRC was indeed interested in facilitating specific types of relationships between groups and fostering the production of academically rigorous research that was of specific use to advocates.[25]

At the NCMR, some participants opted out of scheduled conference events to hold a small rally decrying the fact that *Democracy Now!*, a news program featuring Amy Goodman, was not broadcast in St. Louis. Wandering away from the conference site of a downtown hotel, the activists set up a protest with banners and signs near a highway off-ramp. Concerned that drivers were flying by without noticing the protest, one Prometheus organizer spontaneously decided to get their attention by writing "Democracy Now!" across her belly with a marker and flashing her bare breasts and stomach at the cars. Whether or not this worked to capture the attention of the passers-by, her action seemed on some level a protest against the tone of the conference itself; she seemed to translate some of her frustration at the conference into an oppositional and "improper" bodily response. (*Democracy Now!* staff, including Goodman, looked on, and I do not know whether or how they reacted internally to this addition to their rally.) Of course, this mode of expression would certainly be off-limits if, for example, a congressional meeting about LPFM were to go badly. This indicates that maintaining decorum at NCMR was not her highest priority and, in fact, this breach in her composure may have served to mark a boundary between herself and the "media reformers."

Commenting on Prometheus's status in the terrain of work to promote media democracy, the same activist said, "Big nonprofits should be asking existing community media [outlets] working on getting media reform issues out [in] to their communities [to help them], not [addressing] a generic American public that doesn't exist . . . The movement for a democratic media should not be run out of DC. Nonprofit policy groups only have ground to stand on because of the success of groups at the grassroots level."[26]

In fact, Prometheus organizers are quite thoughtful about the issue of their position in the spectrum of groups working on media democracy, making an effort to reflect on their goals and situate their organization accordingly. Another Prometheus activist said, "Radicalism is not extreme sports, to me. I'm working to advance goals within liberal reforms that are consonant with a more radical vision. I have radical ideals, but I'm also a pragmatist."[27] This issue of positioning can feel like a balancing act for Prometheus at times, as their organization seeks to display radical activist ideals and maintain credibility with radical and grassroots groups, while working within an increasingly bureaucratic nonprofit organizational framework, as well as within the legal and bureaucratic framework governing LPFM. Additionally, they are not immune from criticism from more radicalized elements of the microradio activism community, as some microradio proponents (such as Stephen Dunifer) deride efforts to incorporate low-power radio into a legal, regulated context.[28] The same Prometheus activist who said that "radicalism is not extreme sports" wryly proclaimed that "Dunifer is a great anarchist and a terrible businessman."[29] He doubtless admires anarchism more and respects people for adherence to ideals. Yet in order to accomplish practical goals, he was willing to compromise some of his most extreme beliefs; in fact, he felt that there was a greater good at stake and that working

toward practical and attainable goals was the best use of his effort. In my observation, Prometheus seemed to navigate these differences by adopting a fairly
tolerant stance toward groups with different views than their own—they not
only work with nonpartisan reform groups but have forged alliances with conservative Christians on the issue of LPFM legislation—and through frequent
reflection on their own goals and position. Still, much boundary work occurred
in the organization in order to demarcate Prometheus from other groups with
whom they work, mainly "Beltway" nonprofits and policy groups. (I do not
mean to suggest that all of these instances of boundary drawing are reflectively
self-conscious; indeed, they are often spontaneous and unmediated means of
managing anxiety about organizational change and maturation.)

The Case of Scholars

Another group with whom media activists may tenuously ally is academics.
Throughout my fieldwork, a current of tension familiar to ethnographers over
how to "give back" to one's "subjects" in exchange for providing access led me
to consider how the projects of academics and activists differ and overlap. Of
course, the question of whether and how to pursue advocacy and involvement
in the issues one studies has been a concern of social science for decades. Some
scholars choose to elide their own presence in studying activism and approach
their subject as nonparticipants, though perhaps sympathetic ones,[30] or as former activist-participants whose role as scholars overlaps very little with activists
or other actors they study.[31] Others, such as anthropologist Kim Fortun, find
themselves contributing actively to activist efforts by using their skills as writers
to aid people they are also studying, supplying mobilization efforts with written
accounts that are clearly not written for a scholarly purpose.[32]

In my scholarship on media activism, I have not maintained a "symmetrical" approach;[33] I have systematically elevated the status of the radio activists
by giving them the most voice and their claims the most analytical attention
in my publications. I also do not claim to have affected a "neutral" stance with
regard to the controversy over whether consolidated, for-profit media is harmful to democratic discourse or whether a robust independent media system is
preferable. That said, the research I conduct does not directly aim to address
this problem, nor offer prescriptive, "upstream" conclusions that would bear
on it, which has perhaps had consequences in terms of my relationship with
activists.[34]

Once I began my most intensive fieldwork period, which included volunteering in the Prometheus office, we discussed ways that I could make myself
useful. Some of my first tasks were to read and organize news files and produce an issue of Prometheus's newsletter. Later, though, the activists became

interested in meshing my skills with their needs, and I wound up volunteering as an "academic liaison"—I surveyed communications literature for work on LPFM, gave Prometheus database and library access through my academic affiliation, corresponded with academics writing on LPFM, helped draft and distribute calls for academic research desired by Prometheus, and occasionally met with scholars on Prometheus's behalf. This represented a compromise in which my resources and expertise could be put to some productive use but without tying my research project to the production of knowledge that would directly benefit Prometheus.

And even though I was essentially given free rein in my research as far as the activists were concerned, they occasionally displayed a playful, reactive stance to my presence, sometimes introducing me as "our anthropologist," calling themselves my "lab rats," and, on one occasion, indicating that they were undertaking a particular project (a workshop to clean and repair two 1970s-era radio transmitters) in order to provide me with something to study (even though I had not asked them to do this). This provided me with a reminder of the issue raised by Pam Scott and her coauthors in which the presence of the researcher has the potential to actively change what she is studying.[35] I would not take at face value the activists' claim that they held the workshop purely for my benefit, of course, but they were aware that I was interested in the pedagogical dynamics of this workshop and the interactions around technical artifacts. Additionally, it is worth considering that the presence of an outsider interested in studying their organization was perhaps another indication to the activists that their organization was maturing or undergoing change. I do not believe that my presence in any way enhanced or legitimated the activists' standing in contexts such as policy advocacy, but having an academic accompany them in these situations could have had the effect of framing their interactions and experiences with other groups as observable, causing a turn toward awareness of being objectified, analyzed, or formalized, not only for the activists, but also for the people with whom they interacted.

The radio activists desired research that would help them advance their goals. Before I began my project, Prometheus had already solicited scholarly research; during my fieldwork, they became even keener to find people to conduct research that could help them make the case that LPFM provided the benefits that they hoped for and believed in. At the five-year anniversary of LPFM (in 2005), the activists had begun to feel pressured to "prove" its merits in order to secure and, hopefully, improve its standing; they were especially nervous that existing metrics for the impact of (commercial) radio stations were inadequate to demonstrate the benefits of LPFM. Prometheus distributed a document that read,

Scholars! Have You Had Enough Of Morose Meta-Mediated Musings? Do you envy the impact that conservative scholars have over the national media policy debate? Are you ready to kick some ass? Then Prometheus needs you! . . . We're media activists, and we know how to make a difference. We've changed federal policy on community radio, and had a big impact in the media ownership debate. Problem is, none of us has more than a BA. We barely know Adorno from A Door Knob. So often we don't know what we're talking about. None of us even has a library card to a decent public or university library.[36]

Here the Prometheus activists mark a boundary between themselves and academics. Obviously, they do know Adorno from A Door Knob, but they are pointing to the need for academic production and credentialing of knowledge, which differs from the expertise they claim. The Adorno–A Door Knob quote also raises the issue of markers of identity between activists and other groups with whom they interact. The activists were occasionally very funny, and, I argue, sometimes used a tone of irreverence (as in the *Democracy Now!* incident) to reinforce an outsider identity vis-à-vis academic, policy and advocacy, or lobbying groups, for whom such outward displays of humor would be less appropriate or likely.

In addition to identity displays, another point of dissonance in terms of activist-academic collaboration is timing. As sociologist Günter Getzinger states, "A crucial problem of transdisciplinary projects is the different 'timing' of decision-oriented systems ('practice' [policy, activism]) and knowledge-oriented systems ('science' [social science; the academy])."[37] Activist solicitation of scholarly assistance was often to aid in time-sensitive policy discussions, whereas the duration of an academic project is often much longer. When I searched for published research on microradio in 2004–2005, the articles I found took up the topic of 1990s microbroadcasting; the most current of them ended with the introduction of LPFM. For the activists, who sought up-to-date work on the impact of LPFM to use in making policy requests or in issuing comments on legislation, academic research ran the risk of being "stale" by the time it was published, often taking years to go through the academic publication cycle. The activists did attempt to scale their needs to the possibilities presented by academic schedules: "You have students that need projects and internships. Instead of having them write another comparative content analysis of Madonna vs. Britney Spears, why not focus your classes on real problems for community radio? Your research might make it into an official FCC rulemaking, and make a real difference!"[38] Here Prometheus suggests to professors that a semester might be a unit of time that is mutually copacetic, trying to dovetail an academic calendar with an activist research need.

Seeta Peña Gangadharan has discussed what she calls the "knowledge production practices" of media activism. She approaches this topic rather literally, taking documents and reports produced by reform- and social justice-oriented organizations as her object of study.[39] Printed documents, or what Bruno Latour and Steve Woolgar theorize as "inscription devices,"[40] are a very important output of academic and scientific labor (and, as Gangadharan notes, reform and activist labor as well).[41] Documents provide, perhaps, a ready point of comparison between academic and activist or reform projects. From my perspective, it is important to recognize that media activists' knowledge production practices extend to technological practice and political organizing, which may not easily lend themselves to direct comparison with knowledge products such as written reports.

Nonetheless, even when the products of academic labor in some ways resemble activists' knowledge products, the academics' work may still fail to translate to nonacademic projects in significant ways. At the 2008 annual academic professional society meeting of the International Communication Association (ICA) held in Montréal, Canada, ICA hosted a preconference meeting with the SSRC on the topic of "Bridging the Scholar-Activist Divide." At the meeting, participants discussed experiences collaborating across these communities of practice. People who worked in nonacademic roles raised the difficulty of understanding academic writing, even going so far as to suggest that it was hard to trust whether engagement of academics with activist-advocacy topics was conducted in sympathy with them because it seemed impossible to determine from the academic products.[42]

Looking at the situation from the vantage point of scholars, Michael Delli Carpini, a senior scholar who has tried to promote academic work on media reform topics as dean of the Annenberg School for Communication at the University of Pennsylvania, stated,

> I would say that "allies" is too strong, because I don't think we've figured out good ways to work together, but I think kind of kindred spirits, would [include] everything from local groups with a national impact like Prometheus, to some of the Washington-based groups . . . My own personal perspective is that . . . scholars and community activists don't always use the same language and aren't always clear with each other . . . And expectations usually get built that are really, really hard to fulfill, that include the idea that academia can provide data and research that would be useful, that the pace of life for activists and academics doesn't allow to happen very easily.[43]

In spite of his acknowledgment that obstacles to collaboration are real, Delli Carpini formed, with scholars at other universities, a loose federation called COMPASS—a rough acronym for Consortium on Media and Policy Studies—in

2004.[44] The goals of COMPASS include placing graduate students in internships and other positions in Washington and potentially developing curricula that would include a public interest focus, likely at the graduate level. However, its goals remain largely inchoate. Delli Carpini reflected at some length on difficulties reconciling differing agendas:

> I think that seeing each other's goals as complementary and overlapping, that can be worked out. I think that mainly requires more interaction, more honest, open, civil interactions, where you're in kind of a trusting space where you can talk freely about what you can bring to this . . . I fervently believe, from years of doing this, that the basic critique of media reformers is right. [And] I believe . . . that [getting] information out, with the imprimatur of good research . . . could play a very powerful role in bringing about reform. And I think that that's the underlying premise of why I think that scholars should be involved in this. And that's not scholars as citizens, you know I can get involved in all kinds of things in my personal life, and be an activist on the side, but I'm talking about what I bring as a scholar, what the field can bring as scholars.[45]

Like the radio activists, Delli Carpini invokes a boundary between scholarly projects and those of activists, and also like the radio activists, he focuses on ways that those projects could be brought in line with one another even while cognizant of difference.

Conclusions, Reflections

In this chapter, I have outlined how activists, scholars, and, to a lesser degree, reformers approach media change, each with their own priorities and strategies. I have also attempted to demonstrate how members of these groups may either enroll or mark distance between themselves and members of other groups, sometimes simultaneously. In essence, both activists and scholars are concerned with both marking difference and effacing boundaries in order to advance what they feel are the most meaningful, constitutive aspects of work to change the media system. Even while they recognize, and indeed highlight, distinctions between their goals and work styles, each of the groups I have discussed also strives to overcome these differences at times, in order to foster, if not collaboration, at least a sense of common cause or common way of seeing.

I want to point out that the insistence on "making a real difference," however it is defined, underscores the similarity in activist and academic projects around media democracy. Like activists, academics occupy a mediating position, making knowledge claims and mobilizing them across networks. As anthropologist Dominic Boyer suggests, a sense of critical agency pervades the work of intellectuals;[46] elsewhere I have suggested that this concept may be useful in understanding activism as well.[47] Normative intervention does not necessarily flow from critical agency, but they are closely related, as an impulse to intervene is predicated on criticality, as well as the not-insignificant belief that social change is possible. Thus even out of the "variegated, even chaotic field of collective action" complementarity may emerge. Differences matter (even greatly), but efforts to strategically efface boundaries between groups may also yield productive alignments and unforeseen transformations.

Notes

1. "Indymedia" refers to a loosely affiliated network of rhizomatic citizen-journalist "Independent Media Centers" (IMCs) devoted to creating and disseminating alternative news content that sprung up around 2000.
2. William Carroll and Robert Hackett, "Democratic Media Activism through the Lens of Social Movement Theory," *Media, Culture & Society* 28, no. 1 (2006): 83–104.
3. I alternate between terms, using "media democracy movement" most frequently, but it is important to note that this is a disputed label. Indeed, the issue of whether this is actually "a" single movement is also contestable, which this chapter also seeks to address.
4. Thomas Gieryn, "Boundary-Work and the Demarcation of Science from Non-Science: Strains and Interests in Professional Ideologies of Scientists," *American Sociological Review* 48, no. 6 (1983): 781–95.
5. See Carroll and Hackett, "Democratic Media Activism," 100.
6. McChesney attributes this quote (paraphrased) to former Federal Communications Commission (FCC) commissioner Nicholas Johnson. Robert McChesney, Russell Newman, and Ben Scott, eds., *The Future of Media: Resistance and Reform in the 21st Century* (New York: Seven Stories, 2005), 11.
7. Carroll and Hackett, "Democratic Media Activism," 84. See also Todd Gitlin, *The Whole World is Watching* (Berkeley, CA: University of California Press, 1980).
8. Philip Napoli, "Public Interest Media Advocacy and Activism as a Social Movement," in *Communication Yearbook* 33, ed. Christina Beck (New York: Routledge, 2009), 391.
9. Carroll and Hackett, "Democratic Media Activism," 88.
10. Todd Wolfson, "The Cyber Left: Indymedia and the Making of 21st-Century Social Movements" (PhD diss., University of Pennsylvania, 2008).
11. Wolfson, "The Cyber Left"; emphasis in original.
12. Philadelphia Independent Media Center, "About," accessed June 13, 2007, http://phillyimc.org/about.
13. Free Press, "Free Press and the Free Press Action Fund," accessed June 13, 2007, http://www.freepress.net/about_us.
14. Faye Ginsburg, "Procreation Stories: Reproduction, Nurturance, and Procreation in Life Narratives of Abortion Activists," *American Ethnologist* 14, no. 4 (1987): 623–36; Hugh Gusterson, *Nuclear Rites* (Berkeley: University of California Press, 1996).

15. Interview by author, January 2003.
16. Interviews by author, July 19, 2006, and October 4, 2006.
17. Interview by author, October 5, 2006.
18. Interview by author, October 4, 2006. I was unable to interview Kennard himself.
19. Ginsburg, "Procreation Stories," 623.
20. Mediageek, "Be The Media: Blogging from the Audience, Hallways and Streets of the 2005 National Conference for Media," May 14, 2005, accessed February 26, 2007, http://www.mediageek.org/btm/archives/2005/05/indymedia_caucu.html.
21. Anarchogeek, "Followup on the National Conference On Media Reform," May 16, 2005, accessed February 26, 2007, http://www.anarchogeek.com/articles/2005/05/16/followup-on-the-national-conference-on-media-reform.
22. Field notes, February 2006.
23. Field notes, September 30, 2005.
24. According to the SSRC, in 2005–7, it received three grants from Ford for this program area, in amounts of $100,000 (for an initial feasibility study), $750,000, and $1.5 million ("SSRC Receives $1.5 Million Ford Grant to Continue Innovative Work on Media Reform," June 22, 2007, http://www.ssrc.org/press/fordgrant062107).
25. See, for example, Ellen Lagemann, ed., *Philanthropic Foundations: New Scholarship, New Possibilities* (Bloomington, IN: Indiana University Press, 1999), on the impact of foundation patronage on academic research.
26. Field notes, March 3, 2005.
27. Field notes, March 8, 2005.
28. See Ted Coopman, "*U.S. v. Dunifer*: A Case Study of Micro Broadcasting," *Journal of Radio Studies* 7, no. 2 (2000): 287–309. See also Eric Klinenberg, *Fighting for Air: The Battle to Control America's Media* (New York: Metropolitan Books, 2007), 256. Craig Cox describes similar conflicts between anarchists and communists (accused by the anarchists of being "reformers") in food co-ops in the Twin Cities in the 1970s in his *Storefront Revolution: Food Co-ops and the Counterculture* (New Brunswick, NJ: Rutgers University Press, 1994).
29. Field notes, April 27, 2005.
30. Steven Epstein, *Impure Science: AIDS, Activism, and the Politics of Knowledge* (Berkeley: University of California Press, 1996); Steven Yearley, *The Green Case: A Sociology Of Environmental Issues, Arguments, and Politics* (London: Harper Collins, 1991).
31. Gusterson, *Nuclear Rites*.
32. Kim Fortun, *Advocacy After Bhopal: Environmentalism, Disaster, New Global Orders* (Chicago: University of Chicago Press, 2001).
33. Pam Scott, Evelleen Richards, and Brian Martin, "Captives of Controversy: The Myth of the Neutral Social Researcher in Contemporary Scientific Controversies," *Science, Technology & Human Values* 15, no. 4 (1990): 474–94.
34. See H. M. Collins and Robert Evans, "The Third Wave of Science Studies: Studies of Expertise and Experience," *Social Studies of Science* 32, no. 2 (2002): 235–96.
35. Scott, Richards, and Martin, "Captives of Controversy."
36. Prometheus Radio Project, "Scholars!," n.d.

37. Günter Getzinger, "Trans-disciplinary Research and Sustainable Technology Design" (paper presented at the sixth Annual Conference of the Institute for Advanced Studies on Science, Technology and Society, Graz, Austria, May 25, 2007).

38. Prometheus Radio Project, "Scholars!," n.d.

39. Seeta Peña Gangadharan, "Building the Case for Change: Knowledge Practices of the Media Reform and Media Justice Movements," in *Communicating for Social Impact: Engaging Communication Theory, Research, and Pedagogy*, ed. Lynn M. Harter, Mohan J. Dutta, and Courtney E. Cole (Cresskill, NJ: Hampton Press, 2009), 161–74.

40. Bruno Latour and Steve Woolgar, *Laboratory Life* (Princeton, NJ: Princeton University Press, 1979).

41. See also Annelise Riles, *The Network Inside Out* (Ann Arbor, MI: University of Michigan Press, 2000) for more on paperwork or so-called network artifacts produced by advocacy organizations.

42. Field notes, May 22, 2008.

43. Interview by author, August 19, 2009.

44. See Robert McChesney, *Communication Revolution* (New York: New Press, 2007), 173–75.

45. Interview by author, August 19, 2009.

46. Dominic Boyer, "The Social Context of Critical Intellectual Agency: The Shifting Fortunes of the German Educated Bourgeoisie and the Criticism of Modern Society" (paper presented at the Society for the Humanities, Cornell University, May 2003).

47. Christina Dunbar-Hester, "Geeks, Meta-Geeks and Gender Trouble: Activism, Identity, and Low-power FM Radio," *Social Studies of Science* 38, no. 2 (2008): 201–32.

CHAPTER 14

From Psychological Warfare to Social Justice

Shifts in Foundation Support for Communication Research

Jefferson Pooley

In its first few decades, US communication research was shaped by a pair of institutional patrons: the federal government and the big foundations. Beginning with the Rockefeller Foundation in the 1930s, on through to the Ford Foundation's 1950s social science spending spree, the philanthropic agenda was, to a large extent, the field's agenda. And the foundations during this period frequently aligned themselves with the federal government—the other giant patron of communication research. One result was that the study of communication was organized, to a remarkable degree, around the question of effective propaganda design. With World War II and the Cold War as backdrops, the communication researcher became, in effect, a social scientific specialist in "psychological warfare."

It is not enough, of course, to leave it there; plenty of other factors, including good-faith enthusiasm for new kinds of quantitative social science, helped give the emerging field its distinctive shape. Still, the thumbnail I've sketched will do for now, since my aim in this chapter is to highlight a contrast. If early communication research was indeed in the persuasion business, then one enabling factor was foundation largesse from Ford and others; the foundations underwrote the field's fixation on changing men's minds, very often in support of military ends. That was then.

Things have changed rather dramatically over the last decade. Ford has self-consciously directed substantial funds to the media democracy movement—over $20 million from 1999 to 2008.[1] Some of that money has supported communication scholarship, with the idea that media scholars, activists, and policy advocates might mutually inform the movement's goals. With this recent support in mind—and with a glance back at the 1930s and 1950s—we might say that the field's foundation patrons have shifted from psychological warfare to social justice.

The claim needs some parsing, of course. But for the moment I want to linger on a strange fact: the Ford Foundation that worked closely with the CIA in the 1950s is the same Ford Foundation that has made dozens of media-democracy grants over the last decade, many of them involving communication scholars. The turnabout is striking on its own terms but comes off as especially startling to those of us reared on a particular story—let's call it the *beholden foundation*—about Ford, Rockefeller, and the others. According to this story, the twentieth-century American foundation has served the interests of big capital by smoothing over the market's rough edges and by managing dissent. Foundations like Carnegie, the account states, supply a veneer of philanthropic legitimacy to policies and initiatives that ultimately benefit the captains of industry whose fortunes they inherited. Ford and the rest, according to the story, have also aided—even spearheaded—sensitive government initiatives, especially in the Cold War years. Social science, all along, has been a favorite tool of the beholden foundation, according to the many scholars who have contributed to the story.

Philanthropy as the robber barons' soft gloves: the claim is made in a large, cross-disciplinary literature. Foundations (to quote book and chapter titles) are agents of "cultural imperialism" and "collaboration"; they supply an "extension of ideology" and "the mask of pluralism."[2] Many of these are well-supported and convincing accounts; there really are a number of documented cases, especially during the early Cold War, when Ford and the others acted to contain dissent and help out the national security state. The history of midcentury communication research that I sketched earlier draws substantially on this work.[3]

It's the strength of the foundation-critique literature that makes the recent Ford work on media democracy so startling. The twentieth-century pattern has not held. In the last decade, Ford has battled, through its funded proxies, the big media companies. And the foundation enlisted communication scholars to aid the effort. One lesson is that another world is possible for foundations too.

Foundations for Change

The philanthropic foundation comes off as an unlikely agent of social change. Foundations are, after all, constrained by law and by restrictions put in place by benefactors. Foundations are also—the big ones at least—hierarchical and many-layered. In theory, authority flows from a board of trustees, through to a board-appointed president, on down to a staff that awards grants and runs programs.

In practice, however, there is often a great deal of officer-level autonomy. Big foundations' official flow charts disguise the on-the-ground freedom that some program officers maintain. It's also true that newly installed presidents, depending on the foundation, are expected to launch initiatives and reshape existing programs—within limits. Crucially, those limits aren't just internal— board oversight, say—but are also set by conditions outside, like the national political climate.[4]

The philanthropic foundation is, in short, a human institution, made up of real people whose convictions matter. The broader conditions of politics matter too. Foundations might be—have been—servants of the state or handmaidens of capital. But they need not be. My case in point is the Ford Foundation's media-democracy agenda over the last ten years. Although substantial grant-making in this area didn't get under way until 1999, the roots of the initiative date back to 1996, when Susan Berresford became the foundation's first female president. Berresford reorganized the foundation's program structure, with special attention to Ford's media-related grant making. Though uninvolved in its day-to-day operations, she was responsible for the original commitment to the media-policy agenda as well as the ongoing financial support. Berresford's patronage mattered.

Becky Lentz was another key figure in Ford's media initiatives. Lentz, a veteran information services professional and midcareer doctoral student at the University of Texas at Austin, took a leave from her graduate studies to head up, beginning in 2001, the Ford "portfolio" responsible for most of the relevant grant making.[5] Lentz was embedded in a network of scholar-activists committed to media democratization as part of a broader social justice agenda. Over her six-year tenure at Ford, Lentz drew on this community for advice and strategic direction. More than anyone else, it was Lentz who gave shape to the foundation's on-the-ground interventions in the media and democracy field. Lentz mattered too.

The initiative wouldn't have happened—at least in the form that it took— without, however, certain enabling conditions. The end of the Cold War in 1989 was especially important. Since the early 1950s, right-wing politicians have assailed (and periodically investigated) the big US foundations, and Ford in particular, for alleged sympathy for socialism and, by extension, the country's enemies. In a Cold War political culture that exposed left-leaning individuals and institutions to sometimes virulent red-baiting, Ford and the others charted an often cautious course.[6] Skittish trustees and predictable flack from the Right led foundations like Ford to tread carefully around initiatives whose social justice goals might be taken up as evidence of disloyalty.[7] After 1989, some of this pressure was lifted.

The end of the Cold War was important for another reason: the blurring of the Left's once-sharp divide between reformers and radicals. The collapse of "actually existing socialism" occurred in the midst of an embrace of market-based solutions to public policy problems. Market fundamentalism, especially in Britain and the United States since the early 1980s, had justified policies that benefitted the wealthy at the expense of the social safety net and the poor. The US ideological spectrum, at least in electoral politics, had already shifted rightward by the time the country's Cold War enemy buckled. In the face of the market juggernaut—and with no real socialist alternative—the traditional enmity between reformers and radicals lost some of its edge. If the word "liberal" was, for the New Left of the 1960s for example, a pejorative, the post-1989 resistance to market fundamentalism served to rally liberals and radicals alike around concepts like strong democracy. The always-fractious Left was to some extent united by a common enemy.

In the years after 1989, the media's role in a healthy democracy took on special importance for this broader Left. An emerging *media democracy* movement enlisted the energies of both radicals and reformers—hard leftists alongside defenders of mainstream journalism.[8] The media democracy question, certainly by the late 1990s, was widely perceived to be a major (perhaps *the* major) front in the battle to halt the market's momentum. The movement's growth was fueled not only by both threats and opportunities (the ongoing efforts to rollback public interest protections) but also by the democratic promise of new technologies like the Internet. The Telecommunications Act of 1996, which loosened a number of public-interest limits on media companies, started a wave of industry consolidation. Wall Street demands for high profits led to increasingly underfunded newsrooms dependent on handouts from public relations firms. The creeping commercialization of the Internet, alongside uneven access to its benefits, also galvanized activists, scholars, and policy advocates to join the effort. The movement had attracted enough broad-based public support to stop, in 2004, the Federal Communications Commission (FCC) from further relaxing ownership limits.[9]

Defensive efforts like these were joined by a number of alternative media experiments, some of which, like the various Indymedia sites, harnessed new digital technologies. Other projects have drawn on "old" technologies like radio: since the late 1990s, a number of groups fought, and ultimately won, FCC approval for low-power FM (LPFM) stations.[10] Since at least 2003, major movement actors have campaigned to establish a "net neutrality" principle of Internet regulation, to prevent big media companies from discriminating among web content providers. Some of the same groups have sought to carve out more space, especially online, for the public domain in the name of creativity and shared culture.[11] On the international stage, activists who coalesced around the UN-sponsored World Summit on the Information Society (WSIS) in the late 1990s have articulated a "right to communicate" alongside other human rights claims.[12]

Dozens of US-based groups—some, like the Media Access Project, venerable but resurgent, and many others, like Reclaim the Media, recently founded—make up a loose coalition of public interest nonprofits that work on one or more of these issues. Though US media reform efforts have been under way, with varying intensity, since at least the 1930s, the surge of activity since the mid-1990s is unprecedented.[13] There is, to a significant degree, movement *self-consciousness*, and growing public awareness of, and involvement in, the movement's campaigns.[14] There are real fissures, to be sure, reflecting tactical differences, clashes over priorities, competition for scarce funds, and disputes between Washington, DC-based policy advocates and grassroots activists. Indeed, the movement's name itself is contested terrain, with word choice—media *reform* versus media *justice*, for example—fraught with symbolic import.[15] (The broader post-1989 rapprochement of reformers and radicals that I alluded to earlier was partial and tentative, and remains so.) Still, many of the constituent groups engage in a mix of reform-oriented advocacy and alternative media projects. The National Conferences for Media Reform—there have been four since 2003—gather together thousands of actors from all corners of the movement.

The Ford Foundation, as I detail later, has been the single largest funder of the media democracy movement, at least since 1999. Ford dollars have seeded efforts across the movement's typical divides—from radical media justice work by and for the undervoiced to inside-the-Beltway lobbying. For now, I want to emphasize a different point: the Ford initiatives were only feasible in the context of a preexisting movement for media reform—even if the movement that Ford encountered was atrophied from funding neglect, with no popular constituency. Foundations are pliable, up to a point. Individuals like Lentz exercised autonomy, but it was freedom opened up by a changed social backdrop: new post-1989 political conditions and the reawakening media democracy movement itself. Ford may have enabled media reform, but media reform enabled Ford first.

Ford and the Media Democracy Movement, 1999–2008

When Susan V. Berresford assumed the Ford presidency in 1996, the foundation's media grant making centered on *content*.[16] Since the late 1970s, the foundation had been funding documentary filmmakers and other programmers, whose work typically appeared on public television or radio. *The Eyes on the Prize* (1987) civil rights series and the urban public school film *Stand and Deliver* (1988) were emblematic of the effort. All told, the foundation spent over $120 million on media content from the late 1970s up through 1996, the year Berresford became president.[17] At the pre-Berresford Ford, content was king.

Berresford, a 25-year Ford veteran whose officer and management roles had centered on urban and women's issues, changed this.[18] As part of a foundation-wide reorganization, Berresford folded the cross-program media content initiative, the Media Projects Fund (MPF), into a new Media, Arts, and Culture (MAC) unit. MAC was housed within a new Education, Media, Arts and Culture (EMAC) program—one of three overarching divisions in Berresford's streamlined Ford.[19] Though it is easy to get lost in the acronyms, the move was crucial for a number of reasons. First, the prominent place of media in the new Ford structure signaled a fresh commitment to communication issues.[20] Second, media grant making was now housed in a dedicated unit, free to articulate its own goals. Under the pre-Berresford system, media funds had been dispersed to support other, nonmedia programs and projects.

Third and most important, the new MAC unit explicitly widened its mandate beyond content for public broadcasting.[21] Here a key role was played by Andrea Taylor, a former journalist and founding director of the Media Projects Fund. Before she left the foundation in 1996, Taylor advised Berresford to take up media policy issues in the aftermath of the Telecommunications Act of 1996.[22] Media policy, activism, and scholarship were now on the agenda.

After 1996, the foundation began to make relatively small-scale, exploratory grants outside its traditional content-for-public-media focus. In 1997, for example, MAC launched a News Media and Diversity initiative, which included substantial funding for the study of racial bias in journalism.[23] It was only in 1999, however, that the foundation established a funding "portfolio" devoted to policy and analysis, focused on Media Policy and Technology.[24] The idea was to build an "enabling policy environment" for public interest media in recognition of the "systematic erosion" of legal and regulatory protections since the 1980s. One irony of the new Ford effort was that the foundation had, back in the mid-to-late 1970s, helped *nurture* the market-oriented reasoning that justified the regulatory rollback of the 1980s and early 1990s—before abandoning media policy altogether in the late 1970s.[25]

To plan the new media policy portfolio, Ford in 1999 recruited Gigi Sohn, then director of the Media Access Project, a Washington public interest law firm that Ford had supported in the 1970s.[26] As a full-time Ford consultant, Sohn also oversaw the new portfolio's exploratory grant making.[27] By 2000, new language had been added to the mission statement of the MAC unit, indicating "support [for] the development of media policy."[28] That year, the foundation handed out 37 policy and advocacy-related grants, totaling $4.7 million—a big uptick from 1999, when the foundation spent $2 million on ten projects. The year before, in 1998, the foundation hadn't made *any* policy-related grants.[29]

The 2000 spending did not signal a complete change of course: Ford continued to spend more on public media and journalism review subsidies than on policy—$6.7 million in 2000—but the balance was beginning to shift. Indeed, if the dollars spent on the ongoing news and diversity initiative—$5.4 million—are combined with the policy grants, Ford's spending in 2000 was over $10 million. Among the policy grants was a highly symbolic $250,000 award to the United Church of Christ's Office of Communication, the Ford-supported group that, in the mid-1960s, had sparked the modern media reform movement.[30]

Sohn left Ford in early 2001 to cofound and direct Public Knowledge, a Washington nonprofit focused on intellectual property issues. The new director of the MAC unit within EMAC, Margaret Wilkerson, selected Becky Lentz, an outsider to the DC policy community, as the portfolio's program officer. (Wilkerson was a former professor of African American studies at UC Berkeley who had served as a program officer within another EMAC unit since 1998.)[31] Wilkerson's choice of an outsider was not accidental; she was seeking someone who would reach out to marginalized constituencies and engage with scholars in the policy arena. As director of MAC—the unit that housed the media policy portfolio—Wilkerson supported Lentz's efforts to develop a social justice agenda. Lentz also credits the vice president of the overarching EMAC division, Alison Bernstein, with backing her initiatives.[32]

At the time of her hire, Lentz had been working on a midcareer doctorate at the University of Texas at Austin, after many years working on telecommunication issues in industry and government. Lentz's mentor and main dissertation advisor at Texas was John Downing, a well known communication academic who writes on media justice and alternative media issues.[33] Before joining Ford, Lentz had conducted research for the university's Telecommunications and Policy Institute, and her dissertation (completed in 2008, soon after her departure from Ford) focused on the history of regulatory debates over new communication technologies.[34]

Lentz directed Ford's media policy initiative over the next six years, from 2001 to 2007.[35] By all accounts, she was the central figure in the foundation's involvement in the media democracy movement that flourished over these same years.[36] Ford's annual reports during this period provide detail on the dozens of direct grants made by Lentz's Electronic Media Policy portfolio. All told, Lentz dispersed over $20 million dollars during her six-year tenure—making Ford the media democracy movement's most important bankroller by far.[37]

More significant than the dollar figure, arguably, was the *range* of grant making under Lentz. When the Ford intervention picked up around 1999 under Sohn, the media reform community was relatively insular and centered on a small number of chronically underfunded, Washington, DC-based policy groups focused on legal and regulatory issues. Many of these groups were formed in the 1970s with Ford's support but were forced to scramble for scarce dollars in the 1980s and early 1990s after Ford stopped funding media policy work.

Under Sohn, Ford had already begun to fund these Washington nonprofits again. But with Lentz's appointment in 2001, the Ford grants also began to flow to two other constituencies that had been largely absent from media reform circles before 2000: media justice advocates and academics. The other striking feature of Ford funding over the last decade is that in each arena—policy, grassroots activism, and scholarship—radical groups and individuals were funded alongside reformists and mainstream liberals.

It is helpful to divide Lentz's tenure at Ford into two periods, the first stretching from her arrival in September 2001 to February 2004, when Ford gave formal approval to the portfolio under the new "Electronic Media Policy" name.[38] (Until then, the portfolio had existed in Ford's version of purgatory, with funding but no official sanction; it was, says Lentz, "never clear whether the foundation would continue to commit funds.")[39] The second period ran from the approval in 2004 until Lentz's departure in 2007.[40] In the first period, Lentz continued to fund media policy groups. But she also awarded a series of grants to support conferences and information-gathering reports, which in turn informed her funding strategy for the field. Over these years her goal became nothing less than the self-conscious seeding of a bona fide social movement.[41] Recall that in 2001 she had encountered a reform movement centered on a small, Washington, DC-based policy community without a popular constituency and with very weak ties to university-based researchers. With input from the gatherings and reports that she commissioned, Lentz developed a plan to cultivate both grassroots media activists and committed scholars, with the aim of joining these to the existing policy community within an overarching social movement.[42]

An early initiative to fund a grassroots, beyond-the-Beltway conference at the Highlander Research and Education Center in Tennessee turned out to be a pivotal moment in the history of media activism. The choice of Highlander, the venerable labor and civil rights organizing school, was deliberate and signaled Lentz's interest in connecting media policy-making to social justice traditions. Held in August 2002, the Highlander Media and Society Summer Camp—which came to be known as the Highlander Media Justice Gathering—gave birth to the "media justice" terminology that would, over the following years, become the key self-descriptor for media activists working from a social justice perspective.[43] At Highlander and thereafter, newly christened "media justice" activists would identify with the civil rights movement and with historically marginalized communities more broadly. By design, about half of the 21 Highlander participants were people of color, and issues of race—linked as an advocacy issue to the predominantly white policy-making community—were prominent.[44] According to the widely circulated report authored by the conference organizer, Nan Rubin, a "key strategic decision" was made to shift the terms of media organizing from "'Media Democracy,' to 'Media Justice,'" in part to "put our efforts on the same level as other social justice and human rights organizing, and give us a new vocabulary to work with in terms of defining our various goals."[45] On the strength of the label, the nascent personal networks formed at Highlander, and Ford funding to come, activists would soon be referring to a full-fledged media justice movement.[46]

Lentz, by helping to spark self-consciousness in the geographically scattered media justice community, had also inadvertently hardened an already existing divide between grassroots activists and the Washington policy community. Her work over the next two years, in collaboration with select grantees, was to try to bridge these two constituencies. The tension between the two camps was (and is) complex, deriving from the policy community's legal-technical focus, real and perceived ideological differences, racial and generational gaps, competition over scarce resources, a national versus local frame, and center-periphery inequities.[47] Already at the Highlander gathering, media justice activists were defining themselves against the Washington public interest groups.[48]

The Media Justice Network, founded in 2003 by over a dozen activist groups representing communities of color, soon issued "A Declaration of Media Independence." In an unmistakable reference to the Washington reform groups, the declaration stated, "We are interested in more than paternalistic conceptualizations of 'access,' more than paper rights, more than taking up space in a crowded boxcar along the corporate information highway."[49] Aliza Dichter, an activist and researcher supported by Ford, observed soon after that the Media Justice Network "has established itself in contrast and opposition to the existing field of media reformers and advocates, calling for a movement that is grounded in a power analysis of race, class and gender."[50]

A November 2003 article in *The Nation* by Makani Themba-Nixon, one of the Media Justice Network founders, and Rubin, the main organizer of the Highlander gathering, became an often cited founding document for the media justice community.[51] The article, titled "Speaking for Ourselves," carried a charged subtitle: "A movement led by people of color seeks media justice—not just media reform." Themba-Nixon and Rubin, reflecting the emerging media justice frame, stressed the injuries inflicted by media coverage of marginalized communities and point to a "growing group of activists" who are "developing race-, class- and gender-conscious visions for changing media content and structure." The article referenced not only the Highlander gathering but also the Youth Media Council's successful 2002 campaign against a San Francisco–based Clear Channel station, which soon became a mnemonic touchstone for the movement.[52] Cyril Malkia, the Youth Media Council's young, queer African American director, emerged as a major figure in the media justice community.[53]

Media justice advocates, including Themba-Nixon and Rubin, also sought to claim the legacy of the United Church of Christ's landmark civil rights activism of the mid-1960s. The claim was especially significant since the culminating court case in the UCC campaign established public interest groups' legal standing before the FCC and hence is typically cited as the founding moment in the modern media reform movement. "Nearly forty years ago," Themba-Nixon and Rubin open their article, "a few determined civil rights activists at the United Church of Christ and the NAACP in Jackson, Mississippi, decided to take on the treatment of blacks by the television. They drew a straight line from the racism they faced on the streets to the racism they faced in their living rooms when they turned on the TV." The "lobbyists and scholars leading the current efforts at media reform," they continue, are focused on campaigns "which are a far cry from the issues of racism and unfair treatment that launched the earlier movement," referring to the UCC. Media justice activists, they conclude, are "going back to the movement's roots."[54]

Some of the tension between policy advocates and media justice activists came out in reference to Free Press, the successful media policy nonprofit founded in 2002 by media scholar Robert McChesney and Josh Silver. Free Press, which played a prominent role in organizing resistance to the FCC's proposed relaxation of media ownership rules in 2003, had burst on the scene and quickly occupied the movement's "media reform" mindspace. Even though the fight against the FCC mobilized a broad coalition across the media democracy movement—and ended in a successful 2004 court challenge—Free Press's self-appointed centrality attracted sustained criticism from media justice advocates.[55] The Free Press–organized National Conferences for Media Reform became "flashpoints for questions of voice and representation within the movement."[56] It is no accident that the Themba-Nixon and Rubin *Nation* article ran alongside a cover story on the FCC fight coauthored by McChesney.

Soon after her arrival at Ford in 2001, Lentz had sponsored a pair of interview-based stock-taking and information-gathering studies, which helped lay the groundwork for her own 2004 internal Ford proposal for an "Electronic Media Policy" portfolio. The aim of these studies was to identify strategies to inform her plan to catalyze and support a full-fledged, media-oriented social movement. Among other things, the studies needed to address the divisions between the media justice and policy communities and identify strategies to incorporate university-based scholars into an umbrella movement. In 2002, Lentz awarded a grant to the OMG Center for Collaborative Learning to direct a "Listening Project," an expansive study of the existing field. The report, published in 2004 as *The Making of a Social Movement?*, was explicitly oriented around finding common ground among the movement's fractured constituencies: policy advocates, scholars, grassroots organizers, and funders.[57] OMG, which based the report on interviews with 71 stakeholders from 59 organizations spanning the movement's spectrum, employed carefully chosen language to signal inclusiveness.[58] The report not only refers to "existing tensions . . . particularly apparent between those organizations doing local organizing (primarily the media justice and activist crowd) and those working in Washington, DC," but also frames the division as surmountable in the service of the larger movement's goals.[59] In order to "fully maximize the movement's potential," the report calls for "constructive conversations and forums," capacity-building for activist groups, the cultivation of a popular constituency for media issues, and more diversity in the movement's leadership—in order to "strengthen and catalyze a movement."[60]

The "Listening Project" report, in its effort to build "bridges across real and imaginary boundaries that exist in the field," also called for new intermediary organizations.[61] In 2003, Lentz provided the seed money for one such intermediary, the Center for International Media Action (CIMA). The New York–based CIMA, while clearly rooted in the media justice community, had as its explicit mission to connect and support "diverse voices and actors in media reform, media production and media accountability."[62] Lentz commissioned CIMA's Aliza Dichter to interview participants in, and review documents from, the promising but ultimately ineffective media reform efforts of the 1990s. In her 2005 report Dichter drew many of the same lessons as the "Listening Project," with particular attention to the movement's past missteps.[63]

These two Ford-funded reports were joined by a third study coauthored by media justice advocate Nan Rubin, published in 2003 and sponsored by National Network of Grantmakers. The report, directed at the foundation community, was devoted to building a "persuasive and compelling argument for increasing donor and foundation funding for a wide range of media activities."[64] Especially in this early stretch of her tenure, Lentz says she devoted about a third of her time to educating the philanthropic community, since the bulk of funding had been devoted to content.[65] As founder of the Working Group on Electronic Media Policy at a funders' consortium, the Grantmakers in Film and Electronic Media (GFEM), Lentz organized three Ford-hosted sessions bringing together funders and movement actors in early 2005.[66] She served, too, as the first chair of the Technology Funders Collaborative, an international grantmaking group on IT issues, and commissioned a 2003 report on grantmaking strategies.[67] All of this frenetic fact-finding and strategy development in Lentz's initial years at Ford culminated in a Program Officer Memo (POM)—an internal Ford proposal to formalize her portfolio. Though the POM was not formally approved until early 2004, Lentz had already been disbursing media reform grants in accordance with the strategy outlined in the memo, drawing on an annual budget of three to four million dollars—a funding level that would remain more-or-less constant throughout her six-year tenure.[68] The POM is, in effect, a persuasive document—a pitch to Lentz's superiors at Ford, especially Wilkerson and Bernstein.[69] The memo opens with a muscular account of the "systematic erosion of policies that protect the public interest," in the federal communication policy-making arena. The deregulatory Telecommunications Act of 1996—the legislation that led to the portfolio's creation in 1999—makes an appearance in the first paragraph, and the already-iconic 2003 FCC ownership rule changes are invoked as a "recent example" of waning public interest protections.[70] Lentz highlights the disparity between industry lobbyists and the "small ecology of under-funded institutions" devoted to the public interest.[71] She observes that most media-related philanthropy underwrites content creation and neglects "more systemic issues": "policies that shape and govern the production, distribution, exhibition and exchange of information and ideas in society using electronic media resources."[72] To support her case, Lentz briefly summarizes the other major foundations' initiatives and concludes that Ford is "unique" in its policy-related grant making.[73]

Throughout the memo, Lentz carefully navigates internal Ford politics. She pays homage to Ford's legacy of public media support and invokes the foundation's mid-1960s grants to the United Church of Christ.[74] She also acknowledges Ford's two other New York–based media portfolios, directed by fellow program officers, and argues that her portfolio "complements" these others "by building an enabling policy environment for media in the public interest which include but are not limited to public interest media such as PBS and NPR."[75] Her new name for the portfolio—"Electronic Media Policy"—was chosen in part to claim turf distinct from the two others.[76] Lentz's decision to stress social justice not only reflected her own commitments but also dovetailed nicely with Ford's longstanding attention to social justice initiatives.[77] Lentz maneuvered adroitly within the opportunity structure that she inherited at Ford.

The memo observes that there is no widespread popular constituency for media policy reform and invokes the nascent media justice community that Lentz had helped cultivate. She refers to the Highlander gathering, citing *The Nation* article, as the "'coming out party' for media justice work in the U.S." The memo mentions the issues raised at Highlander and after, including the lack of racial and age diversity among movement leaders, and calls attention to the media justice community's relative marginalization:

> Until very recently, the dominant voices in the emerging field of electronic media policy reform have been highly specialized public interest lawyers and high profile academics or journalists who interact mostly with Washington and university elites as well as national press. Non-experts, ordinary citizens, and grassroots groups have had little voice in this field because public interest advocacy has been monopolized by these legal and technical professionals. Also until very recently, few social justice organizers, labor organizations, arts and culture institutions, civil rights coalitions, and environmental justice groups have taken up issues in this field because the "harms" of deregulatory media policies have not been adequately explained or publicized.[78]

In keeping with the "Listening Project" report, the memo's essential thread is a call to "support the evolution of a consensual definition of the public interest to unite disparate efforts." Until advocates find a "common language and a shared cause," writes Lentz, the movement's efforts will "continue to be disconnected, fragmented, and under-funded."[79]

With these arguments as the backdrop, the memo proposes three goals for the portfolio: (1) to strengthen public interest advocacy institutions; (2) to activate and unite diverse constituencies; and (3) to build strategic knowledge.[80] The first goal is targeted at supporting advocacy organizations, including capacity-building for outside-the-Beltway organizations. The second goal focuses on the field uniting—"more engagement between social justice advocates and media reform groups." The last goal is centered on research, with the explicit aim to support university-based scholarship that builds "a sustainable case for public interest values such as diversity, freedom of expression, and universal access to electronic media."[81] The memo, in short, is a blueprint for Lentz's more expansive vision for a broad-based social movement—a vision that self-consciously stretches the funding agenda in place during the brief, Washington-centric Sohn period.

The approval of the POM memo marked the beginning of what I am calling Lentz's second phase, which lasted until her departure from Ford in 2007. Though many of the second-phase initiatives, and the thinking behind them, were already in place before the POM approval, the bulk of the funding and activity occurred after the memo was officially endorsed.[82] Since the fact-finding reports and Lentz's memo placed a special emphasis on intermediary grantees, I highlight three major grant recipients, each of which passed along Ford dollars to specific groups and projects: the Media Justice Fund, the Media Democracy Fund, and the Social Science Research Council.[83]

Lentz had seeded the Media Justice Fund (MJF) with $500,000 back in 2003—in concert with the founding of the Media Justice Network in the aftermath of Highlander—and supplied another $2.4 million to the entity through 2007.[84] The MJF, which closed its doors at the end of 2009, was operated by the Funding Exchange, a coalition of 16 community foundations that support a range of progressive activism.[85] Relative to other Ford efforts, the MJF prioritized smaller grants to grassroots social justice groups, many devoted to empowering voiceless communities in specific regions.[86] The Fund's explicit commitment to social and media *justice* signaled its radical, small "d" democratic orientation; in keeping with the media justice framework, the MJF claimed to work in the "spirit" of the landmark 1966 United Church of Christ case.[87] According to an evaluative report, the MJF "broadened the social justice movement infrastructure, and has been especially successful at involving marginalized communities and populations in work that has been the historical domain of a fairly insular circle of Beltway-focused actors."[88] The Fund's typical grants ranged from $15,000 to $25,000, awarded to progressive groups like the low-power FM radio advocate Prometheus Radio Project and the People's Production House.[89]

Lentz has also supported the Media Democracy Fund (MDF), a collaborative effort involving many other liberal and progressive foundations. The fund was started by Helen Brunner of the Albert A. List Foundation, who convinced List—then spending out its endowment—to seed a "Media Action Fund" in 2003.[90] The fund was relaunched in 2006 as the Media Democracy Fund, with Ford supplying over half of its $1.2 million budget.[91] Under Brunner's widely praised leadership, the fund has supported some of the same grassroots advocacy groups that received MJF funding, in addition to established, Washington, DC-based policy groups like Free Press and the Future of Music Coalition.[92]

The third and final grant recipient I touch on here is the Social Science Research Council (SSRC), which has since 2005 received $2.4 million to fund its Necessary Knowledge for a Democratic Public Sphere program, directed by Joe Karaganis in cooperation with the Ford-funded Center for International Media Action.[93] As we have seen, the idea of drawing scholars into the media reform movement's orbit was an early Lentz goal, reflected in commissioned studies and a pair of scholarly convenings (in 2003 and 2006).[94] The purpose of the SSRC grants was to stimulate cooperation between legal and media scholars and the broader media democracy movement, inclusive of media justice activists.[95] Academics' slow research pace, notoriously dense writing style, and perceived indifference to on-the-ground developments were obstacles that the SSRC program was designed to challenge.[96] The Ford grants have supported an online Media Research Hub, dozens of collaborative academic-activist grants, student internships with activist groups, papers and reports on media policy and activism, and scholars' participation in the broader National Conferences for Media Reform.[97] One 2008 collaborative grant, for example, brought University of Louisville researchers together with Kentucky Jobs for Justice to study Internet access in minority Louisville neighborhoods.[98]

These three intermediary grant recipients (MJF, MDF, and the SSRC) represent a fraction of the overall Ford spending on media democracy issues since 2000. Dozens of direct grants were awarded over this period, to grassroots activist groups, Washington policy nonprofits, and university-based academics alike.[99] The Ford funding was strikingly ecumenical, by ideological, tactical, and topical measures.

The media democracy movement flourished in no small part thanks to Ford intervention. The funding mattered most, of course, but so did the alliance-building incentives written into the grants. Lentz's success depended, in turn, on the growing movement; it is impossible, of course, to tease out causality. Still, there's something remarkable about this turn of events. In the 1950s, recall, Ford underwrote Cold War propaganda research. In the late 1960s and 1970s, the foundation supported a few liberal media reform organizations but funded market-oriented research too. With a changed political climate, an emergent social movement, and the efforts of a few individuals—Lentz and Berresford among them—Ford recast itself as an agent of media justice.

Susan Berresford stepped down as president in 2007, and soon after Lentz left the foundation to finish her dissertation and, in early 2009, to take up a post at McGill University.[100] It is too early to tell whether the new president, Luis Ubiñas, or Lentz's successor as program officer, Jenny Toomey, will maintain Ford's media democracy commitments. As part of a sweeping 2008 reorganization, Ubiñas established nine "core issues," one of which ("Freedom of Expression") is dedicated to media-related issues.[101] Total funding for media, arts, and culture declined from $93.3 million in 2007 to $60.7 million in 2008—a 35 percent drop-off.[102] Still, many media reform groups continued to receive funding in 2008 under Toomey, a former indie rock musician and former director of the Future of Music Coalition.[103] The departures of Berresford and Lentz may augur badly for the media democracy movement—an irony, if true, given the relatively progressive media policy orientation of the Obama administration.

The Ford Record

In the preceding seven decades, media reform had occasionally appeared on the major foundations' agendas, very often linked to communication research initiatives. Consider the role of the Rockefeller Foundation in the 1930s. During the so-called Radio Wars—the years of policy debate between the Radio Act of 1927 and the Communication Act of 1934—educational broadcasters and other civic groups battled the commercial networks over the shape of public interest regulation. The commercial broadcasters prevailed, of course.[104] In the aftermath of the 1934 Act, the Rockefeller Foundation organized meetings and funded efforts to reconcile embittered education advocates and the victorious networks. The Rockefeller-supported Princeton Radio Research Project, as William Buxton has shown, was created to convince ratings-conscious commercial broadcasters that arts and educational programming would in fact draw in large audiences.[105] Rockefeller's cautious, market-driven approach—involving as it did Frank Stanton, then rising through the CBS ranks—failed to change broadcasters' programming choices. But Rockefeller's radio initiatives, at Princeton and elsewhere, soon took on an altogether different function. After Germany invaded Poland in 1939, Rockefeller repurposed its radio research projects into a private propaganda and intelligence network, before it was politically acceptable for the Roosevelt administration.[106] Rockefeller's tepid 1930s reform effort had, in short, issued in war-related propaganda research—and formed the nucleus of the government's sprawling, social science–driven persuasion bureaucracy after Pearl Harbor.

Propaganda was also the major postwar theme of foundation-sponsored communication research. After the war, the Ford Foundation replaced Rockefeller as the principal patron of communication research. A newly flush Ford, relaunched in 1949 as a leading national foundation, established a Behavioral Sciences Program (BSP) in 1951, headed by communication scholar Bernard Berelson. The BSP dispensed millions of dollars to communication-related research, including funds for MIT's CIA-linked Center for International Communications. Most of the Ford spending on communication scholarship in the 1950s, before the BSP was shuttered in 1957, supported often secret, Cold War–related "psychological warfare" research—the unblushing label applied to the many persuasion studies of the period.[107]

Ford would not invest significant sums in university-based communication research again until the recent wave of media democracy funding. Instead, Ford dollars supported the emerging public broadcasting community. Beginning with its 1951 grant to create the Radio-Television Workshop, Ford would go on to play *the* major role in financing public television and radio—with grants for stations, programming, and infrastructure. By 1977, when Ford scaled back its support, the foundation had spent $289 million.[108]

Public broadcasting and propaganda isn't the whole story of Ford and the media in the postwar era. The foundation also backed key organizations in the nascent broadcast reform movement, which had emerged after the landmark 1966 United Church of Christ decision that established "standing" for citizens' groups in the FCC policy-making process.[109] Ford awarded the UCC $160,000 in 1968 and followed up with over $800,000 more through 1977.[110] The

UCC decision spawned a number of media policy groups, many of which—the Citizens Communications Center and Action for Children's Television, for example—received substantial Ford funding in the 1970s.[111]

The 1970s broadcast reform groups gained a seat at the communication policy-making table and won some limited concessions from broadcasters and the FCC.[112] Still, the movement's goals were modest, diluted by the industry and reticent regulators. In part because the Washington, DC-based groups lacked a popular constituency, their reform efforts were effectively contained.[113] One index of their relative impotence was that the FCC's policy orientation shifted markedly, beginning in the late 1970s, toward deregulation and market-based analysis.[114]

Despite Ford's financial support for the 1970s reform movement, the foundation arguably shares the blame for the regulatory setbacks of the 1980s and after. For one thing, Ford dramatically scaled back its media-related grant making in the late 1970s, in keeping with its decision to phase out funding for public broadcasting. As a result, many broadcast reform groups folded, and the few survivors were chronically underfunded.[115] Ford's departure from the media policy field also elevated the influence of the more market-oriented Markle Foundation, which remained an active player throughout the 1980s.[116] Even before its departure, Ford's cautious funding choices had the effect of narrowing the incipient media reform movement. Albert H. Kramer, founder of the Ford-funded Citizens Communications Center, detailed Ford and other foundations' timidity in the broadcast policy realm in a well-supported 1977 report. Kramer criticized Ford's unwillingness to challenge industry interests, as well as its preference for moderate groups with establishment credentials.[117]

Ford, moreover, partially offset its own broadcast reform funding by underwriting, in the early to mid-1970s, much of the research that would, a few years later, inform the FCC's embrace of the marketplace. As Katharina Kopp has documented, the Markle Foundation seeded many of the economist-led, market-oriented research efforts at the RAND Corporation, the Aspen Institute, and the Brookings Institution in the early 1970s. Kopp shows that Ford, though more ecumenical in its grant making, nevertheless joined Markle in funding the RAND, Aspen, and Brookings research.[118] The Brookings-sponsored *Economic Aspects of Television Regulation*—the highly influential 1973 deregulatory treatise—was funded by Ford, for example.[119] The foundation, perhaps unwittingly, had undermined its own media reform grant making—before abandoning the field just as the marketplace paradigm was in ascendance.

Conclusion

Ford's late 1990s turn to media policy issues was, in a sense, a revival of its decades-long commitment to mass media themes. But the recent wave of media democracy funding was, above all, a *break* with its past—an implicit repudiation of the Cold War propaganda research and the mixed record in broadcast reform. From a media justice perspective, the foundation's twentieth-century interventions in media policy and communication research had been accommodationist at best, and very often much worse. With past performance as our guide, we would expect more of the same.

The lesson of Ford's recent history is that past performance should *not* be our guide. Lentz—with the notable help of Ford figures like Alison Bernstein, Andrea Taylor, and Margaret Wilkerson; other funders including Charles Benton and David Haas; and key movement allies like Gene Kimmelman and Nan Rubin—managed to commit the foundation to media justice principles. Yet there is a small but growing literature that attacks foundation support for media democracy on just these grounds. Michael Barker, for example, points to foundations' "historical hegemonic role" in his high-octane denunciation of media reform philanthropy.[120] Observes Bob Feldman, another critic, "Since [foundations'] creation, an important goal has been to channel all protest and dissent into activities that do not threaten the wealth and power of the large corporations, or their access to the resources and markets of the world." Why, asks Feldman, "would the liberal foundations want to fund the left?"[121]

Barker and Feldman catalog foundations' misdeeds, citing scholarship from the beholden foundation tradition I invoked earlier.[122] Barker, noting that foundation endowments derive from "the world's most rapicious [sic] capitalists," asserts that there is an "inherent contradiction of progressive activists receiving significant support from liberal elites." Both critics concede that Ford and others have recently funded radical media justice groups but argue that foundations are acting on "ulterior motives" (Barker) to co-opt "formerly radical" (Feldman) organizations. Writes Barker, "although liberal foundations effectively exist to maintain the capitalist status quo, this does not prevent them from supporting a limited number of activists who are seeking radical social change. In fact, sponsoring radicals is integral to their overall mission, as arguably it allows them to keep a close eye on the ideas of radicals, while simultaneously enabling them to improve their progressive PR credentials (thereby helping deter critical investigations of their work)."

Having established liberal foundations' "antidemocratic credentials," Barker concludes that Ford and the others must be behaving badly again.[123]

The Ford case shows, to the contrary, that there is nothing like an iron law of foundation conservatism. It is true that foundations are risk-averse, but windows of progressive intervention are possible, given the right confluence of people and enabling conditions. The claims of Barker and Feldman—and by extension the beholden foundation tradition as whole—depend on an argumentative bait and switch in which a reading of the past substitutes for current analysis and future prognosis. Ford's Cold War history should not blind us to the foundation's media justice present.

Notes

1. The estimate is based on the Electronic Media Policy portfolio's annual budget of $3–4 million from 2000 through 2007. Becky Lentz, interview with author, May 10–11, 2010; *The Makings of a Social Movement? Strategic Issues and Themes in Communications Policy Work* (Philadelphia: OMG Center for Collaborative Learning, 2004), 2. Note that a larger figure occasionally cited, more than $30 million over these years, includes grants from other Ford portfolios not under review in this chapter. "Plugging in the Public Interest," *Ford Reports* 37, no. 2 (2007): 14. Precise figures are difficult to determine, since grant making is not specified by portfolio in Ford's annual repots.

2. Robert F. Arnove, ed., *Philanthropy and Cultural Imperialism: The Foundations at Home and Abroad* (Bloomington: Indiana University Press, 1982); Joan Roelofs, "Foundations and Collaboration," *Critical Sociology* 33, no. 3 (2007): 479–504; Edward H. Berman, "The Extension of Ideology: Foundation Support for Intermediate Organizations and Forums," *Comparative Education Review* 26, no. 1 (1982): 48–68; and Roelofs, *Foundations and Public Policy: The Mask of Pluralism* (Albany: State University of New York Press, 2003).

3. For an overview, see Jefferson Pooley, "The New History of Mass Communication Research," in *The History of Media and Communication Research: Contested Memories*, ed. David Park and Jefferson Pooley (New York: Peter Lang, 2008), 43–69.

4. For a rich treatment of the complexity of foundations' evolution, sometimes against the grain of founders' motivation, see Barry D. Karl and Stanley N. Katz, "Foundations and Ruling Class Elites," *Daedalus* 116, no. 1 (1987): 1–40, esp. 36–39.

5. At Ford, portfolios are specified budget lines administered by individual program officers.

6. See, for example, David Morrison on Ford's abandonment of its TV research agenda in the 1950s in the wake of congressional criticism. Morrison, "Opportunity Structures and the Creation of Knowledge: Paul Lazarsfeld and the Politics of Research," in *The History of Media and Communication Research: Contested Memories*, ed. David W. Park and Jefferson Pooley (New York: Peter Lang, 2008), 179–204.

7. Most of the Ford presidents up through the 1970s—including H. Rowan Gaither and McGeorge Bundy—were themselves avowed Cold War liberals and committed anti-Communists.

8. Two strong overviews of the movement are Robert A. Hackett and William K. Carroll, *Remaking Media: The Struggle to Democratize Public Communication* (New York: Routledge, 2006); and Robert W. McChesney, Russell Newman, and Ben Scott, eds., *The Future of Media: Resistance and Reform in the 21st Century* (New

York: Seven Stories Press, 2005). For an excellent survey, see Philip M. Napoli, "Public Interest Media Activism and Advocacy as a Social Movement: A Review of the Literature," McGannon Center Working Paper Series (2007), accessed January 14, 2010, http://fordham.bepress.com/mcgannon working papers/21. (A revised version appears in *Communication Yearbook*, vol. 33, ed. Christina S. Beck [New York: Routledge, 2009], 385–430.) For an overview of the advocacy groups involved in this and earlier media reform struggles, see Milton M. Mueller, Christiane Page, and Brenden Kuerbis, "Civil Society and the Shaping of Communication-Information Policy: Four Decades of Advocacy," *The Information Society* 20, no. 3 (2004): 169–85.

9. See Ben Scott, "The Politics and Policy of Media Ownership," *American University Law Review* 53, no. 3 (2004): 645–77.

10. See Christina Dunbar-Hester, this volume.

11. See John L. Sullivan, this volume.

12. See Cees J. Hamelink, this volume. For a historical overview of the "right to communicate" movement, see Lauren B. Movius, "Global Debates on the Right to Communicate," *Global Media Journal—American Edition* 7, no. 13 (2008), accessed December 8, 2009, http://lass.calumet.purdue.edu/cca/gmj/fa08/graduate/gmj-fa08-grad-movius.htm.

13. Gene Kimmelman, the longtime consumer advocate currently serving in the Obama administration, points out that the recent wave of the media reform movement has important roots in the consumer movement—organizations like Public Citizen and Consumers Union—that mobilized on issues like the AT&T divestiture in the early 1980s. These groups remain important players in the current media reform movement. Gene Kimmelman, interview with the author, April 19, 2010; and Milton Mueller, Brenden Kuerbis, and Christiane Page, *Re-inventing Media Activism: Public Interest Advocacy in the Making of U.S. Communication-Information Policy, 1960–2002* (Syracuse, NY: Convergence Center, Syracuse University, 2004), 32–33.

14. There is an ongoing debate about whether the media reform coalition qualifies as a bona fide social movement; see Napoli, "Public Interest Media Activism," 23–25.

15. Ibid., 9–19. See also the superb discussion of movement frames in Hackett and Carroll, *Remaking Media*, 78–82.

16. The account that follows draws on two Ford-related sources of information: the foundation's annual reports from 1996 through 2008 and various Ford-commissioned or -funded reports that reflect on the foundation's media grant making. My data include only US grants.

17. From 1977 to 1988, media production funds were disbursed from an independent program within Ford. A Media Projects Fund (MPF) was created in 1988 to better integrate media-making with the foundation's other programs. The MPF used one-to-one internal matching grants with other Ford programs and spent $88.5 million over its eight-year existence. See Joe Karaganis and Waad El-Hadidy, *Freedom of Expression at the Ford Foundation* (New York: Social Science Research Council, 2007), 5–6; and Laura Forlano and Becky Lentz, *Conversations on Media, Technology, Society & Culture: Convening Report: Media and Communications at a Crossroads* (New York: Ford Foundation, 2007), 14–16.

18. Peter Frumkin, "Private Foundations as Public Institutions: Regulation, Professionalization, and the Redefinition of Organized Philanthropy," in *Philanthropic Foundations: New Scholarship, New Possibilities,* ed. Ellen Condliffe Lagemann (Bloomington: Indiana University Press, 1999), 88.

19. Karaganis and El-Hadidy, *Freedom of Expression at the Ford Foundation,* 6–7.

20. Forlano and Lentz, summarizing the 2006 remarks of Alison Bernstein, the vice president in charge of EMAC: "Something very important happened in 1996. Susan Beresford [sic] became the first woman President of the Ford Foundation and committed herself to revisiting and reinventing Ford's resources and energies around media." *Conversations on Media,* 15.

21. According to Ford's 1996 annual report, MAC "will continue to support media productions" but under the rubric of a broader goal: "analyses of the media's contribution to the well-being of a diverse citizenry." *1996 Ford Foundation Annual Report* (New York: Ford Foundation, 1997), 75. Based on a one-year listening tour, Berresford's inaugural "President's Message" claimed that leaders and average citizens around the world expressed worry that a "growing technological culture . . . will not adequately serve the common good or the disadvantaged" (vii).

22. Lentz, interview with author. See also "Honoree Andrea L. Taylor," the HistoryMakers, accessed February 11, 2010, http://www.wvhistorymakers.com/andrea taylor. Taylor, an African American, worked in finance before serving as president of the media-oriented Benton Foundation and later as director of North American Community Affairs at Microsoft.

23. In 1997, Ford gave $2.2 million to at least eight different analysis and monitoring projects on minority news coverage at the Aspen Institute, the University of Missouri, and the Poynter Institute among others. Ford spent another $1.2 million on grants to groups like the National Association of Black Journalists to promote diversity in the newsroom. *1997 Ford Foundation Annual Report* (New York: Ford Foundation, 1998), 127, 137. These grants were funded out of Jon Funabiki's News and Journalism portfolio. Lentz, interview with author.

24. Forlano and Lentz, *Conversations on Media,* 10–11. The new Media Policy and Technology portfolio (later renamed Electronic Media Policy) joined two preexisting portfolios in News and Journalism (responsible for the diversity initiative, among other grants) and in Public Interest Media Production and Infrastructure (which directed public broadcasting and content grant making). According to Lentz, it was Taylor who suggested the "Media Policy and Technology" name. Lentz, interview with author.

25. See the discussion that follows.

26. On Sohn's recruitment, see Bill McConnell, "MAP's Sohn Takes Ride to Ford Foundation," *Broadcasting and Cable,* March 1999, 2; and "Gigi B. Sohn," Advisory Committee to the Congressional Internet Caucus, November 15, 2007, accessed February 11, 2010, http://www.netcaucus.org/biography/gigi-sohn.shtml. See also Harold Feld, "Tribute to Becky Lentz," Wetmachine blog, October 25, 2007, accessed February 11, 2010, http://www.wetmachine.com/item/892. On Ford and the Media Access Project (though mostly funded by the Markle Foundation) in the 1970s, see Katharina Kopp, "The Role of Private Philanthropic Foundations in

Communications Policy Making: Defining 'the Public Interest'" (PhD diss., University of Pennsylvania, 1997), 190–93.

27. As a "project specialist" rather than a full program officer, Sohn did not have formal authority to recommend grants, but in practice she administered the nascent portfolio. Lentz, interview with author.

28. *2000 Ford Foundation Annual Report* (New York: Ford Foundation, 2001), 64.

29. *1998 Ford Foundation Annual Report* (New York: Ford Foundation, 1999), 124–25; and *1999 Ford Foundation Annual Report* (New York: Ford Foundation, 2000), 134–35.

30. *2000 Ford Foundation Annual Report*, 148–50. The Ford grant funded a media organizing guide produced by the UCC's Office of Communication. Saskia Fischer and Margot Hardenbergh, *Media Empowerment Manual: A Guide to Understanding Media Power and Organizing for Media Justice in Your Community* (Washington, DC: Office of Communication, United Church of Christ, 2004). The 2000 grantmaking also included two internal grants, for $160,000 total, to develop the foundation's "media policy portfolio" and a "network of media policy scholars." *2000 Ford Foundation Annual Report*, 149.

31. *2001 Ford Foundation Annual Report* (New York: Ford Foundation, 2002), 21.

32. It is not "accidental that they hired an outsider," states Lentz. "Their goal was not to do business as usual . . . I had support for doing things differently." Lentz, interview with author.

33. Because of her Ford role, Lentz did not complete her dissertation until 2008, the year she left Ford. Though Downing had by then moved from UT Austin to Southern Illinois University at Carbondale, he remained cosupervisor (with UT's Karin Wilkins) of Lentz's dissertation, and is singled out in Lentz's acknowledgments as a key figure in her doctoral training. Roberta G. Lentz, "'Linguistic Engineering' and the FCC Computer Inquiries, 1966–1989" (PhD diss., University of Texas at Austin, 2008), v.

34. E.g., Becky Lentz, *Internet Service Providers in Rural Texas: Rebels With a Cause* (Austin, TX: Telecommunications and Policy Institute, 1998). In her dissertation ("'Linguistic Engineering' and the FCC Computer Inquiries, 1966–1989"), Lentz analyzed the so-called Computer Inquiries, the debate at the FCC, spanning three decades, on how to reconcile regulated telephony with unregulated computer technologies.

35. Lentz's official tenure as program officer spanned September 2001 to September 2007, though she remained at Ford through mid-March 2008 as a Senior Ford Fellow, while also serving as a Visiting Scholar at New York University.

36. See, for example, Forlano and Lentz, *Conversations on Media*, 10–13; and Feld, "Tribute to Becky Lentz."

37. See note 1.

38. Becky Lentz, "Program Officer Memo: Reclaiming the Public Interest in Electronic Media Policy," Ford Foundation, February 2004.

39. Lentz, interview with author.

40. According to Lentz, it was Ford practice at the time to restrict program officers to two three-year terms in order to draw expertise from the field in the service of more-informed grant making. One effect of the de facto six-year tenure is that

program officers cannot accrue undue (or at least lasting) power over their funding fiefdoms. Lentz, interview with author.

41. Says Lentz, "I wanted to build a field; that was the goal—so that there would be institutions and leaders there for the longer term to keep advocating for public interest policy." Lentz, interview with author.

42. Lentz, "Program Officer Memo."

43. Nan Rubin, *Highlander Media Justice Gathering* (New York: Ford Foundation, 2002).

44. The plan was that the "gathering would NOT be only the 'usual suspects' (heavily weighted to white males over 50) associated with progressive media, but would include some of the younger, energetic thinkers . . . The issues of race and class, always underground, were also brought to the surface as major elements that had to be considered, difficult as they might be. The noticeable lack of people of color within media advocacy organizations points to some serious shortcomings in our political perspectives, and in our ability to build popular support within communities of color." Ibid., 3, 6.

45. Ibid., 9.

46. Indeed, the Highlander report already refers to a future "Media Justice Movement," 8. Lentz credits the report for helping convince the foundation that funding for media justice projects was warranted. Lentz, interview with author. A well-informed, interview-based overview of the media justice movement is Dharma Dailey, *A Field Report: Media Justice through the Eyes of Local Organizers* (New York: Funding Exchange, 2009).

47. The best short summary of the tensions involved is Joe Karaganis, *Cultures of Collaboration in Media Research* (New York: Social Science Research Council, 2009), 3–5. Karaganis distinguishes between two "geographies" of activism, one in a "consumer-rights-based model of policy advocacy; the other emerging from predominantly civil-rights-informed concerns with accountability, representation, and voice in the media. Media Reform and Media Justice became the shorthand for these two orientations. Among adherents of the latter, the distinctions sometimes carried a critique of the technocratic, policy-focused approaches to social change characteristic of DC-based advocacy" (4).

48. Rubin, *Highlander Media Justice Gathering*, 1.

49. "A Declaration of Media Independence," November 11, 2003, quoted in Fischer and Hardenbergh, *Media Empowerment Manual*, 16–17.

50. Aliza Dichter, "Where Are the People in the 'Public Interest'? U.S. Media Activism and the Search for a Constituency," *Media Development* 4 (2004), accessed November 5, 2009, http://www.waccglobal.org/en/20041-media-reform/612-Where-are-the-people-in-the-public-interest-US-media-activism-and-the-search-for-constituency.html. In a 2005 Ford-supported stock-taking of the false starts in 1990s media activism, Dichter cites similar complaints about the policy groups. Aliza Dichter, *Together, We Know More: Networks and Coalitions to Advance Media Democracy, Communication Rights and the Public Sphere, 1990–2005* (New York: Social Science Research Council, 2005), 12.

51. Makani Themba-Nixon and Nan Rubin, "Speaking for Ourselves," *The Nation*, November 17, 2003, 17–19.

52. Ibid., 17–18. On the Youth Media Council campaigns, see Neil F. Carlson, *The Role of Grassroots Organizers in Challenging Media Consolidation in the U.S.* (New York: Ford Foundation, 2005), 16–17; Seeta Peña Gangadharan, "Proof Positive: How Researcher/Activist Collaborations Can Build Your Case for Change," in *Whose Media? Our Media! Strategic Communication Tools to Reform, Reclaim and Revolutionize the Media*, ed. Isobel White (San Francisco: SPIN Project, 2008), 62–63; Fischer and Hardenbergh, *Media Empowerment Manual*, 12; and Rubin, *Highlander Media Justice Gathering*, 36.

53. Cyril's Youth Media Council (renamed the Center for Media Justice in 2008) hosts, for example, the Media Action Grassroots Network (MAG-net), which is, in effect, the successor coalition to the moribund Media Justice Network. Cyril, a participant at the Highlander gathering, was a featured speaker ("Media Justice 101") at an important 2007 media justice conference in Knoxville, Tennessee. See *Media Justice or Media Control? A Conference Organized by the Appalachian Community Fund in Collaboration with the Fund for Southern Communities* (Knoxville, TN: Appalachian Community Fund, 2007), 3–6; and Nina Gregg, this volume. See also Malkia Cyril, "A Framework for Media Justice," in *Alternatives on Media Content, Journalism, and Regulation*, ed. Seeta Peña Gangadharan et al. (Tartu University Press: Tartu, Estonia, 2007), 55–56.

54. Themba-Nixon and Rubin, "Speaking for Ourselves," 17. It is interesting to note that the UCC's Office of Communication has recently rebranded itself as "The UCC's Media Justice Advocacy Arm," accessed February 7, 2010, http://www .uccmediajustice.org.

55. See Karaganis, *Cultures of Collaboration*, 5; Aliza Dichter, "Where Are the People in the 'Public Interest?'"; and Lentz, interview with author. Dichter, codirector of the media justice–oriented Center for International Media Action, included a thinly veiled attack on Free Press in her remarks at a Ford-sponsored symposium in 2005: "Even an email list of 200,000 activists ready to sign petitions needs to be backed up by sustained grassroots and community organizing so people will continue to fight for media rights after that action alert has passed." Quoted in Carlson, *The Role of Grassroots Organizers*, 18.

56. Karaganis, *Cultures of Collaboration*, 5; and Dunbar-Hester, this volume. Ironically, it was Lentz who first suggested to McChesney that he convene such gatherings. Lentz, interview with author.

57. As Lentz recalled, the report "revealed a lot of splits about how people were seeing their work." Lentz, interview with author. One of the Listening Project's three goals was to "Provide a space to talk across the apparent boundaries in the field that have been created by ideology, practice and perspective and articulate a clear vision for the field." *The Makings of a Social Movement?*, 4. On Ford funding and the role of Lentz, see ibid., i, 4.

58. Take, for example, the goal to "work across areas to strategically advance the broader public interest and social justice agendas." "Public interest" and "social justice" are code words for policy and media justice, respectively. Ibid., ii, 5. The interviewees are listed on 32–35.

59. Ibid., v, 2. The report, for example, notes that those who "identify with the media justice framework are led by people of color, who embrace a grassroots-directed

approach to change and are critical of the 'top-down' approach they associate with media reform," but quickly adds, "In truth, current media advocacy and communications policy work at the national level has not focused on these issues, but it has clearly targeted some of the structural concerns that underlies some of the media issues that a number of local communities, including communities of color and low-income people, face" (v). In an effort to encourage mutual understanding, the report describes four "theories of change," all of which seek common goals, 6–7.

60. Ibid., v–vi, 14–15, 19.
61. Ibid., 14, 16.
62. "Our Values," CIMA, http://mediaactioncenter.org/values; see also "Our Principles," CIMA, accessed February 8, 2010, http://mediaactioncenter.org/principles. The group is currently dormant.
63. Dichter, *Together, We Know More.* The report was part of a Ford-funded Social Science Research Council initiative, discussed later.
64. Nan Rubin and Sharon Maeda, *Funding Media for Social Change* (New York: National Network of Grantmakers, 2003), 1. The study was part of a Media-Works Initiative, "which grew out of the Working Group on Funding Media of the National Network of Grantmakers" (1). See ibid., 41, for a list of the steering committee. The report makes reference to a "new national network focused on Media Justice . . . comprised of activists of color, many of them young people" (24).
65. Lentz, interview with author.
66. On the GFEM sessions, see *Securing Our Rights to Public Knowledge, Creativity and Freedom of Expression: Funders Briefing Hosted At the Ford Foundation, January 7, 2005—Complete Transcript* (New York: Ford Foundation, 2005); and Neil F. Carlson, *The Role of Grassroots Organizers.* In her efforts to mobilize the foundation community, Lentz worked closely with David Haas of the William Penn Foundation and chair of GFEM's steering committee. Haas had awarded GFEM a grant that enabled the group to hire a staff person who, among other things, helped with the Ford-hosted sessions. Lentz, interview with author.
67. Lentz, "Program Officer Memo," 17–18; and Edward M. Lenert, *Mapping Social Entrepreneurship and the Role of Charitable Foundations in Electronic Media: 1946–1996* (New York: Ford Foundation, 2003).
68. Lentz, interview with author; and *The Makings of a Social Movement?*, 2.
69. Lentz, "Program Officer Memo"; and Lentz, interview with author.
70. Lentz, "Program Officer Memo," 1–4, 7. The POM also notes that "Ford-funded public education and advocacy efforts" (9) helped win the 2004 appeals court decision to throw out the rule changes.
71. Ibid., 8.
72. Ibid., 2.
73. Ibid., 5. At the time, the Markle Foundation—the longtime communication policy funder—was being criticized for neglecting its media-policy roots, among other things. See Jim Rutenberg, "A Foundation Travels Far From Sesame Street," *The New York Times*, September 6, 2002.
74. Ibid., 6.
75. Ibid., 1, 6. The other two portfolios are News and Journalism and Public Interest Media Production and Infrastructure (which funds public radio and television).

76. Lentz, interview with author. In the POM, Lentz observed that, inside Ford, she has "been working closely with David Winters in the Human Rights unit to build a global working group on intellectual property" and recorded her participation in the foundation's "Freedom of Expression" working group. Lentz, "Program Officer Memo," 18. Lentz was also careful to deploy the phrase "freedom of expression" internally at Ford. In 2003, Bernstein's EMAC division had been renamed as Knowledge, Creativity, and Freedom (KC&F). At one of the early 2005 Ford-hosted GFEM sessions linking potential grantees and funders, Alison Bernstein, head of KC&F, acknowledged Lentz's strategic language choice: "I want to pay particular tribute to Becky Lentz . . . I see Becky's hand and head all over this organizational meeting, including the title, which is a complete plagiarism from our program called Knowledge, Creativity and Freedom." (The session's title was "Securing Our Rights to Public Knowledge, Creativity and Freedom of Expression.") *Securing Our Rights to Public Knowledge*, 2. Bernstein, recalls Lentz, "couldn't disown it then." The "freedom of expression" term became, adds Lentz, something that she "had to market," since it was linked to human rights—the "dominant discourse" at Ford. Lentz, interview with author.

77. Lentz says that she referred to "media justice" internally, in part "so I could get people interested," given the preexisting Ford interest in social justice. She also set out to collaborate with other units in order to "link [her portfolio] to other departments, so it doesn't look so different." Lentz, interview with author.

78. Lentz, "Program Officer Memo," 11, 13.

79. Ibid., 13, 8.

80. Ibid., 10. Technically, the memo proposes an "initiative"—the bulk of funding, with these three goals—as well as a much smaller "exploration" devoted to "Advancing Public Interest Values in Global Electronic Media Policy Making," 1, 10.

81. Ibid., 14.

82. One reason that many of the large, three-year grants came after the POM was approved is that the portfolio's previously unofficial status had made multiyear awards difficult to justify. Lentz, interview with author.

83. One rationale for using intermediaries was that Ford's grantmaking practices made it difficult to award a large number of small grants. Lentz, interview with author. The use of intermediary funders is a time-honored Ford practice. In the early years of the modern, postwar Ford Foundation, a number of self-governing "Funds" were created, most famously the civil liberties–oriented Fund for the Republic.

84. See Ford Foundation annual reports, 2003 through 2007; and Lentz, "Program Officer Memo," 14. Lentz had hired Nan Rubin, the Highlander organizer, to serve as a consultant and link to the media justice groups. Lentz needed a funding intermediary because Ford's grantmaking structure doesn't allow the many small grants the initiative required. Another program officer mentioned the Funding Exchange, and Rubin proceeded to negotiate the relationship between Ford and the new fund. Lentz, interview with author. For most of its existence, the Media Justice Fund was directed by Hye-Jung Park. See Catherine Borgman-Arboleda, *The Media Justice Fund of the Funding Exchange: Final Evaluation Report* (New York: Funding Exchange, 2008), which includes detailed case studies, funding figures, and lessons informed by a number of interviews. See also Dailey, *A Field Report*; Rubin and

Maeda, *Funding Media for Social Change*, 26; and the extensive documentation available on the Funding Exchange's website, http://www.fex.org/mjf.

85. It is unclear why the MJF closed, though Lentz referred to a funding impropriety. Lentz, interview with author.

86. For a case study of an MJF–supported initiative, see Nina Gregg, this volume.

87. See "About The Media Justice Fund," Funding Exchange, accessed January 14, 2010, http://www.fex.org/content/mjf.php?pid=47.

88. Borgman-Arboleda, *The Media Justice Fund*, 1.

89. Ibid., 4, 12.

90. Rubin and Maeda, *Funding Media for Social Change*, 26; Theler Pekar, "Straight From the Source: Garnering Funds to Support Media Activism," in *Whose Media? Our Media!*, 68; and Lentz, interview with author.

91. See Ford Foundation annual reports, 2005 through 2008. See also "Media Democracy Fund Launched," Funders Network on Transforming the Global Economy, November 9, 2006, accessed February 8, 2010, http://www.fntg.org/news/index.php?op=readarticleid=1352. The MDF is administered by the Proteus Fund. See "About Media Democracy Fund," Media Democracy Fund, accessed February 8, http://www.mediademocracyfund.org/about.

92. For a complete list of the fund's grantees, see "Our Grantees," Media Democracy Fund, accessed February 8, 2010, http://www.mediademocracyfund.org/our-grantees. Gene Kimmelman and Lentz are both effusive in their praise of Brunner; Lentz notes that Brunner "was there before everybody." Lentz, interview with author; and Kimmelman, interview with author.

93. See Ford Foundation annual reports, 2003 through 2007. See also Forlano and Lentz, *Conversations on Media*, 53–59; and "SSRC Receives $1.5 Million Ford Grant to Continue Innovative Work on Media Reform," SSRC, June 22, 2007, accessed January 14, 2010, http://www.ssrc.org/press-releases/view/356. For an overview of the SSRC effort, see Karaganis, *Cultures of Collaboration in Media Research*.

94. Ford-commissioned studies of media-reform scholarship include Mueller, Kuerbis, and Page, *Re-inventing Media Activism*; and Napoli, "Public Interest Media Activism." On the scholarly convenings, see Forlano and Lentz, *Conversations on Media*, 3. Gigi Sohn had, in 2001, granted $270,000 to Leslie Harris and Associates to operate the Digital Media Forum, whose mission was to invite collaboration among media reform groups and scholars. The effort faltered, in part due to advocates' complaints about the grantee's work for industry. *2001 Ford Foundation Annual Report*, 165; and Lentz, interview with author.

95. As Karaganis observes, the SSRC's mandate involved a difficult but deliberate balancing act that often involved turning down well-articulated requests from the highly organized policy community. Karaganis, *Cultures of Collaboration in Media Research*, 8–9.

96. Ibid., 8, 17–18. Karaganis said, "Nearly everyone—including the academics—viewed academia as isolated from and, most of the time, irrelevant to civil society activity. The near unanimity on this point profoundly shaped our sense of the program's mission and potential contribution" (3).

97. See the Media Research Hub at http://www.mediaresearchhub.ssrc.org. See the SSRC program's background papers at http://www.ssrc.org/programs/pages/necessary-knowledge-for-a-democratic-public-sphere/program-background-papers; and a detailed report on the collaborative grants, *SSRC Collaborative Grants in Media Communications, 2005–2008* (New York: SSRC, 2008).

98. *SSRC Collaborative Grants*, 37–38.

99. For a comprehensive (though broader) listing, see Karaganis and El-Hadidy, *Freedom of Expression At the Ford Foundation*, 42–57. University-based and other research grantees received over $5 million during this period; see the list in Forlano and Lentz, *Conversations on Media*, 60–89.

100. *2007 Ford Foundation Annual Report* (New York: Ford Foundation, 2008).

101. The articulation of "freedom of expression" was, arguably, a direct outgrowth of the discursive maneuvers Lentz made while at Ford.

102. Due to endowment losses, Ford's overall giving declined in 2008, but by a smaller 12 percent. See *2007 Ford Foundation Annual Report*, 30; and *2008 Ford Foundation Annual Report* (New York: Ford Foundation, 2009), 11, 23, 38.

103. See "Jenny Toomey," Ford Foundation, http://www.fordfoundation.org/regions/united-states/team/jenny-toomey; and Kimmelman, interview with author. Toomey's Future of Music Coalition was a grantee of Lentz's portfolio. See *2004 Ford Foundation Annual Report* (New York: Ford Foundation, 2005), 124; and *2005 Ford Foundation Annual Report* (New York: Ford Foundation, 2006), 130.

104. See Robert W. McChesney, *Telecommunications, Mass Media, and Democracy: The Battle for the Control of U.S. Broadcasting, 1928–1935* (New York: Oxford University Press, 1993). As William Buxton describes, the Carnegie Corporation and John D. Rockefeller supported a moderate reform group over the other, more radical educational broadcasting advocate during the "Radio Wars." Buxton, "The Political Economy of Communications Research," in *Information and Communication in Economics*, ed. Robert E. Babe (Boston: Kluwer, 1994), 154.

105. Buxton, "The Political Economy of Communications Research."

106. See Brett Gary, "Communication Research, the Rockefeller Foundation, and Mobilization for the War on Words," *Journal of Communication* 46, no. 3 (1996): 124–47.

107. See Christopher Simpson, *Science of Coercion: Communication Research and Psychological Warfare, 1945–1960* (New York: Oxford University Press, 1994); Timothy Glander, *Origins of Mass Communications Research During the American Cold War* (Mahwah, NJ: Lawrence Erlbaum, 2000); and Ron T. Robin, *The Making of the Cold War Enemy: Culture and Politics in the Military-Intellectual Complex* (Princeton, NJ: Princeton University Press, 2001).

108. See the detailed account in *Ford Foundation Activities in Noncommercial Broadcasting 1951–1976* (New York: Ford Foundation, 1976). See also Marilyn A. Lashner, "The Role of Foundations in Public Broadcasting, I: Development and Trends," *Journal of Broadcasting* 20, no. 4 (1976): 529–47; and Lashner, "The Role of Foundations in Public Broadcasting, II: The Ford Foundation," *Journal of Broadcasting* 21, no. 2 (1977): 235–54.

109. *Office of Communication of United Church of Christ v. FCC*, 359 F.2d 994 (D.C. Cir., 1966). There is a growing literature on the UCC case and its aftermath. The

classic treatment is Robert B. Horwitz, "Broadcast Reform Revisited: Reverend Everett C. Parker and the 'Standing' Case," *The Communication Review* 2, no. 3 (1997): 311–48. See Napoli, "Public Interest Media Activism," 6, for a comprehensive list of publications. The post-1966 broadcast reform movement had significant roots in earlier reform efforts.

110. *1968 Ford Foundation Annual Report* (New York: Ford Foundation, 1969); and Richard Magat, *The Ford Foundation At Work: Philanthropic Choices, Methods, and Styles* (New York: Plenum Press, 1979), 80.

111. See, for example, *1972 Ford Foundation Annual Report* (New York: Ford Foundation, 1973), 19; and *1974 Ford Foundation Annual Report* (New York: Ford Foundation, 1975), 11, 29. Other policy groups, including the Media Access Project, were supported by the Markle Foundation. See Lenert, *Mapping Social Entrepreneurship*, 16. A key figure in Ford's grant making in public broadcasting and media policy was Fred Friendly, the former CBS newsman. Friendly served as the foundation's "advisor" on broadcasting from 1966 to 1980 and chaired an important 1973 internal task force on new communication technology. See *1973 Ford Foundation Annual Report*, 29–30; and Forlano and Lentz, *Conversations on Media*, 9–10, 15. Friendly also created and oversaw Ford's Media and Society Seminars from 1974–1980, which centered on legal questions around journalism. *The Seminars on Media and Society 1974–1980: A Summary and Casebook* (New York: Ford Foundation, 1980).

112. For an overview, see Anne Wells Branscomb and Maria Savage, "The Broadcast Reform Movement: At the Crossroads," *Journal of Communication* 28, no. 4 (1978): 25–34; Theodore J. Schneyer, "An Overview of Public Interest Law Activity in the Communications Field," *Wisconsin Law Review* no. 3 (1977): 619–83; and Mueller, Kuerbis, and Page, *Re-inventing Media Activism*, 35–50.

113. Willard Rowland makes this argument convincingly. Rowland, "The Illusion of Fulfillment: The Broadcast Reform Movement," *Journalism Monographs* 79 (1982): 1–41.

114. Rowland, "The Illusion of Fulfillment"; Timothy R. Haight, "The 'S. 1' of Communications," in *Telecommunications Policy and the Citizen: Public Interest Perspectives on the Communications Act Rewrite*, ed. Haight (New York, NY: Praeger, 1979), 241–66; and Thomas Streeter, "Policy Discourse and Broadcast Practice: The FCC, the US Broadcast Networks and the Discourse of the Marketplace," *Media, Culture and Society* 5, nos. 3–4 (1983): 247–62.

115. Lenert, *Mapping Social Entrepreneurship*, 49–51, quoting Jeff Chester; Mueller, Kuerbis, and Page, *Re-inventing Media Activism*, 51–64; and Napoli, "Public Interest Media Activism," 31–32.

116. As Katharina Kopp observes, by 1980 Ford had "completely abandoned the field and left it to the more conservative influence of the Markle Foundation." Kopp, "The Role of Private Philanthropic Foundations," 309.

117. Albert H. Kramer stated, "In general, the pattern that emerges confirms the view that organizations dealing in highly controversial attempts to redistribute control of the decision-making processes affecting the media or to challenge the basis of the commercial media, that is advertiser support, have been underfunded, gone without funding, or had to undergo incredible tests of stamina before receiving

funding." Kramer, "The Role of Foundations in Broadcasting and Cable Communications Policy Development," in *Research Papers Volume II: Philanthropic Fields of Interest, Part II—Additional Perspectives* (Washington, DC: Department of the Treasury, 1977), esp. 1320–30.

118. On Ford funding of research supporting deregulatory arguments, see Kopp, "The Role of Private Philanthropic Foundations," 84–85, 93, 108, 118–20, 195, 201–2, 264–70.

119. Roger G. Noll, Merton J. Peck, and John J. McGowan, *Economic Aspects of Television Regulation* (Washington, DC: Brookings Institution, 1973).

120. Michael J. Barker, "The Liberal Foundations of Media Reform? Creating Sustainable Funding Opportunities for Radical Media Reform," *Global Media Journal—Australian Edition* 1, no. 2 (2008), 1.

121. Bob Feldman, "Report From the Field: Left Media and Left Think Tanks Foundation-Managed Protest?," *Critical Sociology* 33, no. 3 (2007): 429.

122. See Roelofs, *Foundations and Public Policy*; Arnove, *Philanthropy and Cultural Imperialism*; Donald Fisher, "The Role of Philanthropic Foundations in the Reproduction and Production of Hegemony: Rockefeller Foundations and the Social Sciences," *Sociology* 17, no. 2 (1983): 206–33; and a recent special issue of *Critical Sociology* 33, no. 3 (2007).

123. Barker, "The Liberal Foundations of Media Reform?" 2, 8, 10; and Feldman, "Report from the Field," 444.

CHAPTER 15

Media Democracy in Action
Truth Emergency and the Progressive Media Reform Movement

Mickey Huff and Peter Phillips

There is nothing so strong or safe in an emergency of life as the simple truth.
—Charles Dickens[1]

The late New York University media scholar Neil Postman once wrote that "Americans are the best entertained and quite likely the least well informed people in the Western world."[2] That was 25 years ago, and after two-plus decades of more deregulation and the growth of conglomerates in the media that trend has continued. From Tyra Banks's shifting figure and the Balloon Boy hoax, to the celebrity death of Michael Jackson and the Obama Beer Summit, Americans are fed a steady "news" diet of tabloidized, trivialized, and outright useless information laden with personal anecdotes, scandals, and gossip.

Topics and in-depth reports that matter little to most people in any meaningful way are increasingly given massive amounts of attention in the corporate media. In recent years, that pattern has only become more obvious. For instance, CNN's coverage of celebrity Anna Nicole Smith's untimely death in early 2007 is arguably one of the most egregious examples of an overabused news story. The magnitude of corporate media attention paid to Smith's death was clearly out of sync with the coverage the story deserved, which was at most a simple, passing mention. Instead, CNN broadcast "breaking" stories of Smith's death uninterrupted, without commercials, for almost two hours, with commentary

The authors would like to give thanks to Project Censored interns Frances A. Capell, Andrew Hobbs, and Nolan Higdon for their research assistance and contributions.

by lead anchors and journalists. This marked among the longest uninterrupted "news" broadcasts at CNN since the tragic events of September 11, 2001. Anna Nicole Smith and 9/11 are now strange bedfellows, milestone bookends of a deranged corporate news culture.[3]

While news outlets were obsessing over Smith's death, most big media giants were missing a far more important story. The US ambassador to Iraq misplaced $12 billion in shrink-wrapped one-hundred-dollar bills that were flown to Baghdad. This garnered little attention due to the media's morbid (even voyeuristic) infatuation with Smith's passing. This is clearly news judgment gone terribly awry, if not an outright retreat from journalistic standards. The once trivial and absurd are now mainstreamed as "news." More young people turn to late night comics' fake news to learn the truth or tune out to so-called reality shows often scripted as Roman Holiday spectacles of the surreal. This hyper-reality creation of corporate media in the twenty-first century has led to what Postman presciently warned about: an infotainment society.[4]

Mass coverage of trivial events in corporate media continued in 2009. British tabloid *News of the World* published an exclusive photo of Olympic gold medalist Michael Phelps smoking marijuana from a bong in February 2009 with the headline "What a Dope." The incident occurred nearly three months after the swimmer won eight gold medals for the United States at the 2008 Olympics in Beijing. Phelps quickly apologized to the public for his "regrettable behavior." Did anyone ask, is this really a newsworthy issue? Why instead was there not a discussion about the almost one-and-a-half-million marijuana user arrests in 2006 and 2007?[5]

Photos of Jessica Simpson performing at a Florida Chili Cook-off looking a bit heavier than usual surfaced during the week of January 26, 2009. The purportedly unflattering shots of a curvier-looking Simpson immediately made news headlines. Was she picking up eating habits from her NFL star quarterback boyfriend? Or was she simply hungry for publicity? During a pre–Super Bowl interview, President Obama even noted that Simpson was "in a weight battle." Again, why is this a news story and why is the leader of the free world commenting on it? Why was there not a discussion about the worsening problems of hunger, or poverty, or obesity in America?[6]

The United States not only is becoming a nation of obese people but also is on the verge of another phenomenon, the equivalent of cultural and mental obesity. We, in America, are a nation awash in a sea of information, yet we have a paucity of understanding. We are a country where over a quarter of the population know the names of all five members of the fictitious family from *The Simpsons* yet only one in a thousand can name all the rights protected under the First Amendment to the US Constitution. Journalistic values have been sold out to commercial interests and not even our core, national, and constitutionally protected values are sacred. Far too often, important news stories are underreported or ignored entirely by corporate news outlets, especially on television, where over 70 percent of Americans get their news—even though only an astounding 29 percent say it is accurate. In short, Americans are living in a state of truth emergency.[7]

Truth Emergency: Keeping the Facts at Bay

The truth comes as conqueror only because we have lost the art of receiving it as guest.

—Rabindranath Tagore[8]

What are some of these truths, that not knowing them creates a literal state of emergency for human society? Here are two of many possible examples. A 2008 report from the World Bank admitted that in 2005, over three billion people lived on less than $2.50 a day and about 44 percent of these people survive on less than $1.25.[9] Complete and total wretchedness can be the only description for the circumstances faced by so many, especially those in urban areas of so-called developing nations. Simple items Americans take for granted like phone calls, television, inoculations and even food are beyond the possible for billions of people.

In another ignored but related story, Starvation.net logged the increasing impacts of world hunger and starvation. Over 30,000 people a day (85 percent children under 5) die of malnutrition, curable diseases, and starvation.[10] The number of deaths has exceeded 300 million people over the past 40 years.[11] These stories should be alarming headlines, certainly more significant than celebrity tripe and tabloid hype.

Continuing on the theme of human poverty and its ramifications, farmers around the world grow more than enough food to feed the entire world adequately. Global grain production yielded a record 2.3 billion tons in 2007, up 4 percent from the year before, yet billions of people go hungry every day. The nonprofit GRAIN described the core reasons for continuing hunger in a recent report, *Making a Killing from Hunger*. It turns out that while farmers grow enough food to feed the world, commodity speculators and huge grain traders like Cargill control the global food prices and distribution. Starvation is profitable for corporations when demand for food push the prices up. Cargill announced that profits for commodity trading for the first quarter of 2008 were 86 percent above 2007. World food prices grew 22 percent from June 2007 to June 2008, and a significant portion of the increase was propelled by the $175 billion invested in commodity futures that speculate on price instead of seeking to feed the hungry.[12] This results in erratic food price spirals, both up and down, with food insecurity remaining widespread.

For a family on the bottom rung of poverty, a small price increase is the difference between life and death, yet no American presidents have declared a war on starvation. Instead they talk about national security and the continuation of the War on Terror as if these were the primary issues for their terms in office. Given that ten times as many innocent people died of starvation than those in the World Trade Center on September 11, 2001, why is there no war on starvation? Is not starvation, especially if preventable, a form of inflicted terror by those who profit from it or even stand by and do nothing? Where is the Manhattan Project for global hunger? Where is the commitment to national security though unilateral starvation relief? Where is the outrage in the corporate news media with pictures of dying children and an analysis of those that benefit from hunger? Could the same not be said for those who die due to lack of health care coverage, to the tune of 45,000 a year?[13]

While news stories on the realities of global hunger remain undercovered in the United States, topics closer to home are often ignored as well. For example, racial inequality remains problematic in the United States. People of color continue to experience disproportionately high rates of poverty, unemployment, police profiling, repressive incarceration, and school segregation. According to a recent civil rights report from UCLA, schools in the United States are currently 44 percent nonwhite, and minorities are rapidly emerging as the majority of public school students. Latinos and blacks are the two largest minority groups. However, black and Latino students attend schools more segregated today than during the civil rights era. More than 50 years after *Brown v. Board of Education*, schools remain separate and unequal. The UCLA study shows that public schools in the Western states, including California, suffer from the most severe segregation in the United States, rather than Southern schools, as many people believe.[14]

This new form of segregation is primarily based on how urban areas are geographically organized—as Cornel West so passionately describes—into vanilla suburbs and chocolate cities.[15] Schools remain highly unequal, in terms of both money and qualified teachers and curriculum. Unequal education leads to diminishing access to colleges and future jobs for the afflicted demographics. Nonwhite schools are segregated by poverty as well as race. These "chocolate," low-income public schools are where most of the nation's dropouts occur, leading to large numbers of virtually unemployable young people of color struggling to survive in a troubled economy.

Diminished opportunity for students of color invariably creates greater privileges for whites. White privilege is a concept that is challenging for many whites to accept. Whites like to think of themselves as hard-working individuals whose achievements are due to deserved personal efforts. In many cases this is partly true; hard work in college often pays off in many ways. Nonetheless, many whites find it difficult to accept that geographically and structurally based racism remains a significant barrier for many students of color. Whites often say racism is in the past and that Americans need not think about it today. Yet inequality stares back at society daily from the barrios, ghettos, and from behind prisons walls.

For these factual stories to not be reported by major media outlets is clearly a matter of censorship and top-down information control. The aforementioned are two riveting examples of a failure of the free press to accurately inform the public about critical issues facing our global and national society. Sadly, there are many more examples.

Fourth Estate Sale: Censorship, the "Free" Press, and Truth Emergency

Freedom of the press is guaranteed only to those who own one.

—A. J. Liebling[16]

The corporate media in the United States like to think of themselves as the official, most accurate source for news reporting of the day. *The New York Times* motto of "all the news that's fit to print" is a clear example of this perspective. However, with corporate media coverage dependent on fewer reporters as a result of downsizing that increasingly focuses on a narrow range of celebrity updates, news from official government and institutional sources and sensationalized crimes and disasters, the self-justification of being the most fit or trusted is no longer valid for American journalism. This shift away from fact-based, socially relevant reporting constitutes a principal form of censorship at the base of this ongoing truth emergency.

There is a growing need to broaden understanding of censorship in the United States. The dictionary definition of direct government control of news as censorship is no longer adequate. The private corporate media significantly undercover and/or deliberately censor numerous important news stories every year. The corporate media ignore valid news stories, even when based on university-quality research. It appears that certain topics are simply forbidden inside the mainstream media today. To openly cover these news stories would stir up questions regarding "inconvenient truths" that many in the US power structure would rather avoid. One group raising these questions is Project Censored, which has covered inconvenient truths, exposed junk news patterns, and called for a more independent, research-driven, transparent, and fact-based system of reporting since 1976.

Some of these taboo truths include civilian death rates in Iraq, the post-9/11 erosion of civil liberties, levels of violence by side in the Israeli-Palestinian conflict, the coup in Haiti, election fraud in the United States, and questions concerning the very events and subsequent official investigations of 9/11. Here are some more details of the ongoing truth emergency.

Researchers from Johns Hopkins University and a professional survey company in Great Britain, Opinion Research Business (ORB), report that the United States is directly responsible for over one million Iraqi deaths since our invasion in 2003. In a January 2008 report, ORB concluded that "survey work confirms our earlier estimate that over 1,000,000 Iraqi citizens have died as a result of the conflict which started in 2003 . . . We now estimate that the death toll between March 2003 and August 2007 is likely to have been of the order of 1,033,000."[17] A 2006 Johns Hopkins study found that US aerial bombing in civilian neighborhoods caused over a third of these deaths and that over half the deaths are directly attributable to US forces.[18] As John Tirman, executive director and principal research scientist at MIT's Center for International Studies, writes, "We have, at present between 800,000 and 1.3 million 'excessive Deaths' as we approach the six-year anniversary of this war."[19]

Some common themes of recently censored stories include the systemic erosion of human rights and civil liberties in both the United States and the world at large. The corporate media ignored the fact that habeas corpus can now be suspended for anyone by order of the president. With the approval of Congress, the Military Commissions Act (MCA) of 2006 allows for the suspension of habeas corpus for US citizens and noncitizens alike. While media, including a lead editorial in *The New York Times*, have given false comfort that American citizens will not be the victims of the measures legalized by the act, the law is quite clear that "any person" can be targeted. The text in the MCA allows for the institution of a military alternative to the constitutional justice system for "any person" regardless of American citizenship. The MCA effectively does away with habeas corpus rights for all people living in the United States deemed by the president to be enemy combatants.[20] In September 2009, President Obama quietly pledged to continue the program as it was instituted by the Bush administration with little fanfare.[21]

Additionally, under the code name Operation FALCON (Federal and Local Cops Organized Nationally), three federally coordinated mass arrests occurred between April 2005 and October 2006. In an unprecedented move, more than 30,000 "fugitives" were arrested in the largest dragnets in the nation's history. By 2008, the number grew to 54,000. Unfortunately, most of those arrested were not, in fact, violent criminals, according to the government's own statistics. The operations, coordinated by the Justice Department and Homeland Security, directly involved over 960 agencies (state, local, and federal) and are the first time in US history that all the domestic police agencies have been put under the direct control of the federal government. As of July 2009, the sixth effort of the FALCON raids has increased the number of "dangerous fugitive felons" arrested to more than 91,000 (of which only 991 were murder suspects, and only 2,269 were gang members, even though these were the very groups agents were claiming to round up).[22]

Finally, the term "terrorism" has been dangerously expanded to include any acts that interfere, or promote interference, with the operations of animal enterprises. The Animal Enterprise Terrorism Act (AETA), signed into law in 2006, expands the definition of an "animal enterprise" to any business that "uses or sells animals or animal products."[23] The law essentially defines protesters, boycotters, or picketers of businesses in the United States as terrorists. This is a clear infringement of First Amendment rights.

Most people in the United States believe in the Bill of Rights and value personal freedoms. Yet in the recent past, the corporate media have failed to adequately inform the public about important changes concerning civil rights and liberties. Despite the busy lives people lead, they want to be informed about serious decisions made by the powerful and rely on the corporate media to keep abreast of significant changes. When corporate media fail to cover these issues, what else can it be called it but censorship? These are issues of considerable concern for the public at large. Conclusions on such matters can only be arrived upon after scrupulous analysis of all known facts. Given that all the facts about these stories are not widely reported, if at all, this leads to a significant crisis for any democracy.

On October 25, 2005, the American Civil Liberties (ACLU) posted to their website 44 autopsy reports, acquired from American military sources, covering the deaths of civilians who died while in US military prisons in Iraq and Afghanistan in 2002–2004. The autopsy reports provided proof of widespread torture by US forces. A press release by the ACLU announcing the deaths was immediately picked up by the Associated Press (AP) wire service, making the story available to US corporate media nationwide. A thorough check of LexisNexis showed that at least 99 percent of daily papers in the United States did not pick the story up, nor did the AP ever conduct follow-up coverage on the issue.[24]

Not only do daily newspapers fail to cover the inconvenient truths presented by their own wire service, but the wire service itself is filled with internal bias. The AP is a nonprofit cooperative with 3,700 employees and 242 bureaus worldwide that deliver news reports 24 hours a day, 7 days a week to 121 countries in 5 languages, including English, German, Dutch, French, and Spanish. In the United States alone, the AP reaches 1,700 newspapers, and 5,000 radio and television stations. The AP reaches over a billion people every day via print, radio, or television.[25]

Bias and censorship is also evident in stories concerning the ongoing Israeli-Palestinian conflict. Researchers from the organization If Americans Knew conducted research on the AP's reporting of the conflict. The study, a statistical analysis of the AP newswire in the year 2004, compared the number of Israeli and Palestinian reported deaths. In 2004 there were 141 reports of Israeli deaths in AP headlines and lead paragraphs, while in reality there were 108 Israeli deaths. During this same period, the AP reported 543 Palestinian deaths, when in fact 821 Palestinians had been killed. The ratio of Israeli conflict deaths to Palestinian deaths in 2004 was one-to-seven, yet the AP reported deaths of Israelis to Palestinians at a two-to-one ratio.[26]

The AP is a massive institutionalized bureaucracy that feeds news stories to nearly every newspaper and radio or TV station in the United States. They are so large that top-down control of individual stories is practically impossible. However, research clearly indicates a built-in bias favoring official US government positions.

Reform Media Reform: Pursuit and Reporting of Truth Emergency Issues

Reformers who are always compromising, have not yet grasped the idea that truth is the only safe ground to stand upon.

—Elizabeth Cady Stanton[27]

There is a literal truth emergency in the United States regarding not only distant wars, torture camps, and doctored intelligence but also issues that most intimately impact our lives at home.

George Seldes once said, "Journalism's job is not impartial 'balanced' reporting. Journalism's job is to tell the people what is really going on." Michael Moore's top-grossing movie *Sicko* is one example of telling the people what is really going on. Health care activists know that US health insurance is an extremely large and lucrative industry with the top nine companies "earning" $30 billion in profits in 2006 alone. The health-care industry represents the country's third-largest economic sector, trailing only energy and retail among the one-thousand largest US firms.

In spite of recent health care reform, at least 16 percent of Americans still have no health insurance whatsoever and that number will not soon decline, as insurance costs continue to rise two to three times faster than inflation. The consequences are immediate and tragic. Unpaid medical bills are now the number one cause of personal bankruptcy in the country, and a recent Harvard Medical School study estimates that nearly 45,000 Americans die prematurely each year because they lack coverage and access to adequate care.[28] That's 15 times the number of people killed on September 11, 2001. In fact, 2,266 veterans died in 2008 due to lack of health coverage.[29] For a nation awash in "Support the Troops" rhetoric, bumper stickers, magnets, and other paraphernalia, it seems odd that the US press largely ignored the Harvard Medical School study that reported this troubling statistic. Despite these findings, Congress opted against a public option or single-payer bill, even though a majority of the public and health practitioners support these policies. Corporate media has largely shut out these approaches from the discussion, often even when dealing with veterans' affairs.

In terms of elections, political analysts have long counted on exit polls as a reliable predictor of actual vote counts. The unusual discrepancy between exit poll data and the actual vote count in the 2004 election challenges that reliability. However, despite evidence of technological vulnerabilities in the voting system and a higher incidence of irregularities in swing states, this discrepancy was not scrutinized in the corporate media. They simply parroted the partisan declarations of "let's move on" instead of providing any meaningful analysis of a highly controversial election.

The official vote count for the 2004 election showed that George W. Bush won by three million votes. But exit polls projected a victory margin of five million votes for John Kerry. This eight-million-vote discrepancy is much greater than the margin of error. That margin should, statistically, have been under 1 percent. But the official result deviated from the poll projections by more than 5 percent—a statistical impossibility.[30]

Tens of thousands of American engaged in various social justice issues constantly witness how corporate media marginalize, denigrate, or simply ignore their concerns. Activist groups working on exposing issues like 9/11 Commission problems, election fraud, impeachable offenses, war propaganda, civil liberties abuses, torture, and many corporate-caused economic and environmental crises have been systematically excluded from mainstream news and the national conversation, leading to a genuine truth emergency in the country.

A growing number of media activists are finally joining forces to address this truth emergency by developing new journalistic systems and practices of their own. They are working to reveal the common corporate denominators behind the diverse crises we face and to develop networks of trustworthy news sources that tell the people what is really going on. Activists know we need a journalism that moves beyond forensic inquiries into particular crimes and atrocities, one that exposes wider patterns of corruption, propaganda, and illicit political control to rouse the nation to reject a malignant, corporate status quo.

An international truth emergency, now in evidence, is the result of missing fact-based, transparent, and truthful reporting on fraudulent elections, compromised 9/11 investigations, and illegal preemptive wars, compounded by top-down corporate media propaganda across the spectrum on public issues. Glenn Beck was able to say on national Fox News television in June 2009 that the 9/11 truth movement openly supported the shooting at the United States Holocaust

Memorial Museum that month. Beck claimed that 9/11 truth proponents saw shooter James von Brunn as a "hero." Beck's statement is completely without factual merit and represents a hyperrealist slamming of a movement already slanderously prelabeled by the corporate, and even much of the progressive media, as "conspiracy theorists." These ad hominem attacks are no substitute for factual reporting and fair coverage. Journalists are supposed to be trained to ferret out conspiracies against the public, not to shy away from them for fear of being attacked.

Conspiracies tend to be actions by small groups of individuals rather than massive collective plots by entire governments. However, small groups can be dangerous, especially when the individuals have significant power in huge public and private bureaucracies. Corporate boards of directors meet in closed rooms to plan their profit-maximizing strategies. If they knowingly make plans that hurt others, violate laws, undermine ethics, or show favoritism to friends, they are involved in a conspiracy.

In addition to attacking, labeling, and reporting falsehoods, critics of unofficial investigations into 9/11, election fraud, and other controversial issues lump together all the questions, lines of inquiry, or both as if each had equal validity. Obviously, they do not. This, however, allows critics to dismiss fact-based, transparent inquiries into major problems with official explanations of these crucial matters by focusing on only the most absurd claims. These fallacies including overgeneralizations, straw persons, appeals to questionable authority, and red herrings that distract from actual fact-based investigations.

Here is another case in point: former Brigham Young University physics professor Steven E. Jones and over 1,200 scientific professionals in the fields of architecture and engineering have now concluded that the official explanation for the collapse of the World Trade Center (WTC) buildings is implausible according to laws of physics.[31] Especially troubling is the collapse of Building 7, a 47-story building that was not hit by planes, yet dropped in its own "footprint" at nearly free-fall speed in the same manner as a controlled demolition.

To support his theory, Jones and eight other scientists conducted chemical research on the dust from the World Trade Center. Their research results were published in a peer-reviewed scientific journal, *Open Chemical Physics Journal*. The authors found traces of thermite. Thermite is a pyrotechnic composition of a metal powder and a metal oxide, which produces an aluminothermic reaction known as a thermite reaction and can be used in controlled demolitions of buildings. This data raises significant questions that should be explored, regardless of what one believes. This should be a part of our political discourse, given how much of the policy in the past nine years has been based on assumptions about 9/11. In a free society, this type of inquiry would be a matter of civic principle, not national ridicule—which is what it has largely been, when not ignored outright by corporate media. To challenge the official narrative of 9/11 in the United States is akin to denying the existence of God, the ultimate blasphemy or heresy in a theocratic culture.

These are some of the reasons we are in a truth emergency, which is predicated on the inability of many to distinguish between what is real and what is not. Corporate media, Fox in particular, offer "news" that creates a hyperreality of real-world problems and issues. Consumers of corporate news media—especially those whose understandings are framed primarily from those media alone—are embedded in a state of excited delirium of knowinglessness. This lack of factual awareness of key issues leaves people politically paralyzed. The real free press is supposed to inform and embolden citizen action, not distract and misinform to the point of a dysfunctional democracy.

To counter knowinglessness, media activists need to include truth emergency issues as important elements of radical-progressive media reform efforts. We must not be afraid of corporate media labeling and instead build truth from the bottom up, with all available facts. Critical thinking and fact finding are the basis of democracy, and we must stand for the maximization of informed participatory democracy at the lowest possible level in society. In order to maintain democracy, the free press must thrive. We the people must become the media. Our survival as a free society depends on it.[32]

Words from Our Revolutionary Sponsors

In a time of universal deceit, telling the truth is a revolutionary act.
—George Orwell (attributed)[33]

The purpose of the free press, as enunciated by key founders of America, was to keep the citizenry informed, engaged, and in dialogue with one another about the crucial issues of the day. The health of any democracy can be diagnosed by the degree to which information flows freely in the culture. Anything that interferes with that free flow of information is a form of censorship, which acts to derail, distort, and deny the efficacy of any true democratic experiment.

Thomas Jefferson and James Madison supported a vigorous public arena of discourse, debate, and competing ideas. In short, they wanted to encourage the process of dialogue and free expression as vehicles to achieve the best of democratic possibilities. In his first inaugural address, Jefferson said, "If there be any among us who would wish to dissolve this Union or to change its republican form, let them stand undisturbed as monuments of the safety with which error of opinion may be tolerated where reason is left free to combat it."[34] We need honest, open dialogue if democracy is to survive.

Madison warned, "A popular Government without popular information or the means of acquiring it, is but a Prologue to a Farce or a Tragedy or perhaps both. Knowledge will forever govern ignorance, and a people who mean to be their own Governors, must arm themselves with the power knowledge gives."[35] The free press is a centerpiece of knowledge; without it we are relegated to ignorance.

"Life, liberty, and the pursuit of happiness" are not just words on parchment. They are the very concepts that make us humane in the modern world. The media, the supposed free press, should be encouraging robust dialogues while fighting for the future of all Americans, not just for the insurance companies, banks, big pharma, and the military-industrial complex. In keeping with the founders' notions of natural rights and intent in providing for the general welfare, we would do well to note that health care is a human right, workers have the right to the fruits of their labor, environmental degradation is a crime against humanity, and war is terrorism. These positions should all be part of national discourse in a truly free press. Where are these voices in the corporate media cacophony?

Instead, the privileged institutions of corporate media are daily miring the public in cynicism (reports of personal scandals, rumors of rampant corruption, and congressional stagnation), rationalizing the populace into deep denial (claiming the recession is over while key public indicators on unemployment, wage losses, and foreclosures refute this), and leaving taxpayers footing a multitrillion-dollar tab for Wall Street bailouts and illegal wars (TARP, Iraq, Afghanistan, but nothing left for the public at home). A truly free press would herald these vile decrees and deeds as those of charlatans and demagogues. We must be the change we wish to see and we must not rely on spoon-fed, top-down, corporate media propaganda. We must become the media in the process of sharing knowledge with each other on the road to a better world. Since the corporate media are not in the business of news and are not beholden to empirical truths—rather, only to shareholder profits and their own bottom line—they should not be trusted.

If a failing corporate media system ensconced in hyperreality creates an excited delirium of knowinglessness, that system must be declared incapable of accurately informing the citizenry. The public must turn to independent journalism based in muckraking traditions, with transparent, fact-based reporting that asks the tough and critical questions of itself and its leaders. An actual free press would provide factual knowledge and encourage us to engage with each other in our local communities on a daily basis in the quest to solve societal problems.[36]

This is possible with our collective efforts, so long as we simultaneously reject the projected imaginings of the corporate media profiteers and their industry of illusion. This must be the crucial focal point of media reform, which actually is more of a media revolution. The health and meaningfulness of our cultural dialogue, as well as the future of our republic, may well depend on how swiftly and significantly we address the current truth emergency and what we do about it.

Notes

1. Richard Alan Krieger, *Civilization's Quotations: Life's Ideal* (New York: Algora Publishing, 2002), 80.
2. Neil Postman, *Amusing Ourselves to Death: Public Discourse in the Age of Show Business* (New York: Penguin Books, 1985), 106.
3. For reports about skewed corporate media coverage of Anna Nicole Smith's death, see "Anna Nicole Smith And Our National Media Embarassment," *Think Progress*, February 9, 2009, accessed March 1–9, 2010, http://thinkprogress.org/2007/02/09/anna-nicole-media-embarassment; and Ryers Online Editorial, "Anna Nicole Smith Coverage Becoming Too Much?" February 15, 2007, *RyersOnline*, accessed March 1–9, 2010, http://www.ryersonline.ca/blogs/83/Anna-Nicole-Smith-coverage-becoming-too-much.html. For more on "junk food news," see Peter Phillips, Mickey Huff, and Frances A. Capell, "Infotainment Society: Junk Food News for 2008/2009," *Daily Censored*, June 8, 2009, accessed March 1–9, 2010, http://dailycensored.com/2009/06/08/infotainment-society-junk-food-news-for-20082009.
4. For more on undercovered stories at the time, see Peter Phillips and Andrew Roth, *Censored 2008* (New York: Seven Stories Press, 2007), chap. 1; and Peter Phillips and Andrew Roth, *Censored 2009* (New York: Seven Stories Press, 2008); or see *Censored 2008* and *Censored 2009* stories online at http://www.projectcensored.org/top-stories/category/y-2008 and http://www.projectcensored.org/top-stories/category/y-2009, respectively.
5. Georgina Dickenson, "14-times Olympic Gold Medal Winner Michael Phelps Caught with Cannabis Pipe," *News of the World*, February 1, 2009, http://www.newsoftheworld.co.uk/news/150832/14-times-Olympic-gold-medal-winner-Michael-Phelps-caught-with-bong-cannabis-pipe.html; "Phelps Acknowledges Photo of Him Smoking a Bong," FOXSports.com, February 2, 2009, http://msn.foxsports.com/other/story/9160136/Report:-Picture-shows-Phelps-using-bong; and "Michael Phelps escapes pot charges," *Vancouver Sun*, February 16, 2009, http://www.vancouversun.com/sports/Michael+Phelps+escapes+charges/1295645/story.html. For marijuana arrests, see Paul Armentano, "Marijuana Arrests Set New Record," Project Censored, accessed March 1–9, 2010, http://www.projectcensored.org/top-stories/articles/20-marijuana-arrests-set-new-record.
6. "Please Stop Calling Jessica Simpson Fat," NBC Bay Area, February 6, 2009, http://www.nbcbayarea.com/around_town/the_scene/Stop-Calling-Jessica-Simpson-Fat.html; "Jessica Simpson Shocks Fans with Noticeably Fuller Figure," FOXNews.com, January 27, 2009, http://www.foxnews.com/story/0,2933,483204,00.html; Marcus Baram, "Obama Talks Football, Troop Withdrawal, Malia and Sasha's School, and Jessica Simpson," *Huffington Post*, February 1, 2009, accessed March 1–9, 2010, http://www.huffingtonpost.com/2009/02/01/obama-talks-football-troo_n_162971.html.

7. For further reading on some of the themes here, see Rick Shenkman, *Just How Stupid Are We? Facing the Truth About the American Voter* (New York: Basic Books, 2008), 13–14; and "Press Accuracy Rating Hits Two Decade Low Public Evaluations of the News Media: 1985-2009," Pew Research Center for the People and the Press, September 13, 2009, http://people-press.org/report/543. For more on the "truth emergency" concept and movement, see http://truthemergency.us, the website for the conference co-organized by the chapter authors in January 2008.

8. Rabindranath Tagore, *The English Writings of Rabindranath Tagore*, ed. Sisir Kumar Das and Nityapriçya Ghosha (New Delhi: Sahitya Akademi, 1994), 169.

9. Cited in Adam W. Parsons, "World Bank Poverty Figures: What Do They Mean?" Share the World's Resources, September 15, 2008, accessed March 1–9, 2010, http://www.stwr.org/globalization/world-bank-poverty-figures-what-do-they -mean.html.

10. Mark R. Elsis, "The Three Top Sins of the Universe," Starvation.net, February 9, 2002, accessed March 1–9, 2010, http://www.starvation.net.

11. Ibid.

12. *Making a Killing from Hunger* (Barcelona: GRAIN, 2008), 2–3, accessed March 1–9, 2010, http://www.grain.org/articles_files/atg-16-en.pdf.

13. David Cecere, "New Study Finds 45,000 Deaths Annually Linked to Lack of Health Coverage," *HarvardScience*, September 17, 2009, accessed March 1–9, 2010, http://www.harvardscience.harvard.edu/medicine-health/articles/new -study-finds-45000-deaths-annually-linked-lack-health-coverage.

14. Gary Orfield, *Reviving the Goal of an Integrated Society: A 21st Century Challenge* (Los Angeles: Civil Rights Project at UCLA, 2009).

15. Cornel West, quoted in Juontel White, "Political Leadership in the Black Community: Cornel West and Tavis Smiley Give Lecture at USC," *Black Voices*, November 16, 2006, accessed March 1–9, 2010, http://www.blackvoicesonline.com/home/index .cfm?event=displayArticle&ustory_id=c6224b88-e419-47f9-bb1b-dc76dadb60e5.

16. A. J. Liebling, "Do You Belong in Journalism?" *The New Yorker*, May 4, 1960, 109.

17. "Update on Iraqi Casualty Data," Opinion Research Business, January 2008, accessed March 1–9, 2010, http://www.opinion.co.uk/Newsroom_details.aspx ?NewsId=120.

18. Gilbert Burnham et al., "Mortality after the 2003 Invasion of Iraq: A Cross-sectional Cluster Sample Survey," *The Lancet* 368, no. 9545 (2006): 1421–28.

19. John Tirman, "Bush's War Totals," *The Nation*, January 28, 2009, accessed March 1–9, 2010, http://www.thenation.com/doc/20090216/tirman. See also Phillips and Roth, *Censored 2009*, 19–25.

20. See Phillips and Roth, *Censored 2008*, 35–44.

21. For President Obama's continuation of this policy at Guantanamo Bay, see "Obama Won't Change Terror Detention System: Report," Reuters, September 23, 2009, accessed March 1–9, 2010, http://www.reuters.com/article/topNews/idUSN2342 27672009092 4?feedType=RSS&feedName=topNews.

22. See Phillips and Roth, *Censored 2008*, chap. 1; see also "Operation FALCON 2009: Federal and Local Cops Organized Nationally," US Marshals Service, July 9, 2009, accessed March 1–9, 2010, http://www.usmarshals.gov/falcon09/index .html.

23. See Phillips and Roth, *Censored 2008*, chap. 1; and David Hoch and Odette Wilkens, "The Animal Enterprise Terrorism Act is Invidiously Detrimental to the Animal Rights Movement (and Unconstitutional as Well)," *Vermont Journal of Environmental Law*, March 9, 2007, accessed March 1–9, 2010, http://ccrjustice .org/learn-more/faqs/factsheet:-animal-enterprise-terrorism-act-%28aeta%29.

24. "U.S. Operatives Killed Detainees During Interrogations in Afghanistan and Iraq," American Civil Liberties Union, October 24, 2005, accessed March 1–9, 2010, http://www.aclu.org/intlhumanrights/gen/21236prs20051024.html.

25. "Facts and Figures," *Associated Press*, accessed March 1–9, 2010, http://www .ap.org/pages/about/about.html.

26. *Deadly Distortion: Associated Press Coverage of Israeli and Palestinian Deaths* (Portland, OR: If Americans Knew, 2006), accessed March 1–9, 2010, http://www .ifamericansknew.org/media/ap-report.html.

27. Elizabeth Cady Stanton, introduction to *The Woman's Bible* (New York: European Publishing Co., 1895).

28. Sanjay Gupta, "It Can Happen to You," CNN.com, January 30, 2008, accessed March 1–9, 2010, http://www.cnn.com/HEALTH/blogs/paging .dr.gupta/2008/01/it-can-happen-to-you.html.

29. Andrew P. Wilper et al., "Health Insurance and Mortality in US Adults," *American Journal of Public Health* 99, no. 12 (2009): 2289–95.

30. See Phillips, *Censored 2006* (New York: Seven Stories Press, 2005), 48–52.

31. "1000+ Architects & Engineers Officially Demand New 9/11 Investigation," InfoWars.com, January 18, 2010, accessed March 1–9, 2010, http://www.infowars .com/1000-architects-engineers-officially-demand-new-911-investigation.

32. For more on the themes developed in this article, see Peter Phillips and Mickey Huff, *Censored 2010* (New York: Seven Stories Press, 2009).

33. David J. Palmisano, *On Leadership: Essential Principles for Success* (New York: Sky Horse Publishing, 2008), 129.

34. See Thomas Jefferson, "First Inaugural Address," March 4, 1801, accessed March 1–9, 2010, http://press-pubs.uchicago.edu/founders/documents/v1ch4s33.html.

35. James Madison, letter to W. T. Barry, August 4, 1822, accessed March 1–9, 2010, http://press-pubs.uchicago.edu/founders/documents/v1ch18s35.html.

36. For more on the concept of hyperreality, see Jean Baudrillard, "Simulacra and Simulations," in *Selected Writings*, ed. Mark Poster (Palo Alto, CA: Stanford University Press, 1988), 166–84; see also John Tiffin and Nobuyoshi Terashima, eds., *Hyperreality: Paradigm for the Third Millennium* (New York: Routledge, 2001).

Contributors

Mark Andrejevic is associate professor of communication studies at the University of Iowa. His books include *iSpy* (2007) and *Reality TV: The Work of Being Watched* (2004); he has also written several journal articles and book chapters on reality TV and interactive media. His recent research focuses on surveillance and monitoring in the digital economy.

Patricia Aufderheide is professor of communication and director of the Center for Social Media at American University. Her books include *Documentary: A Very Short Introduction* (2007), *The Daily Planet* (2000), and *Communications Policy in the Public Interest* (1999). She serves on the board of directors of Kartemquin Films, a leading independent social documentary production company, and on the editorial boards of a variety of publications, including *Communication Law and Policy* and *In These Times*.

Mari Castañeda is associate professor in the department of communication at the University of Massachusetts Amherst. She is currently coediting two books and serving as chairperson of the National Association for Chicana and Chicano Studies. Her current research interests include Latina/o media and cultural production, transcultural political economy of media, and new technologies policy. She is the faculty adviser to Student Bridges, a student-initiated outreach program that expands pathways to higher education for residents from Holyoke, Massachusetts, a predominantly Latino, postindustrial city located thirty minutes from the University of Massachusetts Amherst campus.

Jessica Clark is the director of the Future of Public Media project at American University's Center for Social Media, and a Knight Media Policy Fellow at the New America Foundation. She is coauthor, with Tracy Van Slyke, of *Beyond the Echo Chamber* (New Press, 2010). At the Center for Social Media, she both directs and commissions research, offers expert commentary on the evolution of public media for a range of national conferences and outlets, and organizes events such as the Beyond Broadcast conference. She has researched, created, and fought for independent media for more than a decade in various contexts, including as a writer and editor of *In These Times.*

Nick Couldry is professor of media and communications and director of the Centre for the Study of Global Media and Democracy at Goldsmiths College, University of London. He is the author and coauthor or coeditor of several books, including *Why Voice Matters: Culture and Politics After Neoliberalism (2010), Media Events in a Global Age (2009), Media Consumption and Public Engagement* (2007), *Listening Beyond the Echoes* (2006), *MediaSpace* (2004), *Contesting Media Power* (2003), *Media Rituals* (2003), and *Inside Culture* (2000).

Christina Dunbar-Hester is assistant professor of journalism and media studies at Rutgers University. She completed her PhD at Cornell University in Science and Technology Studies in 2008, where her dissertation was an ethnographic study of contemporary activism around low-power FM radio in the United States. Her work has appeared in *Social Studies of Science, New Media & Society,* and *Science, Technology & Human Values.*

Mickey S. Huff is associate director of the Media Freedom Foundation and Project Censored and associate professor of history at Diablo Valley College. In addition to his contributions to *Censored 2009* and *Censored 2010,* he also contributes to *AlterNet, Counterpunch,* and *Z Magazine.* He teaches courses on US Media History, Sociology of Media and Censorship, Propaganda, and Media Studies. He is also a composer and musician.

Margaret Gallagher is an independent researcher and writer specializing in gender and media. She has worked as a consultant for the United Nations and its agencies, the European Commission, international development agencies, and broadcasting organizations. Widely published on women, media, and development, her works include *Gender Setting: New Agendas for Media Monitoring and Advocacy* (2001) and *Who Makes the News? Global Media Monitoring Project 2005* (2006). She serves on the editorial boards of *International Communication Gazette, Feminist Media Studies, Media Development,* and *Communication, Culture and Critique.* She is a member of the Governing Board of the Panos Institute, London.

William Gamson is a past president of the American Sociological Association and professor of sociology at Boston College. He is author or coauthor of several books, including *Shaping Abortion Discourse* (2002), *Talking Politics* (1992), *The Strategy of Social Protest* (1990), *What's News* (1984), *Conceptions of Social*

Life (1984), *Encounters with Unjust Authority* (1982), *Untangling the Cold War* (1971), and *Power and Discontent* (1968). He codirects the Movement/Media Research Action Project (MRAP), a national network of social researchers and community activists.

Nina Gregg is an organizational consultant working with social justice and nonprofit organizations on governance, planning, evaluation, and leadership transitions. She lives on a farm in Blount County, Tennessee. Nina taught communication and media studies at the University of Pittsburgh, Western Maryland College (now McDaniel College), and Maryville College. She was guest editor of the "Communication and Social Change" issue of *Electronic Journal of Communication/La Revue Electronique de Communication* (2004). She received an undergraduate degree from Princeton University and graduate degrees (MA and PhD) from McGill University. Since 2006 she has been Coordinator of US Activities for the International Charter of Human Responsibilities.

Cees J. Hamelink is professor emeritus of international communication at the University of Amsterdam and professor emeritus of media, religion, and culture at the Free University in Amsterdam, Netherlands. He is presently professor of health and human rights at the Vrije Universiteit, Amsterdam, and professor of knowledge management at the University of Aruba. Among the 16 books he has authored are *The Ethics of Cyberspace* (2000), *World Communication* (1995), *The Politics of World Communication: A Human Rights Perspective* (1994), *The Technology Gamble* (1988), *Finance and Information* (1983), and *Cultural Autonomy in Global Communications* (1983). He is editor-in-chief of the *International Communication Gazette*, honorary president of the International Association for Media and Communication Research (IAMCR), and founder of the People's Communication Charter.

Sue Curry Jansen is professor of media and communication at Muhlenberg College. She is the author of *Censorship* (1991) and *Critical Communication Theory* (2002). She served on the board of the short-lived but far-sighted Cultural Environment Movement.

Brian Martin, international director of Whistleblowers Australia, is professor of social sciences at the University of Wollongong, Australia. He is author, coauthor, or editor of 15 books, including most recently *Justice Ignited* (2007), *Nonviolence Speaks* (2003), *Nonviolence versus Capitalism* (2001), *Random Selection in Politics* (1999), *The Whistleblower's Handbook* (1999), *Information Liberation* (1998), and *Suppression Stories* (1997). He is also author of more than two hundred articles or chapters examining nonviolent action, dissent, and scientific controversies.

Peter Phillips is former director of Project Censored and professor of sociology at Sonoma State University. His books include 13 annual editions of *Censored* and *The Progressive Guide to Alternative Media and Activism* (1999, 2001). In addition to contributing articles to academic publications, he also publishes widely in the popular press, including *Newsday, Z Magazine, Briar Patch*, and hundreds of independent newspapers. His work was recognized by the Union for Democratic Communications with its prestigious Dallas Smythe Award in 2009.

Jefferson Pooley is associate professor of media and communication at Muhlenberg College. He is coeditor, with David W. Park, of *The History of Media & Communication Research* (2008). His research centers on the history of communication studies as the field's emergence has intersected with the twentieth-century rise of the other social sciences. His particular interest is in the field's memories of itself, as these serve to privilege certain approaches while closing off others. He is an active member of the local media reform movement.

Charlotte Ryan teaches sociology at the University of Massachusetts at Lowell. Her books include *Rhyming Hope and History: Social Movement Scholarship and Activism*, with David Croteau and William Hoynes (2005), and *Prime Time Activism: Media Strategies for Grassroots Organizing* (1991). With William A. Gamson, she codirects the Movement/Media Research Action Project (http://www.mrap.info). Her research focuses on how social movement and community-based organizations integrate communication strategies into institutional change strategies.

John L. Sullivan is associate professor of media and communication at Muhlenberg College. Recent publications include an analysis of representations of creative production in DVD extras in *Knowledge Workers in the Information Society*, edited by Katherine McKercher and Vincent Mosco (2007), and an intellectual history of Leo C. Rosten's work on Hollywood motion picture production in *Production Studies: Cultural Studies of Media Production*, edited by Vicki Mayer, Miranda Banks, and John Caldwell (2009). Focusing on the political economy of cultural production, he is currently researching labor consciousness among free software communities and writing a textbook on media audiences.

Lora Taub-Pervizpour is associate professor and chairperson of the Department of Media and Communication at Muhlenberg College. She directs the

RJ Fellows program, an honors program focused on social change. A recent publication growing out of her social justice commitments appears in *Story Circle: Digital Storytelling Around the World* (2009). She has been engaged in collaborations with young people making media for more than a decade in communities as diverse as San Diego, California, and Sao Paulo, Brazil. In Allentown, Pennsylvania, she codirects HYPE (Healthy Youth Peer Education), a youth leadership development program that mobilizes new digital media as tools for advocacy and community change.

Index

Name

Subject